"Whiteness Just Isn't
What It Used To Be"

SUNY series, INTERRUPTIONS:
Border Testimony(ies) and Critical Discourse/s

Henry A. Giroux, Editor

"Whiteness Just Isn't
What It Used To Be"

White Identity
in a Changing South Africa

Melissa E. Steyn

State University of New York Press

Published by
State University of New York Press Albany

For information, address State University of New York Press,
90 State Street, Suite 700, Albany, NY 12207

Production by Diane Ganeles
Marketing by Anne Valentine

Library of Congress Cataloging-in-Publication Data

Steyn, Melissa E.
    Whiteness just isn't what it used to be: white identity in a changing
South Africa/Melissa Steyn
        p. cm—(SUNY series, interruptions—border testimony(ies) and critical
discourses)
    Includes bibliographical references and index.
    ISBN 0-7914-5079-1 (alk. paper)—ISBN 0-7914-5080-5 (pbk.: alk. paper)
    1. Whites—South Africa—Attitudes. 2. Whites—South Africa—
Psychology. 3. South Africa—Race relations. 4. South Africa—
Politics and government—1994–5. South Africa—Social conditions—
1994– I. Title. II. Interruptions

DT1768.W55 S84 2001
305.8 ' 034068—dc21   00-053154

10   9   8   7   6   5   4   3   2   1

For Reg, and my two lovely daughters

Contents

The interregnum is not only between two social orders but between two identities, one known and discarded, the other unknown and undetermined.

—Nadine Gordimer, *Living in The Interregum*

A new identity is always post-some-old-identity.

—Kwame Anthony Appiah, "Cosmopolitan Patriots"

But what if I should discover that the very enemy himself is within me, that I myself am the enemy that must be loved—what then?

—Carl G. Jung, *The Vision Seminars*

Preface

❧

A Narrative of Whiteness

[M]ore like a snake shedding its skin than like death: the old constriction is sloughed off with difficulty, but there is expansion . . . some growth, and some reward for struggle and curiosity. Yet, if we are women who have gained privilege by our white skin *or* our Christian culture, but who are trying to free ourselves *as* women in a more complex way, we can experience this change as loss. Because it is: the old lies and ways of living, habitual, familiar, comfortable, fitting us like our skin, were *ours*.

—Minnie Bruce Pratt, "Identity: Skin Blood Heart"

He was a slightly-built, middle-aged white man, probably about fifty-five years old, dressed in a checked shirt and gaudy yellow shorts. The broad Afrikaans accent with which he spoke English was barely audible from behind his hands. He was trying to speak through his sobs, which shook his entire body.

In the two days of the antiracism workshop we were attending in Cape Town early in 1992, I had been grappling with an issue of my identity that had confused me all my life—Was I really Afrikaans, as my family background claimed, or was I an "English-speaking South African" adopted into this culture through my educational background and political history? The issue had become pertinent in some of the workshop exercises that required us to work in groups with our "own" cultures, and I had had to make a choice. The warm rapport I felt with this man and a few of the other Afrikaners in the group had helped me recognize that I should acknowledge my roots and work with the Afrikaans delegates. Now, he sat torn with a grief that had been repressed for fifty years, and that he would not have acknowledged before the political changes that were taking place in our country. I was confronted with a powerful symbol of what white identity meant for those of us who had grown up in Apartheid South Africa.

He was recounting an early memory. As a little boy on the farm in the Northern Transvaal where he grew up, he had loved his African nanny. He had loved to snuggle his head between her full breasts; he had loved the songs she sang to him in her language; he had loved the food she fed him. But as he grew up, his friends had taunted him for his affection for her, as she was "net 'n kaffirmeid" (just a nigger servant girl). He had learned to deny his love for his first friend in life, and to call her names to prove his indifference. Now he was articulating a deep sense of loss and waste, anger at a social system that had raised him on lies and damaged his humanity. He had feelings of personal shame for not having somehow managed to transcend his social conditioning. To a greater or lesser extent, all the white people in the room identified with his pain. We had all been damaged, ironically, by sociopolitical structures that had been designed to protect us, deeply humbled by the historical outcome of an arrogant system originally intended to entrench our white superiority and entitlement. We were grateful that the nightmare was finally ending, whatever our fears for the future.

This image of a grown man crying at early memories of himself and his country has remained with me as the moment at which I most clearly understood that I was working to counter racism as much for myself, as for the "others" against whom my country had perpetrated such great injustice. It was my own racialization that I needed to unravel. At that stage, it seemed to me that my task was to deconstruct the distorted understandings I had inherited of members of other races. I wanted to learn, and to encourage in those I taught, an appreciative approach to African culture.

As a native South African, I cannot remember a time when I was not aware of being "white." Race was the defining factor in any South African's life. White people lived in nice houses, went to good schools, did the work that mattered, had culture, and decided political issues. Other South Africans worked in our houses, on the roads, on the farms. They were laborers, although some were terrorists, to be feared. During weekends most dark-skinned men would disappear into the townships, and we would enjoy the white beaches, the white cinemas, the white parks, and our private swimming pools. Our maids would prepare our food (except in some homes where the worthy woman of the house would not have black hands work with the food, although such hands could wash the dishes after the meal); they would sleep in a room at the back of the house, use the back door and separate ablution facilities, and eat with separate cutlery and from tin plates and mugs. These things were common to practically all white households, even working-class homes, English and Afrikaans, give or take a few differences in cultural nuances.

The divisions between the English and Afrikaans groups, born of a long history of competition for control of the land between two colonizing groups, were still evident; the slow-to-heal wounds of the Boer War still smarted. I remember an old Afrikaner man who maintained that if someone were to line up a black man and an Englishman against a wall, and instruct him to shoot, he would shoot the Englishman first. My father, initially as a journalist, and then as a politician, had aligned himself with General Smuts, an internationally respected Afrikaner thinker. Despite having been a Boer general in the war, he had endeavored to take the white people in the country along a more united, reconciliatory path. My father became a leader in the South African Party, later called the United Party, which supported Britain and its allies in the two world wars. In opposing the strong nationalistic pressures within the Afrikaner culture, and refusing (in my childhood years) to join the Nationalist Party that was developing the policy of Apartheid he fiercely criticized, my father was often accused of being a traitor to his people. He taught our family to identity as South Africans. This would indicate that we had transcended the English/Afrikaans dichotomy, something that his own exceptional bilingualism served to model. We went to English schools, and did not, as many of our friends, belong to the Voortrekkers, a militaristic-type youth organization that inculcated Afrikaner Christian Nationalist ideology. In my early childhood we attended Sunday school in the Dutch Reformed Church, the church that helped to shape and perpetuate Afrikaner attitudes about being a chosen people with a special destiny in Africa. Later, because the sermons were becoming steadily more overtly political and pro-Apartheid, we switched to a series of English Protestant churches. None of them could assuage my spiritually displaced mother's guilt for leaving the church of her people, which still was the axis around which her numerous siblings centered their lives.

"South Africans are not colonialists," my father would say. "We don't carry other passports; there is no 'back home' for us in Europe. This is where we belong." The official history that was taught in our

schools stressed that the early Dutch settlers had arrived at the
Cape and moved into the interior of the country at the same time as
the African tribes they encountered were moving south. The land
was as much ours as it was theirs.

The question that begged an answer, of course, was whether the
"nonwhite" people in the country also qualified for the designation
South African. That our discussions actively entertained the idea
that whites did not have sole proprietorship of the land was a measure of what I understood to be the progressive thinking in my
home. The official policy of the United Party was a federal system, in
which there would be separate parliaments for each racial group.
The concept of one-man-one-vote espoused by the "far-left" and the
"communists" was as impractical and dangerous as Apartheid itself.
I was much older before I slowly started recognizing how racist my
"enlightened" father really was, and could see how little difference
there had been between the government and its official opposition
in the white political system.

As children growing up in a politically charged society, our con-
versations during breaks in our whites-only schools were often
about issues such as what kind of representation "nonwhites"
should be "allowed" to have. None of us had any idea of what African
people themselves thought about these issues other than trading
stereotypes and information imbibed from highly biased, rigorously
censored media. The ANC (African National Congress) had been
banned and Nelson Mandela incarcerated early in my childhood. I
didn't even know what he looked like—we never as much as saw a
photograph of him after the Rivonia trials, when he was convicted of
conspiracy against the state. But then African views didn't seem
particularly relevant to the discussion, really, except in an academic
way for those of us who strongly advocated against Apartheid. And
even the most liberal of us were raised on stories of the bloody decolonization process led by African Nationalist movements to our
north as an object lesson of what could await us, despite the many
differences between South Africa and the rest of the continent.

These differences were often the topic of conversation, bolster-
ing the belief that black rule could never come to our country—an
event that popular discourse held would inevitably bring disaster.
The country would lose the benefit of generations of white industry, expertise, and civilization. Africans themselves would of course
be the greatest losers, descending into the chaos that was Africa
without European leadership, and into abject poverty without the
driving force of European capitalism. It had ensured our country's

prosperity (along with the fact that we were a Christian nation, and the only democracy in Africa, and had one of the finest legal systems in the world).

Sorting through the combination of lies and half-truths given me as my heritage has been, and still is, a slow and painful task. It has involved trusting some impulses that ran contrary not only to my socialization, but also to what has at times been sensible, and, on occasions, even safe. I know that moments that seemed insignificant have had a lasting effect on me. One such moment was the first time I ventured into our maid's room one afternoon as a little girl. I suppose I was curious, and feeling bold. A white child just knew that one was not supposed to go into "their" places. The inside of her room was certainly very strange to me—its musty smell; the inside walls only roughly plastered; the extreme frugality compared with our house, which it adjoined. I had never seen newspaper used as a tablecloth before. The bed was raised on bricks to thwart any attempts the "tokoloshe" (a small impish man who in African belief can cast spells) may make to get at her while she slept. She sat holding her daughter's hand while we chatted, exchanging some asides in Xhosa to her child.

"She's a real mother." Intimations of depths to her personhood, of a life quite separate from our home that I had unquestioningly assumed to be all that defined her, broke into my consciousness. Drawn by this sense of an alternative world that she protected, of a subtle yet profoundly subversive knowledge that I now secretly shared, I subsequently spent many hours in her room. The habit became a topic with which my parents entertained guests at dinner parties. But the visits always left me with an unformulated discomfort about the incongruence of the relationship of her life to ours. At some level I intuited that the version of reality my parents were giving me did not tell the whole truth.

Another such moment was when I was older, in my early adolescence. We were moving, and I arrived home from school before my mother. I was to supervise the movers. A young "colored" man and I struck up a conversation. "Will I be raped?" The messages about the dangers of dark men, ingrained by socialization, tugged against my awkward impulse to reach out. He was doing his Junior Certificate, as I was, but by a correspondence course, while working to support his studies. It was a shock to realize that this stranger and I shared interests as equals—we exchanged opinions on *Macbeth,* our prescribed text—and yet we lived in such different worlds. We sensed that we were testing what lay beyond the social taboos. I have always remembered that he said my name in a way that was quite the most appealing I had yet heard it said. Feeling the excitement, but as yet unfamiliar with my own budding sexuality, I was somewhat taken aback at myself. But not as shocked as my friends at school were when I told them the next day, repeating the exact inflection of his voice. I certainly never told my parents about those wayward feelings of attraction.

Later in my life, my eldest brother's daughter was killed in a tragic accident. I flew to Johannesburg for the funeral. My brother had married a conservative Afrikaans woman, and the funeral was held in the local Dutch Reformed Church. The grief-stricken African woman who had been her nanny drove in the car with me to the service. At the church I learned that there was a separate section where she, along with the other Africans who worked on my brother's farm and had wanted to attend the service, were to sit. The section was separated from the main pews by a glass partition. The injustice of the situation raged in my body throughout the service. The church was full of white people who had hardly known the little girl, but whom I uncharitably suspected of attending the funeral for the spectacle. Yet the one person besides the immediate family, whose grief was deep and genuinely inconsolable, was not fit to sit in the church pews. My outrage reached snapping point when the "dominee" (the minister) sanctimoniously came to commiserate with me at the graveside, and I could not hold back my bitterness. Speaking my mind at that unorthodox time and place gave some measure of relief. Yet shame, guilt, and anger seem to have accompanied me throughout my white life.

One of the most difficult things has been to learn to break "the law of the father," learning to stand up to the men who, in my cultural background, were the seat of authority. The father of my childhood provided a role model for living against the grain of one's background. On the other hand, however, my father had joined the fold in his later career as a politician. His maverick political career had served to entrench white power. His vision had never really embraced a system that was truly inclusive. Increasingly, the political history of the country was shaped outside of Parliament, in the underground movement.

I was "saved" from active political involvement by the fact of my very early marriage, after which my life centered on trying to provide a stable home environment for my two daughters. Those years were full of inner conflict for me—caught between the need to admire my father despite his increasingly conservative position, trying to main-

tain my marriage to a man whose "typical" white South African attitudes on race and gender were cozily in accord with the ethos of the
sleepy rural area in which we were farming. I was stuck with my
own inability to come to a clear position or do more than make symbolic gestures of rebellion. I was (somewhat) comfortable with being
considered mad for my weird ideas, after all, it was true that I *did*
read philosophy.

We were poor by most Western standards, living in a small, uncomfortable house with no electricity (and, for a time, no hot water),
surviving for the most part on what the farm could produce. Yet we
were living a life of privilege compared with the abject poverty of the
laborers who worked on our farm. One Christmas, I received a message that the woman who worked in our home had been beaten up
by her drunk husband and was bleeding.

"You're NOT to go down there," my husband forbade me, when I
wanted to go and tend to her in her cottage. "They're all drunk.
You'll get yourself killed. And I'm not going either."

On all holidays most of the laborers were drunk. This always
made perfect sense to me, given their life prospects. That was one of
my "crazy" ideas—it was obvious that "coloreds" were just congeni-
tally degenerate, lacking in ambition and moral fiber.

"If she makes it till the day after tomorrow when they're all
sober again, I'll take her to the hospital."

I stood in her little shack for a long time. Her slightly retarded
eighteen-month-old child, naked except for a torn vest, sat on the
mud floor, swaying to and fro and moaning softly. The child's unconscious mother lay on a bare mattress, covered by a dirty blanket. A
few objects, some of which I recognized from my home, were placed
on the rickety table, the only piece of furniture in the house. My very
existence seemed anchored upon this woman's misery. As I cleaned
her wounds, my stomach churned with the sense that so much was
so desperately wrong. Short of razing the farm to the ground, nothing I could do seemed significant. I felt so helpless at the enormity of
it all, paralyzed by my own internalization of the network of personal and cultural relationships that I believed held my life in place.
The personal cost of really answering the challenges the incident
seemed to put to me, just felt too high to pay.

Only in the late 1980s once I was on my own, and had moved
back to Cape Town, did I feel free to pursue my impulses with a mixed
sense of urgency and relief. I knew very well I was reconnecting with
myself after a long detour; a reconnection strongly symbolized by
taking back my maiden name. Writing, speaking, and organizing

around intercultural and feminist issues became the focus of my professional life, and restored a sense of personal integrity. Of course, the political situation was changing—at least it was no longer illegal to engage in social activism. This was when I first went into some of the townships to attend workshops and meetings at which grassroots decisions were being made that could feed into the negotiation process. Tense and volatile as the situations in some of the townships were, working along with South Africans of all cultural groups toward a common cause, greatly deepened my insight into what my whiteness had cost me: the sense of community I had been deprived of; the friends I could have had; the freedom I had never known to inhabit my land other than as some sort of psychological squatter. These experiences reinforced the belief that the estrangement between our people need never have been, and bolstered the hope that the country could still be different. Above all, I came to know in a new way, through personal relationships, the deep humanity of the African people I had been raised to fear. Every time I stepped further into the space my society had reserved for those it demonized and dehumanized, I learned more surely what I had intuited as a little girl in the domestic worker's room in our backyard—the normalcy and complexity of lives the societal taboos intended me not to discover on the "other side."

I cannot pretend that when all of South Africa sat glued to televisions, watching Nelson Mandela step out into the sun after twenty-seven years in prison, that I did not feel fear intermingled with my elation that nothing could reverse the process of change anymore. After all the years of having been fed propaganda that depicted Nelson Mandela as an inhumane blood-lusting terrorist, the fear that the long-dreaded "swart gevaar" (black peril) was going to exact its revenge lurked somewhere in the back of most white psyches, even if one believed one had outgrown such misinformation. Only a few years before, I had been kicked out of bed, literally, for saying that sooner or later, the Nationalist government would have to talk to the ANC: I was a bad influence on the children. Reality had done a volte-face.

One of the most emotional experiences of my life was the night of our democratic elections. I was still trying to comprehend the miracle that this had been the first day of complete nonviolence in many years, despite all the predictions of impending apocalypse. Ever since the introduction of television in South Africa, the national anthem, *Die Stem,* had been played at midnight to a picture of the national flag flapping in the breeze. Like many compatriots, I was watching the election results on television, when, at midnight, *Nkosi Sikelel iAfrika* (God bless Africa), the freedom anthem of the African people, come over the air. Only a few years prior, to sing this song had been a criminal offense; now *Nkosi Sikelel iAfrica* was on national television, heralding in the New South Africa. If there was so much emotion in this moment for me, I could not but be humbled to imagine the feelings of those who had paid really dearly in their struggle for freedom.

The signal was clear that whiteness in South Africa would never be again what it used to be.

Two months after the election I left to study in the United States for two years. Inevitably, physical and psychological distance from home brought about many shifts in my understanding. Reading in postcolonialism, particularly, and working on my thesis confronted my childhood conditioning in a sustained and in-depth manner. Although deeply liberating, the process was also fraught with the feelings of guilt and betrayal that accompany writing from the insider's position. What sustains is the conviction that betrayal of "race" is loyalty to something so much greater.

Personal immersion in another Western society has sharpened my appreciation of the fact that race is certainly not just skin-deep. Indeed, it is generations deep and continents wide. I continue to struggle through the multiple fences of white identity that my heritage constructed to define me. But bits of flesh remain caught in the barbs. A white skin is not skin that can be shed without losing some blood. Yet the further I move from the center of my white conditioning, the more I find community with an ever-growing group of South Africans of all gradations of pigmentation, who care about creating a fairer, more equitable society in which we all can grow in human dignity.

Acknowledgments

༄

I would like to thank my committee at Arizona State University for their interest and warm support at every stage in the conception, planning, and writing of the thesis on which this book is based. Tom Nakayama, my committee chair, encouraged and guided my reading and thinking, and yet invested a great deal of trust in my own desires; Fred Corey challenged my writing in rigorous and stimulating ways; and Garry Rolison enriched my thinking in the area of "race" and ethnicity. I am indebted to them all, but especially to Professor Nakayama whose support has extended well beyond that of the original project. His encouragement and initiative were largely responsible for the publication of the work. I would also like to thank Judith Martin and Belle Edson who helped me along the road. A special thank you goes to my friends and family who distributed the questionnaire for me, in particular, Lafras Steyn, Robin Wilding, Judy Bekker, Valerie Morris, Damian Ruth, Melanie Steyn, Marthinus Steyn, Suzanne Stevens, Anna Stevens, Janet Jackson, Vincent Maphai, Judy Dick, and Margaret Gehner. Several persons read the manuscript as part of the research process, providing "member checks" of the substance of the thesis. In this regard I am very grateful to Cathy Barrett, Simon Bekker, Terri Grant, Janet Jackson, Charles Malan, Alison Moultrie, Damian Ruth, Suzanne Stevens, Heather Vallance, and Robin Wilding for their time and interest. My greatest debt is, of course, to the respondents who were willing to self-disclose about such a contested issue as "race" at this stage in South Africa's history.

The Fulbright Program funded my studies in the United States. I should like to express heartfelt appreciation for the opportunity provided by the scholarship. I should also like to acknowledge the

University of Cape Town for arranging special conditions of leave, and my colleagues at the Professional Communication Unit, University of Cape Town, for generously agreeing to my absence.

My deepest appreciation, however, goes to my family and close friends whose ample hearts made it possible for me to take leave from responsibilities at home to devote two years to what I wanted most—the chance to pursue my studies overseas: Mikki for her friendship and invaluable comments; Lafras, for loving and unstinting support; my mother, whose love underwrites all that I do; Suzanne, for believing in me and the work that matters to me; my father, for making me aware of the world as a political place; Reg, whose coming into my life has made it all make sense; but especially Anna, whose daily courage and selfless love are a gift to all who know her. Their love and encouragement inform every page.

Introduction

⌒

The time for the healing of wounds has come.
The moment to bridge the chasms that divide us has come.
The time to build is upon us.

—Nelson Mandela, inaugural speech, 1994

In April 1994, South Africa captured the world's imagination as a country that turned its history around, from a path that was leading to almost certain civil war, to a negotiated future based on national reconciliation. Prior to this, South Africa had the undesirable distinction in the contemporary world of being the white supremacist Apartheid society, legally structured along the axis of race, with a legacy of deeply troubled intercultural and interracial relations. The histories of the political processes, and the stories of the lives that drove, welcomed, and resisted the processes of change, display the full range of human possibilities for good and evil, inspiring rage, elation, sadness, and triumph. Increasingly, academic analyses, biographies, autobiographies, and fictional accounts of this history, informed by many different perspectives, take their place on shelves in bookstores both locally and abroad.

The social revisions brought about by the political realignment of the different population groups in relation to each other are far-reaching, complex, and multiple. Not least among these is the renegotiation of identities. South Africans, willingly or unwillingly, successfully or unsuccessfully, are engaged in one of the most profound collective psychological adjustments happening in the contemporary world. Situated in an existential moment that combines unique intersections of thrownness and agency, they are selecting, editing, and borrowing from the cultural resources available to them to reinterpret old selves in the light of new knowledge and possibilities, while yet retaining a sense of personal congruence. As they exert their imaginations to create coherent accounts that will render their past and future roles consistent with a positive self-regard, that will give meaning and security to their new position-alities, and will provide frameworks for their relationships with others, they invent and recombine fantasy and fact in both new and predictable ways. This is one of those moments in a historical process where change is so far-reaching, but also so accelerated, that one may catch the process of social construction "in the act," as South Africans shape narratives of social identity that will provide bearings in previously uncharted waters.

This moment of "gappiness"[1] in identity is true for all social groupings in contemporary South Africa. The focus of this study, however, is on how white South Africans are shaping a sense of self in the emerging society. This book joins the rapidly expanding liter-ature that examines the social construction of Western racialized whiteness,[2] that explicates its implications, and accentuates its con-testedness. The particularities of South Africa's historical process, which include the nation's demographic profile, the extremely racialized nature of the society, and the recent disruption of old power structures within the country, make a study of whiteness in this context very revealing. People who staked much of their iden-tity on their privileged whiteness are now subordinated politically, in a country that is redefining itself as African, within the African context (Ginwala, 1991; Steyn and Motshabi, 1996; Magubane, 1999; Mamdani, 1999; Mbeki, 1999). Many of the underpinnings of white identity are being challenged; moorings that still largely hold whiteness in place in Euro-American contexts have been removed. In such a situation of ambivalence and personal confusion, it is rea-sonable to expect that the meaning of whiteness will be highly con-tested ideologically, and will undergo notable changes.

Although the specific interest of this book is the New South Africa, the implications of the study extend well beyond the borders of that territory. The economic, cultural, and psychological interdepen-dence of people from European stock with their "others" in territories that they now cohabit is a reality of the contemporary world. One of Western imperialism's achievements has been to bring the world closer together (Said, 1994, p. xxi). But it is also a reality that in post-colonial times the relationships between such groups have been, and still are, undergoing realignments. The South African experience is affiliated to larger global dynamics, as history increasingly tussles with the white hegemony established in modern colonial times. In its extremity the South African situation has always been instructive, and the dramatic nature of the changes in the privileged position of "whiteness" in recent years is no exception. Indeed, if it is true that some element of trauma or bafflement needs to be present to dislodge sedimented racial identity formations (Rodriguez, 1998), then the social and political unsettlement of contemporary South African society provides an interesting case study of a nation that has been provided with a prime (un)learning opportunity.

South Africa has always been characterized by cultural, racial, and political complexity and diversity. At the time of the 1994 elections, it was estimated that of the 40.7 million people in the country, 76 percent were African, belonging to at least ten major cultural groups, 2.5 percent were Asian, predominantly Indian, 8.5 percent were colored, and 13 percent were whites, who belong to two distinct language groups, English and Afrikaans *(Race Relations Survey,* 1994/5). The complexity within and between cultural groups is intensified by the inequalities brought about by urbanization and modernization, as well as the cultures of affluence and poverty that persist as a consequence of the unequal past.

Relations between the cultural groups carry the imprints of the colonial history out of which the country is emerging (Biko, 1978; Makgoba, 1999; Rex, 1986; Steyn, 1998; Thornton, 1996; Unterhalter, 1995). When South Africa left the British Commonwealth and became a republic in 1961, it shed the last overt layer of its colonial heritage.[3] Anne McClintock (1994), however, points out that from the perspective of postcolonialism "deep settler" societies are problematic, as white settlers have a different relationship with the metropolitan centers than indigenous people. Certainly in the case of South Africa, a system of internal colonialism prevailed. White South Africans held on to European assumptions of racial and cultural superiority, of entitlement to political control and land ownership, and of the right to benefit from their access to the world capitalist system at the expense of an exploited, subjugated nonwhite majority. The results of African labor were everywhere in evidence, despite the people's invisibility within the society through lack of political and cultural representation (Nederveen Pieterse, 1992, p. 107).

Apartheid, arguably the generic form of the colonial state in Africa (Mamdani, 1996) was preeminently a policy designed to protect advantaged whiteness, particularly white Afrikanerdom through rigorous separation of racial groups. The small group of

people of European descent at the southernmost part of Africa held
onto a white identity and maintained a privileged status on a continent that elsewhere rid itself of the overt oppression of white colonizers. Whereas the wealth in other parts of the continent flowed
away from Africa along lines of unequal trade relations with the
erstwhile colonial powers, the presence of a critical mass of settled
Europeans in South Africa served to hold the wealth at "home." The
white elite group[4] (Stone, 1985) was able to maintain power politically, economically, militarily, and culturally. A protracted and finally successful struggle for freedom by the majority people of the
country, bolstered by the effects of growing international isolation
through sanctions, led to the first democratic elections in April
1994. Since then South African society has been undertaking massive reform. The economic wing of this reform was initially referred
to as the Programme of Reconstruction and Development, and later
as GEAR.[5] It can be argued that the process underway, along with
the violence that preceded it, and even the crime that accompanies
it (Steyn, 1998), is the working through of dynamics set in place by
the colonial nature of the initial contact between the racial groups
(see Stone, 1985). The present changes have therefore brought the
society into a further level of postcoloniality as cultural, racial, and
political identities are reframed internally, now on different political
and psychological terms.

　　From a postcolonial perspective, South Africa offers particular
interest. In the other "deep-settler" countries, such as the United
States of America, Canada, New Zealand, and Australia, early conquest brought about white majority rule. White South Africans, by
contrast, have always remained a small minority within the country.
Yet, for the most part, they are a permanent group; although not *abo-
riginal,* they are *sociologically indigenous* (see Stone, 1985) and make
a strong bid to legitimate co-occupancy of the land. Many have a deep
commitment to the country. Most white South Africans (especially
Afrikaners) have held little attachment to the countries of their ethnic origin, unlike white Americans, who tend to retain a stronger
"symbolic" ethnicity (see Waters, 1990). Present levels of emigration
are high,[6] especially among English-speaking whites who fit in easily
within white British colonial diaspora. Nevertheless, white South
Africans, with their powerful economic interests, will remain a permanent presence in the country. In all likelihood they will continue to
influence the course of South African history, unlike the pattern in
most instances of African decolonization, where all but a few whites
returned to the metropolitan areas of their origin.

Within the major European metropolitan centers, as well as in countries where colonial whites attained numerical majority, privileged whiteness has remained (relatively) entrenched and secure. Nevertheless, in very recent times, whiteness, even in these contexts, has been experiencing a challenge. At a theoretical and ideological level, the challenge originates from a growing literature in areas such as postmodernism, postcolonialism, cultural studies, and critical race studies. At a material level, the challenge comes in the form of changing patterns of internal demographics within the metropolitan areas through immigration and the growth of diasporas, as well as shifts in global economic patterns where some of Europe's "others" have gained ground.[7] As the postcolonial critic, Edward Said (1994) comments:

> The world has changed since Conrad and Dickens in ways that have surprised, and often alarmed, metropolitan Europeans and Americans, who now confront large non white immigrant populations in their midst, and face an impressive roster of newly empowered voices asking for their narratives to be heard. . . . [S]uch populations and voices have been there for some time, thanks to the globalized process set in motion by modern imperialism; to ignore or otherwise discount the overlapping experience of Westerners and Orientals, the interdependence of cultural terrains in which colonizer and colonized co-existed and battled each other through rival projections as well as rival geographies, narratives, and histories, is to miss what is essential about the world in the past century. (p. xx)

The recognition of "what is essential" about the manner in which power and privilege operate within the contemporary world has brought about the upsurge of academic interest in whiteness and how it interrelates with its more frequently examined other, blackness. Books and articles in fields as diverse as legal studies, literary criticism, history, cultural studies, anthropology, communication studies, sociology, psychology, music history, art history, dance history, humor studies, philosophy, linguistics, folklore and more, have been published on the topic with increasing frequency (see Fishkin, 1995). The field, which is now recognized as "White/Whiteness Studies," has achieved its coming of age with the publication of several collections, drawing together the work of many eminent scholars on the topic. (See, for example, Delgado and Stefancic,

1997; Fine et al., 1997; Frankenburg, 1997; Hill, 1997; Roediger, 1998.)

These works have "put the construction of 'whiteness' on the table to be investigated, analyzed, punctured, and probed" and brought it to "center stage as the site where power and privilege converged and conspired to sabotage ideals of justice, equality, and democracy" (Fishkin, p. 430). The starting point for the earlier scholarship on whiteness has been to name it as an issue. Scholars drew attention to the way in which race and ethnicity have been studied as social categorizations that affect "others," whereas the manner in which these categorizations constitute white identities, and shape the lives of white people, has been relatively unexamined. (Williams and Chrisman, 1994, p. 17). Dyer's (1988) articulation of the normative nature of whiteness in scholarship can be regarded as a classic description of this professional blindness:

> Looking with such passion and single-mindedness at non-dominant groups has had the effect of reproducing the sense of the oddness, differentness, exceptionality of these groups, the feeling that they are departures from the norm. Meanwhile the norm has carried on as if it is the natural, inevitable, ordinary way of being human. (p. 44)

In falling victim to this blind spot, Western scholarship has itself been an expression of how, certainly until recently, white people in the metropolitan centers have been unaware of the role race plays in shaping their lives, and "by extension how race privileges are accrued" (Hyde, 1995, p. 88). As the privileged group, whites have tended to take their identity as the standard by which everyone else is measured. This makes white identity invisible, "even to the extent that many whites do not consciously think about the profound effect being white has on their everyday lives" (Martin, Krizek, Nakayama, and Bradford, 1996, p.125). In sum, because the racialness of their own lives is edited out, white people have been able to ignore the manner in which the notion of race has structured people's life opportunities in society as a whole (Frankenberg, 1993, p.1). To expose whiteness and render it irreversibly visible was therefore the motive that propelled the current interest in the subject as a critical academic endeavor. Scholars called for whiteness to be particularized (Nakayama and Krizek, 1995), for its history and its consequences to be analyzed, and for it to be delimited and localized (Frankenberg, 1993).

That whiteness achieved this normative invisibility, now so well recognized in the literature that it is regarded by some as a critical commonplace (see Gallagher, 1999; Hill, 1998), reflects the centrality of Western ideological constructs in the modern world as we inherited it. Indeed, the notion of whiteness, and the essential attributes that it is meant to signify, can be considered a core-organizing category in modern Western ideology. The social formations it engendered have been so ubiquitous and so powerful that they came to be taken as common sense, the way things are. But it is exactly the centrality of Western, modernist ideological constructs that is challenged by oppositional contemporary theory, as it struggles to bring the ideology under conscious scrutiny.[8] Most characteristically, this is done by emphasizing issues of marginalization and colonization:

> Oppositional paradigms provide new languages through which it becomes possible to deconstruct and challenge dominant relations of power and knowledge legitimated in traditional forms of discourse. . . . What is at stake here is whether such languages offer a vision and practice for new forms of understanding, social practice, and collective struggle. (Henry A. Giroux, 1997)

It is often noted that the dizzying array of "posts" which now populate academic discourse makes it difficult to find one's theoretical bearings. Yet all the posts do have affinity through a kind of regime fatigue. "In each of these domains," Appiah (1991) explains, "there is an antecedent practice that laid claim to a certain exclusivity of insight, and in each of them the 'postmodernism' is a name for the rejection of that claim to exclusivity" (pp. 341–42). Putting it rather picturesquely, Thornton (1996) sees the postmodern as "the failure of Modernism to keep its promises, just as the postcolonial can be seen as the failure of colonialism" (pg. 138).[9]

In the case of postmodernism, the fatigue is evidenced in the acceptance of, or desire for, the breakdown of the categorizing and exclusionary structures of modernism, along with its grand narratives: the faith in rationality and science, a teleological account of history and progress, and an autonomous, potentially fully conscious individual. In the case of postcolonialism, it is the Western colonialist master narrative, with all its assumptions of the superiority, special entitlement, and unique destiny of European peoples in relation to their colonial others that has been ruptured (though not erased).[10] This includes the continuing systems of knowledge and representation that legitimize and effect contemporary political and cultural neocolonialism and imperialism, both within and between nation states. Revealing the social construction of these narratives within particular situated historical circumstances, showing whose interests the narratives have served, and bringing out the voices of those who have been relegated to the margins by the narratives, facilitates their deconstruction and "saps" their power.[11]

At least two strategies are eminently well suited to achieve the purpose of sapping the power of oppressive discourses. The first is to bring in what Michelle Fine (1994) has called "'uppity' voices, stances, and critiques to interrupt Master Narratives" (p. 75). A great deal of writing in postcolonialism, critical postmodernism, and feminism (see Giroux, 1992; 1993; 1997; 1998; McLaren, 1998) opens up ways of "giving voice to those denizens of the world who will no longer acquiesce in the uncritical celebration of nationalism and empire-building" (Hasian, 1995, p. 6). The second technique is to expose the constructions emanating from positions of domination, constructions which by their nature attempt to elude detection. Fine wryly refers to this process of exposing constructions of self and other as "Listening to elites as they manicure them-Selves through Othering" (p. 75).

A core trope in the powerful master narratives that played out their domination both internationally, and also internally within nation states, through modern colonial times, is the construct of "whiteness." In essence, then, turning the critical gaze on the dark center of whiteness is a necessary, but still embryonic, part of the postcolonial undertaking, an undertaking to which this book hopes to contribute. An early recognition of the relationship between the exposure of whiteness and decolonizing the imagination is present in Dyer's observation: "If we are to see the historical, cultural and political limitations (to put it mildly) of white world domination, it is important to see similarities, typicalities, within the seemingly infinite varieties of white representation" (Dyer, 1988, p. 47). If colonial narratives provided the social identity of whiteness, postcolonial narratives must help to redefine and complicate identities for those interpellated by discourses of whiteness, by bringing them into dialogue with "other" identities.

Complicating identities is how Frankenberg (1993) sees her work: a beginning toward "antiracist forms of whiteness, or at least antiracist strategies for reworking the terrain of whiteness" (p. 7). The task is to consider not only how race shapes the lives and experiences of Europe's "others," but how it shapes the lives and experiences of white people themselves, and how they in turn have shaped, and continue to shape, whiteness itself. The intention in redirecting attention to whiteness in this way is not to recenter an essentialized Western whiteness in reaction to the attention received by the race and ethnicity of "others." This is an acknowledged danger inherent in the focus of Whiteness Studies (Fine et al; 1997, pg. xi). The issue, rather, is to reconceptualize racial polarization as a "white problem" (Nakayama and Martin, 1993) to be located and addressed in the discourses, socialization, political and economic privilege of white people, the racial elite, rather than coming from "the existence of blacks" (Lipsitz, 1995, p. 369). This critical strategy follows the same logic as Ferguson's (1993) feminist strategy of shifting her analysis from the traditional problematizing of the position of women in society to the "man problem," and Wittig's (1992) move to challenge heterosexuality as the "problem" rather than marginalized homosexuality.

The consequence of the earlier work has been that whiteness has now truly been exposed, at least at an academic level. The historical construction of white privilege, the institutional, rhetorical, discursive, performative, and psychological strategies used to maintain its centered positionality, the economic policies used to enforce and secure advantage, the protection offered by legal systems—these issues are now established as part of academe's analytical repertoire.[12]

Numerous of these studies point to discursive, political, and economic factors in the formation of whiteness, and decisively put pay to the colonial notion that there exists a natural and homogenous white grouping "prior to their entry into the arena of social relations" (Mohanty, 1994, p. 203). Increasingly, the debates within Whiteness Studies are shifting as new studies challenge the assertion that whiteness is still invisible, and call for more nuanced analyses of whiteness. Gallagher (1997) for example, has found a growing belief among white students in the United States that they are the parties aggrieved through processes of "reverse" racial discrimination. Similarly, conservative rhetoric, which names whites (especially white men) as the victims of contemporary social practice, leads to the production of "retrogressive white identities" in which solidarity can be established through appeals to alleged white disadvantage (Apple, 1998; Giroux, 1997). Moreover, examinations of less centered groups within the white fold, such as "poor whites" (Wray and Newitz, 1997) and white women (Ware, 1992) reveal a great deal of variation, ambivalence, contradiction, and even fragility within the expectations of white privilege.

Extending this concern with different experiences of whiteness, Giroux (1997) points out that fixing whiteness as "a space between guilt and denial" is paralyzing to those whites who seek liberating subject positions. He takes issue with the theorization of whiteness that makes being white synonymous with being racist, and argues for a more nuanced and layered account of whiteness. Giroux differentiates between whiteness as a racial ideology, and the many subject positions that are open to, and adopted by, white people. Crucially, this disagggregation of whiteness allows for progressive white people to develop solidarity across racial lines, and with other non-racist white people, as they reconceptualize their identities in emancipatory ways (Kincheloe and Steinberg, 1998).

In Britain, Hickman and Walter (1995) have challenged the myth of homogeneity among white people in Britain, a myth created to establish the nation state of Britain. They flay open layers of racism within whiteness in that context, arguing that

> colonial racism stemming from Anglo-Irish relations and the construction of the Irish (Catholic) as a historically Other of the English/British (Protestant) have framed the experience of the Irish in Britain. Anti-Irish racism in Britain has comprised both elements of racism: colonial and cultural; that is, the Irish have been constructed as inferior and alien. (p. 9)

Similarly, Puar (1995) differentiates significant distinctions in positional spaces within whiteness. She describes a subject position that she refers to as "oppositionally active whiteness." It involves learning about

> the different constructions of whiteness and their points of intersection. . . . Oppositionally active whiteness is about manipulating the "terror of whiteness," changing the oppressive discourses of whiteness to discourses of subversion and power, and breaking down oppressor/oppressed dichotomies. (p. 28)

The implication is clear: it is appropriate to think in terms of *whitenesses,* rather than whiteness, just as we now know to speak of *racisms* (Appiah, 1990, Goldberg, 1990), and *patriarchies* (Mohanty, 1994). Whiteness, even when understood as a positionality of power and privilege, and not some internal, immutable essence, does not remain constant in varying circumstances. Specific whitenesses are constituted through concrete social relations and within concrete historical socioeconomic situations, while yet they may have an overall coherence through exercising domination (see Ebert, 1995; Hartigan, 1997). It is through careful comparative and historicizing study, building up an accurate knowledge of similarities, differences, and internal nuances within and between different contexts, that an understanding of the true complexities of white sway can be understood. Unless we study whiteness in this contextual manner, we run the risk, among others, of essentializing constructions of whiteness that are researched at the "center" of whiteness itself, Euro-America, beyond their legitimate scope (see Bonnet, 1998 1998b; Hartigan, 1997). Relatively little work has been done on white diasporas, which, besides being of intrinsic interest in themselves, also can throw light on racial dynamics within the center.

This book examines one context in which whiteness has been particularly virile, namely South Africa. It aims to show that the system of Apartheid was a logical, if extreme, interpretation of the trope of modern Western whiteness. With the collapse of the old legalized white regime, and the concomitant reshuffling of power, whiteness in South Africa is fragmented. Different narratives of what it means to be white are vying for legitimation in the hearts and minds of white South Africans. In this respect, whiteness in South Africa clearly demonstrates a postmodern aspect, an aspect that may become more apparent in other contexts as the white center loses its grip there, too.

The present climate in South Africa, where there is considerable resistance to talking about race as a social category, makes it necessary to say a few words about the wisdom of a study that addresses the issue of racial identity when so many South Africans are intent on dissociating the country from its racialized legacy. The constitution of the New South Africa is founded upon the premise of nonracialism, and this is increasingly part of the discourse of mainstream popular struggle (Mamdani, 1996), as it seeks to establish equality and bridge differences. Nonracialism is also often recast in the mold of liberal color-blindness, with the consequence that middle class South Africans, both black and white, frequently express the belief that drawing attention to race as a societal issue is anachronistic and harmful. To name race is taken to be racist. The most frequent comment I receive when asked about my work is "Aren't we beyond this?" The historical process through which South

Africa has traveled makes it more than understandable that South Africans display shell shock in the presence of discourses on race, ethnicity, and even culture. Yet if the structures of feeling that informed the old South African institutions are to be dismantled, an approach that takes cognizance of the long-term effects of colonialism and the concomitant processes of racialization is essential.[13]

Unless South Africans engage the processes of cultural decolonization and deracialization, and not just of desegregation, the capacity to wield power that is built into notions such as "race, progress, evolution, modernity and development" (Nederveen Pieterse and Parekh, 1995, p. 1) will continue to undermine and subvert the societal goals of human dignity, equality, human rights and freedoms, which the New South African constitution aims to guarantee. Both from reading antiracist literature, as well as from personal experience in running workshops within South Africa, I am convinced that while the processes required to create an ethos conducive to reconciliation and to imagine a new way of life based on a different consciousness are not isometric for whites and blacks, both require a constructive engagement with the past. Whereas black South Africans need to address the internalized effects of oppression, such as dependency, white South Africans cannot move forward unless they confront the extent to which their identities and personal expectations have been shaped through asymmetrical power relations, both internally within South Africa, and globally, through enmeshment within Western historical processes and ideologies. The construction of race has been used to skew this society over centuries. If we prematurely banish it from our analytical framework, we serve the narrow interests of those previously advantaged, by concealing the enduring need for redress. To deal with the expressions of power, we have to call it by its name.

A more nuanced, and therefore more difficult misgiving to come to grips with than the ploy of declaring a moratorium on racial cognizance concerns the capacity of this kind of research to achieve its emancipatory goals. Gallagher (1999) tables a pertinent disquiet on the potential for a study of white racial identity, particularly by someone who shares the background, to reproduce the common sense, dichotomous notions of race that it seeks to subvert.[14] This question can be raised at the methodological level—Are the subjects of research challenged to think in critical ways about their racial categories?—as well as at a theoretical level—Does the knowledge produced by the study create a more nuanced, antiessentialist understanding of race, such that it cannot be "the vehicle through which a sophisticated, critical essentialism is articulated" (Gallagher, 1999)? While it is extremely difficult to know the real effects of one's scholarship, the content of this book, through the narratives of whiteness that it identifies, is a very explicit analysis and theorization of the breakdown of essentialist constructions of whiteness in one particular context. The effect on the respondents is more difficult to judge. Nevertheless, in research, just as in any other arena, the concept of the learning moment is pertinent. Whether a respondent is challenged to reconsider some previously unproblematized assumption as the consequence of grappling with answering a question on his or her understanding what it means to be white, or whether the respondent will use the opportunity to further entrench that assumption, is part of the agency a person brings to the research encounter. Whether the encounter is constructed as a learning moment is, at least in part, a function of who hears the questions, and under which circumstances. A respondent who is heavily in defense or in denial will not be moved to reflection by a research question, no matter how sensitively worded. By the same token, a respondent who is ready to move forward, will, in all likelihood, recognize the challenge.[15]

Putting at least some ownership for the effects of the research process on the participants does not, of course, absolve researchers from their responsibility to reflect deeply on how their personal assumptions are implicated in the way in which they represent social issues:

[A]s theorists and researchers, we are never neutral, dispassionate observers of behavior but are always heavily implicated in the construction of the narratives (petit and grand) that provide insight into the social reality that we inhabit. (Mumby, 1993)

The new understanding of the relationship between knowledge and power brought about by poststructuralist thinking has led to the recognition that any discursive context is political; representation is acknowledged to be power. Critical scholars have become acutely conscious of the implications of who is controlling representation, and for what purposes. Denying self-representation to others, or speaking for them, as if one is "objective," "rational," and "disinterested" has been colonizing in effect (Rosaldo, 1989; Krippendorf, 1989, 1993). As mentioned above, one of the central concerns of postcolonialism is therefore to bring in voices from the margins, and to show the internal differences in what colonizing discourse represents as homogenous and unproblematic. Postmodernism, in turn, also strives to find ways of representation that suggest that closure has not been achieved, means of representation that *dis-* close the situated constructedness of whatever wishes to pass for knowledge.

Fine (1994) points out that people in academia that want to make a difference are placed in a profound contradiction. We may want to use the power we occupy by virtue of being producers of knowledge in the interests of greater freedom and justice. Yet in the very act of writing about research subjects, we collude with structures of domination. Remaining silent may simply avoid responsibility and accountability, allowing the status quo to continue (Alcoff, 1991). Both Alcoff and Fine suggest that in this minefield there is no easy answer—retreat, engagement, silence—all carry ethical implications. They advocate careful analysis of the material and contextual particularities of the situation under study, and rigorous self-analysis.

Indeed, the capacity for self-reflexivity is considered one of the major consequences of, and requirements for, living within the late twentieth century. Anderson (1990) relates this self-consciousness to our growing awareness of the multidimensional quality of human experience. The awareness accompanies the admission that "all explanations of reality are themselves constructions—human, useful, but not perfect," and the ability to "step out" of reality constructs and see them as such (pp. 254–55). Lather (1991) relates self-reflexivity to the context of academic writing:

> to make something available for discussion is to make of it an object. This suspicion of the intellectual who both objectifies and speaks for others inveighs us to develop a kind of self-reflexivity that will enable us to look closely at our own practice in terms of how we contribute to dominance in spite of our liberatory intentions. (p. ix)

Applying this sensitization to research on "whiteness," Nakayama and Krizek (1995) call for scholars to be self-reflexive about the "effects of whiteness on our research and on our personal academic pursuits" (p. 30). They invite scholars to begin to mark and incorporate their whiteness into their analyses, making the positionality from which the representation originates visible. Given this sensitization, I can hardly write as if I were unaware of how, in the act of researching fellow "white" South Africans, I am automatically involved in a process of "othering," a process that may seem to imply that I am in some way separate from, and immune to, the issues of whiteness about which I have asked them to self-disclose. This outsider status that is conferred by the process of research was probably augmented by the fact that my research was being conducted from the United States during a two-year sojourn. Indeed, a perception on the part of respondents that they were being subjected to an uncompromising academic gaze would have been somewhat justified, too. Being removed from "home" across time and distance provided a sense of perspective sense of perspective, and a feeling of freedom to write what I saw in the data, neither of which I could have achieved while imbricated within the emotional and psychological webs of family loyalties and social pressures. Dealing with the intense emotional responses that accompanied writing the thesis on which this book is based was an important part of my personal and academic development. The contradictory emotions were a clear indication of the intersectional, insider-outsider nature of researching of one's "own" group.[16]

As Alcoff (1991) indicates, however, it is difficult even to determine what constitutes the "same" group. In those cases where I am ideologically aligned with the "others" of the respondents, I may be telling on respondents rather than speaking for them. Yet what this alerts me to is the need to resist the temptation to try to create a "pure" identity for myself through the power of academic discourse. I know that there are traces of all the narratives described in this book within me. As a white South African I am greatly implicated in racism and structural privilege; I am part of what I study. In the research I had to name my whiteness, inasmuch the respondents were confronted by theirs the instant they knew the topic of the research. My respondents' texts occasioned a great deal of self-reflection, and the final product displays my learning as much as my analysis. Both of these are part of an ongoing process of grappling with what it means to be white in South Africa.

Complicating the ethical issue even further is the intuition that assumptions of racial affinity, even solidarity (see Gallagher, 1999) were triggered by the insider aspect of my relationship to the respondents. These assuptions played an important part in the dynamics between researcher and researched, contributing to the kind of information the respondents were prepared to share. So, for example, some respondents were clearly confiding in me, some even crying for help, assuming that as an insider I would understand the injustice that they were suffering and that I was well placed to plead their cause in the wider world. Others were suspicious of what they perceived to be an attempt by a race traitor to set them up. ("You just want to go and prove that we're all racist," one of my contacts accused me.) Yet others were pushing me away, distancing themselves from what they clearly perceived to be implied racial collusion on my part, which they regarded as insulting. My interpretation of these reactions to being sounded out on their orientation toward their racialization became part of the data that helped to give shape to the narratives in this book.

The privileged access which researching one's own culture enables, while advantageous in some respects, certainly presents pitfalls attributable to sharing the cultural processes of those one studies (Chock, 1986). Unconsciously, the researcher may reproduce the same assumptions in theoretical discourse that respondents produce in their common sense discourse producing what Geertz (1983) has called "an ethnography of witchcraft as written by a witch."[17] In the final chapter I reflect upon the conclusions to which my analysis led me, and how the narrative that emerged to provide insight into the social reality which we inhabit is a product of my own situatedness as a white South African.

The final section of this introduction concerns the methodology of the study on which the book is based. Exploring the social construction of "whiteness" in contemporary South Africa led me into two phases of research. Both phases involved discourse analysis.[18]

The first phase was conceptual and historical, and is the matter of section one in this book. In this section I have tried to provide enough background to current South Africa to provide the reader with some sense of the "characteristics and composition of the total structure of mind" (Billig, 1988, p. 200) of this region, the patterns of beliefs around questions of race that have shaped this social context. The second phase was empirical, and is covered in section two. In this phase, the patterns of explanations offered by the respondents of their new position in the country are "placed" in relation to the broader precedents outlined in section one, and also in relation to each other. The narratives show positions of varying degrees of resistance and openness to change. Some further discussion of the procedures by which I arrived at these narratives is given at the beginning of section two.

The logistics of the study, which had to be conducted from a different continent, required that I be somewhat innovative in methodology. As I was not able to interview the respondents personally, but felt that the information I wanted could not be obtained through the usual survey techniques, I constructed a short series of open-ended questions that in effect guided respondents to tell their stories. The questionnaire tried, in abbreviated form, to obtain information on early experiences of whiteness and interpretations of these experiences; levels of insight into how whiteness has influenced the respondents' lives; whether their perception of their whiteness is informed by an awareness of how others may perceive them; and how they foresee the future for their whiteness. Nine of the open-ended questions were intended to elicit, as far as possible, full personal responses that would be amenable to qualitative analysis. The final question was an invitation to write anything they felt relevant to the topic, and many respondents used this as a space to expand on some of their comments.

Copies of the questionnaire were posted and faxed to family and acquaintances (fourteen in all) that live in different parts of South Africa, and they were asked to "snowball" the questionnaire to white people in their work environments and social circles. Fifty-nine responses were received, most of which were fully answered. While the sample is clearly a sample of convenience, and does not in any way claim to be a "representative" random sample, an effort was made to obtain a range of responses, in terms of geographical region, language, age, gender, qualification, occupation, and income. An analysis of some of the dynamics of the study and a full breakdown of the sample are given in Appendix 1.

The information in the responses was analyzed in order to identify the discernible "narratives of whiteness" that emerged from a close critical reading. Section two presents these narratives, substantiated with quotations from the responses, and a brief descriptor of the respondent.

The narrative should be regarded as the "unit of analysis" in my study, and some explanation of the way in which I use this term is necessary. The five narratives that are outlined in section two are not personal accounts of sequential events, told by five different individuals. Rather, they are each a metastory, my systematic interpretation of the manner in which the respondents organized their memories, made sense of recent events, imagined the motives of others as they created coherent plot-lines to explain racial relationships, engaged in impression-management, and used the cultural resources available to them to fashion identities under changing circumstances.[19] The narratives I outline, therefore, are not literal "stories," but are the descriptions of the respondents' "world making":

> We [use] the term "story" as a commonsense description of
> ways that people explain how the world got to be the way it
> is and what is happening and is likely to happen. (Walter
> Truett Anderson, 1990, pg. 243)

Narratives in this sense are historical social constructions that
provide a frame of interpretation through which we make sense of
the world and our place in it, and thus constitute our sense of reality.[20] They are the coherent systems of meaning we construct to explain, legitimize, and guide our actions in the world. Our narratives
are therefore part of the struggle for meaning. Through this struggle
we negotiate the social world within the "complex and shifting terrain of meaning" (Mumby, 1993, p. 3) to which we have access as social beings. Such a contested environment allows us to create many
competing renderings of what that world is, using the repertoire of
meanings that are at hand,[21] but it also reveals that the struggle is
charged with vested interests between competing power blocks and
ideological formations.[22]

Of interest to my account of whiteness in contemporary South
Africa is that through a process of "sedimentation," dominant meanings become fixed. A shift in power relations may bring about a "moment of antagonism" when alternative worldviews, contending to fix
meaning in other articulations, render visible the possibility of a different resolution (see Mumby, p. 7, after Laclau). My analysis attempts to uncover alternative, contending narratives that are being
constructed to make sense of whiteness in a situation of political uncertainty, a "moment of antagonism," when the hitherto confidently
dominant construction of whiteness has been unseated.

In analyzing the words of my respondents, and formulating the
emergent versions of world making, I do not pretend to have
achieved an objective resolution of what is "out there" in the responses of the respondents. The constructions I identify are my stories about my respondents' stories of their whiteness, and my attempt to explain how these are tied into the larger social story
(Gergen, 1988). I have not achieved closure, or arrived at "truth
about something already made." I will attempt, pragmatically
rather, "to construct something that works cognitively, that fits together and handles new cases, that may implement further inquiry
and invention" (Schwandt, p. 127).

In this spirit, then, the first chapter provides a thumbnail ge-
nealogy of the social construction of whiteness. Using secondary
sources, this section traces how whiteness came into being as a social

identity at the time of European global expansion and the subsequent period of colonization, particularly in relation to Africa and Africans. This section analyzes the major discourses that were synthesized in creating the discourse of whiteness. This resultant discourse is taken as the "master narrative of whiteness"—the discourse that established the broad contours of white identity, and formed the hegemonic core discourse for subsequent and divergent articulations of whiteness.

The second chapter relates the particular articulations of whiteness that took shape in South Africa. As in the previous chapter, this section draws on secondary sources to identify some of the most salient features of the particularities of South African whiteness, paying attention both to the relationship between the two major white groups, as well as to their relationships with the non white people of the country, who at all times formed the backdrop to discourses about whiteness within the country.

Section two examines the ways in which white South Africans are constructing the meaning of whiteness subsequent to political change. This section analyzes and discusses the responses to surveys that were completed by white South Africans in the first three months of 1996, identifying five major narratives. The final chapter discusses the import of these narratives within South Africa, and then considers some theoretical implications of the findings.

Section One

~

Early Tales

A story is *not* just a story. Once the forces have been aroused and set into motion they can't simply be stopped at someone's request. Once told, the story is bound to circulate; humanized, it may have a temporary end, but its effects linger on and its end is never truly an end.

—Trinh T. Minh-ha, *Woman, Native, Other*

Chapter 1

༄

A Master Narrative of Whiteness

The power to narrate, or to block other narratives from forming and emerging, is very important to culture and imperialism, and constitutes one of the main connections between
them.

—Edward W. Said, *Culture and Imperialism*

Global stories are simultaneously attempts to explain the
world—to create a new global reality—and attempts to further
the aspirations, hopes, political agendas, and ego needs of different groups of people.

—Walter Truett Anderson, *Reality Isn't What It Used To Be*

The mental landscape that enabled the emergence of patterns
of signification that I am calling a "master narrative of whiteness"[1]
was present in myths of Europe's role in world relations, long before
the actual inception of colonial conquest. The broad contours of the
ideology that was to shape Europe's relationship with its others can
be seen in medieval representations of the earth, which placed
Christendom (sometimes identified with Jerusalem) at the center of
maps of the world.[2] These representations gave way in the sixteenth
century to images that unequivocally centered Europe, often portrayed in classical trappings, celebrating not only its Christianity,
but also its commerce, and, in time, its empire:

Global stories are simultaneously attempts to explain the imagery of Eurocentrism succeeded the imagery of
Christendom and passed over into the imagery of European
colonialism. . . . The hierarchical logic and tenor of the

3

iconography remained basically unaltered into the twentieth century, when European monuments commemorating
empire and colonialism continue to display a similar view of
international or intercontinental relations. . . . The myths of
Africa and the other continents correlate with a myth of Europe itself. (Nederveen Pieterse, 1992, pp. 20–23)

During the ancient and medieval periods, European discourses
about black Africans underwent several transmutations. These
shifts depended on the dynamics that were at play within Europe itself, not on changes that occurred within the people being represented, and were largely confabulated in the absence of any real experience of Africa or Africans.[3] The fifteenth century marked the
beginning of renewed direct European contact with Africa. Before
any systematic attempt on the part of the Europeans to impose political and economic domination, this period was one of mutual discovery and often partnership (Davidson, 1994, p. 42). Citing mem-
oirs of early European travelers in Portuguese, Dutch, and English,
Davidson describes encounters that were cast in terms of difference,
but not inferiority:

> [T]hey found much to astonish them in custom and belief:
> that king, and even citizens, could have the possession of
> many wives; that shrines were raised to ancestors who were
> revered as gods; that human sacrifice could be practiced on
> certain though few occasions of ritual solemnity; and much
> else besides. Essentially, however . . . [they] found what ap-
> peared to them neither strange nor perverse, but natural
> and even familiar. They found polities whose concern for
> trade appeared much the same as their own, whose laws
> were seen to be generally respected, and whose sense of in-
> dependence, as well as their will and ability to defend that
> independence, were never in serious doubt. They found
> kings who were held to be divine—sanctioned that is, by
> spiritual as well as temporal authority—in much the same
> meaning of degree as their own kings in Europe. (pp. 42–43)

The beginning of an entirely new relationship between Europe
and Africa was established when "in 1441 ten Africans from the
northern Guinea coast were shipped to Portugal as a gift to Prince
Henry" (Nederveen Pieterse, 1992, p. 28). Although these Africans
were not intended as slaves, a Portuguese trade in African slaves

was soon established. At this stage, the slave trade was not limited to black people. People of European origin were also sold as unfree labor, depending on the needs of production (Boulton, 1995; Guillaumin, 1995; Nederveen Pieterse, 1992). Moreover, discourses about black people were still fluid and varied. For example, Ethiopianism, "a love for black Africans and a preoccupation with a fabulous prince somewhere in Africa" (Nederveen Pieterse, p. 28) was present in Europe into the seventeenth century. Nevertheless, the sixteenth and seventeenth centuries were a period of gradual transition, until, by the eighteenth and nineteenth centuries, discourses of blackness had set into images of condescension and denigration. Blackness had come to be taken as the natural mark of slaves, replacing mechanical artificial systems of branding. Enslavement of Europeans had become an abomination (Davidson, 1994, p. 57). The "familiar European contempt for Africans . . . was an attitude born of the slave trade after about 1650, and later, of the cultures of European capitalism. It has no instrumental existence before" (Davidson, p. 43).

In tandem with these developments in the way Africans were viewed, the whiteness of Europeans had been established.[4] Ostensibly their light skin signified a natural grouping of people, who through a superiority "endogenously determined" (see Guillaumin, 1995), occupied a dominant relationship to darker skinned people.[5] On the contrary, though, the grouping that came to regard itself as the white race was in fact the outcome of asymmetrical social relations, and not their cause (see Guillaumin, 1995). While not particularly unifying across troublesome ethnic boundaries within Europe, the invention of whiteness provided people from Europe with a supranationalism[6] that enabled them to ensure that the emerging social formations brought about by European expansion were articulated to their greatest self-interest. Balibar (1990) explains:

> [T]he European, or Euro-American, nations fiercely competing for the world's economic spoils recognized an identity and an "equality" in this very competition, which they baptized "white." (p. 286)

In other words, Europeans whitened as they expanded and conquered, developing a common identity by using Africans as the main foil against which they defined themselves[7] (Lipsitz, 1995; Segrest, 1994). The significant point is that race was established relationally:

> [B]lackness and whiteness can only be understood as a pair.
> . . . European colonists became whites only in parallel with
> their identification of those they colonized as blacks. (Thiele,
> 1991, p. 184)

A light skin color could then become the signifier that interiorized
and acted as shorthand for other markers of European origin, such
as European language, technological advantage, and Christianity.[8]
For those Europeans who settled in the new territories, whiteness
fixed their privilege in the colonies, often reversing the status they
held in their country of origin (Brantlinger, 1985; Roediger, 1991;
Segrest, 1994). Whiteness ensured that they were inserted into the
economy advantageously, and provided a means of social control
over the indigenous populations and other dark skinned people
where these had been imported as labor (Allen, 1994; Chafe, 1992).

In creating a master narrative of whiteness through the process
of marking African blackness, Europeans drew on the various discursive repertoires available to them. They gave these discourses a
new spin, particularly in terms of the developing Enlightenment
consciousness. As Cohen (1992) puts it: "The racist imagination
turns the world upside down, but it does so through a conservative
appropriation of existing structures and discourses of power" (p. 90).

Reaching back into the various discursive resources available to
them, early European, notably Greek discourses of the savage and
the barbarian, medieval Christian mythology, and the notion of the
chain of being that had been present in Europe in some form since
Aristotle were all recycled (Mudimbe, 1994; Nederveen Pieterse,
1992). The narratives taken from such different domains were able
to complement and supplement each other in the service of the imperial project. In time, interlocking strains of these discourses were
incorporated into the new Enlightenment narratives of the science
of race, which were to emerge.

The next section of this chapter will trace how these discourses
were tailored and co-opted to construct a master narrative of whiteness. At once an instrument of, and backed by, the mighty power of
empire, this is a patterning of discourses that could oust other possible explanatory and constitutive discourses around markers of difference between the peoples enmeshed in colonial encounter. It
could make available particular subject positions to different
groups, and groups within groups, with differing opportunities for
self-definition and agency. Such was the power of this narrative that
it could largely determine the scope of its own hegemony, securing

that people would buy into the social identities offered to them, even securing the extent and nature of possible resistance to these identities (see Bové, 1995). Criss-crossed with contradictions, mutating over time, and varying in different geographical and social contexts, the narrative was able to absorb conflicting evidence, and remain amazingly resilient and long-lived (see, for example, Coombes, 1994). The modernist construction of a homogenous, superior "whiteness" played a central part in colonial discourse. It provided justification for the most horrendous destruction of human life and society, and changed the geographical, cultural, and psychological landscape of the globe.

The Cultured and The Savage

The notion of the savage, so central to colonial discourse, had in fact been around in Europe for centuries prior to Europe's expansion. Savagery was associated with the areas of early Europe that had not yet been cultivated:

As regions dominated by the forces of nature they were mysterious, numinous—the domain of Pan and Bacchus for the Greeks. . . . The middle ages were Europe's time of transition from wilderness to cultivation (culture), and the forests were the domain of beings on the border-line between human and animal, myth and reality, like the *homo ferus* who was raised by wolves, and the *homo sylvestris,* or man of the woods. (Nederveen Pieterse, 1992, p. 30)

In time the distinction between culture, or cultivation, and savagery became blurred with another distinction, namely between *civilitas* and *barbaries* (Nederveen Pieterse, p. 31). While originally this referred to a language difference: the Greeks called all non-Greeks "barbaroi,"[9] the term acquired connotations of "baseness" and "rudeness" and merged with the notion of savageness (Nederveen Pieterse, p. 31).

As European commerce expanded, Europe saw itself as the cultivated center of the world, and it applied the notion of the savage to the non-European regions. Whereas before "humanity minus culture" had ambiguous connotations,[10] it became fixed into "a single and utterly negative meaning" (Nederveen Pieterse, p. 34). Africa, particularly, was "the land of the grotesque—grotesque creatures with grotesque features, grotesque mentalities, and grotesque habits" (Owomoyela, 1996). To secure the distinction between the center and its others, some versions of the narrative postulated that the original primitives from whom Europeans evolved contained the seeds of progress, whereas "modern" savages could never progress.[11] Nederveen Pieterse quotes an *Edinburgh Review* of 1802: "Europe is the light of the world, and the ark of knowledge: upon the welfare of Europe, hangs the destiny of most remote and savage people" (p. 34).

The Enlightenment spin—the faith in reason and the notion of history as progress, with white, cultivated Europe at the helm—is clear from this quotation. Africans, as the signifier of most other of the not-European, were assimilated into reasonless nature, smudged into a semihumanity, arrested in a shadowy past without history, without cultures of their own. African heritage was not worth preserving (Coombes, 1994). Erasing, and then rewriting the cultural memory of the natives was an essential undertaking, even moral duty (Mudimbe, 1994, Van Sertima, 1999), as true cultural creativity and historical agency came with a white skin:

> Since Africans could produce nothing of value; the technique of Yoruba statuary must have come from the Egyptians; Benin art must be a Portuguese creation; the architectural achievement of Zimbabwe was due to Arab technicians; and Hausa and Buganda statecraft were inventions of white invaders. (Mudimbe, 1988, p. 13)

Global historical agency closely equates with imperialism. Commenting on colonial explanations for the Great Zimbabwe ruins, Chrisman (1994) comments:

> The quest to find a "rational" explanation for the existence of the ruins mirrors imperial discourse's attempts to find rationality for its own operation, but the quest is also to mystify these ruins, to inscribe them as a vacant site of indeterminacy. (p. 508)

Whiteness brought the power to define both self and other,[12] a power that whites could *wield* (Frye, 1983) to "justify the process of inventing and conquering a continent and naming its 'primitiveness' or 'disorder,' as well as the subsequent means of its exploitation and methods for its 'regeneration'" (Mudimbe, 1988, p. 20). Africa therefore became subsumed within modernist Western models of history.

History centered the West, and was a legitimating narrative for Europe's mandate for Africa (see Blaut, 1993; Mudimbe, 1988). Generous versions of this historiography postulated the progress Africa would achieve under the tutelage of Europe's emissaries—from primitiveness and paganism on the one hand, to civilization and Christianity on the other—by means of evolution, conversion, and modernization. This is a model of history permeated with the notion of Eurocentric diffusionism, the belief that because of Europe's innate superiority,

> Europe eternally advances, progresses, modernizes. The rest of the world advances more sluggishly, or stagnates: it is "traditional society." Therefore the world has a permanent geographical center and a permanent periphery: An Inside and an Outside. . . . [c]ultural processes. . . . tend to flow out of the European sector and toward the non-European sector. This is the natural, normal, logical, and ethical flow of culture, of innovation, of human causality. (Blaut, 1993, p.1)

The power to define and order to their own liking the world of those they were colonizing predisposed Europeans to only the very most superficial knowledge of the people they were marking as black (Trinh, 1989). Part of the privilege of being white was that one could choose not to hear, not to know. Africans could teach Europe nothing, except, as Mudimbe (1988) puts it, "proof of what was already in their imagination" (p.13), the contents of their "epistemological ethnocentrism" (p. 15). Frye (1983) refers to the "determined ignorance" of whites, and points out the embeddedness of the word "ignore" within "ignorance": "Ignorance is not something simple: it is not a simple lack, absence, or emptiness, and it is not a passive state. . . . [it] is a complex result of many acts and many negligences" (p. 118).

The lack of both self-knowledge, and of grounded knowledge of the people they were creating as the black race, allowed whites to continue creating homogenous, "mythical portraits" both of themselves and of their others:

> Nothing could better justify the colonizer's privileged position than his industry, and nothing could better justify the colonized's destitution than his indolence. The mythical portrait of the colonized therefore includes an unbelievable laziness, and that of the colonizer, a virtuous taste for action. At

the same time the colonizer suggests that employing the colonized is not very profitable, thereby authorizing his unreasonable wages. (Memmi, 1990, p. 145)

Such conceptions, abstracted from reality, were based either on negative comparisons or on absences: Africans had no clothes, no letters, no husbandry, no decent kinship systems, no virtue, no restraint (see Nederveen Pieterse, 1992, p. 35). The European was the presence against which the other was marked. The self-interest that informed such imaginary formations needs no explication. Brantlinger (1985) indicates that the construction of Africans as primitive and unimprovable necessitated that they should have civilized masters. It also realized the "central fantasy of imperialism" by furnishing a continent populated with a natural laboring class (p. 181). The construction also ensured that colonization could continue indefinitely, with whites as entrepreneurs. Whiteness emerged and matured in complicity with capitalism (Bonnett, 1998a; Segrest, 1994) and has always been antisocialist (Allen, 1994, p. 38).[13]

A lack of appreciation of the individual humanity of others, who were valued entirely in terms of their surplus value to whites, meant that there were few restraints in the treatment of the Africans. Outrage in the voice of Magubane (1999) still smolders:

[T]he European Renaissance was not simply the freedom of spirit and body for European men, but a new freedom to destroy freedom for the rest of humanity. It was the freedom for the mercantilist bourgeoisie to loot, plunder and steal from the rest of the world. In the process, African people became not human beings, but chattels valued as so much horsepower. . . . The celebrated period of European Enlightenment brought colonized humanity nothing but darkness, degradation, racism and misery. (pp. 21–22)

Avoidance of dealing with human complexity and normal human interaction factored into whiteness a sinister proclivity for genocide, at a psychological and even physical level. Allen (1994) regards destruction of the social identity of subjugated people as central to the functioning of white identity, whereas Brantlinger (1995) observes:

As the British and other empires expanded during the nineteenth century, "savages" who stood in the path of

"civilization" were dealt with in ways that can only be
called genocidal. (p. 44)

For those intent on expansion, justification for the extinction of
primitive, "dying" races in the encounter with "higher" ones was its
apparent inevitability (1985, 1995); fantasies of genocide were an
integral part of the colonizing imagination. The package deal of
white civilization included the rights of both appropriation and
obliteration.

In sum, Europe's narratives about its own cultural distinction,
as opposed to the degradation of others, formed an important thread
in the net of discourses whiteness knotted around the globe. Before
examining another thread, the discourses of Christianity and hea-
thenism, the last word goes to Magubane (1999):

> The destruction of the humanity of the African, the Euro-
> pean belief in white supremacy, was more degrading than
> anything else. Nothing is more injurious to human relation-
> ships than for one group of people to have absolute power
> over others, as the white world had over Africa and its peo-
> ple. (p. 30)

Christians and Heathens

Reconfigured discourses about the cultured nature of Europeans as opposed to the black savage were important to the shaping
of whiteness. Christian narratives, predictably, also provided discourses about saved souls as opposed to heathens, tropes which
were integrated into the construction of white identity. The biblical
story of Noah's curse of Ham's son—"Cursed be Canaan, a servant of
servants shall he be unto his brethren"—for example, was seen as
an explanation of and justification for slavery. The story provided an
account that assuaged any pangs of conscience brought on by awkward convictions of the equality of humanity before God. By the seventeenth century the explanation included the notion that the curse
had been responsible for the darker skin color of Africans. Nederveen Pieterse (1992) sums it up:

> The view of Africa as a continent condemned to eternal
> servitude was eminently suited to a theological assessment

of slavery. Its attractiveness was that the unity of creation remained intact while an exceptional position was yet justified for Africans. (p. 44)

The white master race was sanctioned by divinity.

Probably more important than any specific narrative that Christianity contributed to the construction of whiteness, however, was the underlying textual field[14] within which such stories were embedded, a field that acted as the silent guard or gatekeeper of meaning construction (Ferguson, 1994) and which legitimized racist thinking. Here we are dealing with a semiotic world, the rhetorical and grammatical practices of Christianity. Typically, Christianity was framed within a moral framework of dualism (Hodge, 1990), where good was symbolized by God, and evil by the devil. These two competing forces struggled for dominion over each person's soul. Although many religions operate within a dualistic framework, Hodge points out that a particular additional element in Western culture is the assumption that: "the forces of good are reflected in reason, rationality, or the rule of law. The forces of evil, on the other hand, are reflected in passion, emotion, chance and nature" (p. 95). The symbolism of light and darkness was probably derived "from astrology, alchemy, Gnosticism and forms of Manicheanism; in itself it had nothing to do with skin color" (Nederveen Pieterse, 1992, p. 24), but during the early Christian period, black came to be the color of the devil. This association gave an innate moral authority to white people.

The greatest advantage of marking people in terms of skin color was that it was permanent, given at birth, and could seem to be the way one was created. Inequality therefore did not need to be analyzed; it could be taken as a condition (see Guillaumin, 1995). The identification of the white self with light, and therefore the good, could be further extended through Manichean allegory—"a field of diverse yet interchangeable oppositions between white and black, good and evil, superiority and inferiority, civilization and savagery, intelligence and emotion, rationality and sensuality, self and Other, subject and object" (JanMohamed, 1985, p. 63). As JanMohamed argues, through metonymic substitution the phenomenologically neutral fact of skin color could be converted into a moral and metaphysical difference:

[M]issionary image-building consisted of a Manichean double face, with on the one hand the demonized image of the

heathen under the devil's spell, and on the other the ro-
manticized self-image of the missionary in the role of sav-
iour. These two stereotypes were interdependent: for the
missions to justify themselves the heathen *had to be* perceived and labelled as degraded creatures stuck deep in
darkness who needed to be brought to the light. The glory as
well as the fund-raising of the missions were in direct proportion to the degradation and diabolism of the heathen.
(Nederveen Pieterse, 1992, p. 71)

Within this sociocognitive perspective framed by Christianity,
"clean," "white," "fair," "light," and "good," were clustered together as
the foundations of both esthetics and civilization, reflected in the in-
junction that "cleanliness is next to godliness." "Soap became both a
symbol and yardstick of civilization" (Nederveen Pieterse, p. 196).
Trying to whitewash what is "dark," "black," "dirty," "sinful," and
"evil" became the definition of the impossible. Showing a complete
disregard for accuracy or truth, such chains of signifiers, fixed in opposition to each other, served the ideological function of furthering
imperialism, often triggering discourses of violence, and aggressive
behavior.

Commenting on the tension between the mission and the village,
Mudimbe (1994) shows how the logic of conversion would draw on
such oppositions. The village, contrary to the virtues encapsulated in
the mission, dwelt in "materialism," "debasement," and "slow moral
progress," caught up in "sorcery" and "enslavement to the appetites
and instincts." The absence of "true" values required "replacement."
Undoubtedly, the real lines of influence were considerably more complex than this; practices and ideas were borrowed from the colonies,
and fed back into the home areas, playing a significant constitutive
role in the self-construction of the centers (Williams and Chrisman,
1994; Coombes, 1994). The colonizer, particularly in the form of the
missionary, however, was represented as a benefactor: "Considerable
emphasis was placed on their ability to destroy evils portrayed as entrenched in African society, and to change moral weaknesses they believed to be inherent in the people and destructive of the common
good of the indigenous race" (Coombes 1994, p. 176).

With varying degrees of sophistication, the missionary societies
were able to deliberately present themselves "as the more humanitarian and philanthropic face of colonialism, through the rhetoric of
'brotherly love' " (Coombes, 1994), thus participating in the imperial
project without losing their moral high ground.

The process of identifying the self with a chain of signifiers that are deemed to be desirable, while identifying those one subjugates with the oppositional chain that one rejects, the mechanism of othering (Trinh, 1989), is fundamentally constitutive of the narrative of white identity. The (ideologically driven) psychological projection attempts to create a pure, homogeneous identity for the self, while simultaneously creating a focus in the other for all the qualities one cannot tolerate in oneself, a kind of inverted self-image (JanMohamed, 1985). The other, perceived as teeming with all the devils one most wants to disassociate from, therefore becomes extremely threatening, and a focus for hate and aggression. Yet this very baseness reflects one's own superiority. JanMohamed (1985) draws attention to this as a process of accumulating "surplus morality," and stresses the affective pleasure colonizers derived from colonialist discourse. Within the moral order thus established, the oppressor is both master and innocent (Memmi, 1990, p.142). Such self-gratification (Trinh, 1989) is clearly a bonus to the economic benefits derived from being white, which Gates (1985) regards as the main reason why whites cling to racism.

Despite providing self-congratulatory strokes, such pure whiteness is inherently unstable (Memmi, 1990). The illusion of a singular, fixed, and essential self is ironically achieved only in relationship (Mohanty, 1994), through projection. Deriving its sense of homogeneity from exclusions, denials, and repressions, the white identity tends toward alienation from its own unconscious desire (JanMohamed, 1985). Despite all pretensions of rationality, the white colonial enterprise testifies to the fears and desires of the white colonizer acted onto, and through, black bodies. The desire for power and domination, which operates in this dynamic, requires no further explication. Guilt for the suffering of the oppressed was displaced onto the victims themselves, the familiar technique of blaming the victim (Memmi, 1990). The absurdity of the ensuing logic is well-illustrated by Brantlinger (1985), who points out that Africans even came to be considered responsible for their own slavery.

Similarly, imaginary constructs of natives absorbed the savage impulses and behavior of settlers. Segrest (1994) writes about early American colonizers:

> [C]olonialists living in cave-like holes dug up and devoured newly buried corpses, one man killing his wife, salting and eating all parts of her body except her head. European settlers in such new worlds probably often found themselves in such desperate situations acting similarly savage and

animal-like, responses which intensified their need to project such characteristics onto the people they encountered. (p. 187)

Nederveen Pieterse (1992) avers that there is in fact no basis for truth in the myth of cannibalism in Africa,[15] but that the accusation of cannibalism served as a central justification for conquest by establishing an enemy image, and a rhetorical device for defining the center and periphery within the colonial Christian moral order. He indicates that the emergence of this fantasy has been attributed to a psychosis of domination (pp. 113–22).

The sexual content of these white projections, originating within a Christian/Western mind/body dichotomy (see Segrest, 1994) has been noted by numerous scholars.[16] Segrest comments:

> British (and other European) explorers projected their disquieting sexual feelings onto the darker, seemingly less inhibited peoples with whom they came into contact. . . . This tendency of Christian men to project sexual desire onto an Other, then to exterminate the "polluted" was already in practice in the witch burnings in Europe. (p. 191)

The more insecure the Victorians were about their sexuality, the more they exoticized and exaggerated the physicality in general (Coombes, 1994), and sexuality in particular, of Africans. "[T]he paranoid fantasy was endlessly repeated: the uncontrollable sexual drive of the non-white races and their limitless fertility" (Young, 1995). Myths abounded about the large penises of African men, and the elongated labia of Hottentot women. Colonialism was locked into a dialectic of attraction and repulsion (Young, 1995). This mixture of disgust and fatal attraction,[17] is evident in the fear of going native (Brantlinger, 1985), revealing an element of racial envy that typifies this trading of places: "[E]nvy is an ambivalent structure of feeling; it involves the desire to possess certain idealized attributes of the Other *and* the desire to destroy them because they signify what is felt to be lacking" (Cohen, 1992, p. 90).

Nederveen Pieterse's (1992) observation is pertinent: "[S]ubliminal sexuality takes on larger, more extravagant forms. Subsequently a connection can arise between the control and repression of one's own sexuality and the control and repression of "others" (p. 172). The sexual dimension of white violence is seldom far beneath the surface, as is obvious from the castrations that often accompanied the lynchings of African American men in the southern United States.

Whether one analyzes the effects of this trading places by means of Lacanian split subject theory,[18] or Derridean deconstruction,[19] the conclusion is the same—the psychological dependence of the oppressor on the oppressed for a sense of identity: "It is the black condition, and only that, which informs the consciousness of white people. It is a terrible paradox, but those who believed that they could control and define Black people divested themselves of the power to control and define themselves" (Baldwin, 1984, quoted in Segrest, 1994). The purer white the identity, the more dependent it is on its black other.[20] The power given to the other in this psychological dynamic is immense, and serves to explain the paranoid need to control, the feelings of fear and threat, that white identity is subject to: "The apparently stable, centered position . . . is . . . profoundly unstable, based on exclusions, and characterized by terror" (Martin & Mohanty, 1987, p. 201).

Ironically, therefore, homogenous white identity is characterized by contradictions and ambivalences, the need to disown what one is dependent on. Memmi (1990) stresses that the presence of subjugated others creates a sense of guilt and potential self-hatred, which no amount of touting one's self-virtue in order to create a sense of legitimacy can completely subdue. As Memmi says, "Deep within himself, the colonialist pleads guilty" (p.123). This guilt can only be assuaged by further denigrating the oppressed to provide self-justification, and to support the unrealistic self-image. The vicious cycle thus established creates in the dominating identity a neediness, a desire to be loved and reassured by those who are subjugated (Trinh, 1989; Memmi, 1990).

In addition to reframing discourses of savagery and Christian mythology to construct a narrative of whiteness, colonialists also drew on discourses that had served to categorize species, such as the chain of being, and gave them a facelift within the new science of race. The Enlightenment pride in its reason seems to contain more than an element of infatuation with its ability to rationalize existing European prejudices, and to justify its imperial ambitions, as the next section shows.

Natural Orders, Norms, and Deviations

The attempt to find (or, more accurately, to stipulate) the natural order of things had informed early European classificatory systems, such as the chain of being, a hierarchical ordering of the universe from the microorganisms to the gods. This raised the issue of what was to count as the transitional zone between the "human" sphere and the "animal." Early European explanations were in terms of mythical beings such as satyrs and centaurs (Nederveen Pieterse, 1990, p. 40). Later Enlightenment explanations were more inclined to place orangutans, or, of course, Africans in this position. Edward Tyson proposed the pygmy; many others considered the Hottentot eminently suitable for this distinction (Nederveen Pieterse, pp. 40–41). The question of the "missing link," allied to the issue of classifying the subspecies of *homo sapiens,* became one of the puzzles of the new science of "race."[21] Opinions varied as to the number and nature of subspecies, but the effect was clear: Africans could be classified out of the *genus homo* and established as a separate species. In both cases the maneuver had the effect of naturalizing Africans into a fundamentally different, and irrevocably inferior, position. Once established as part of the world of animal nature, Africans became legitimate objects of domination through natural science. The humanness of white people was never in question in these schemata, indeed the human was fully equated with whiteness. The debate lucidly indicates the political nature of the concept "human," an issue that will be discussed more fully later in this chapter.

It is a moot question whether the notion of biological race as it came to dominate Western thinking arose as justification for slavery, in spite of abolitionism (Stepan, 1990) or rather as a consequence of the success of abolitionism (Nederveen Pieterse, 1992). Whichever theory is correct, the invention of modern race enabled whites to establish through measurement, description, and theory, a hierarchical human differentiation that could be fixed as biological. The science of race drew on fields such as ethology, ethnology, phrenology, eugenics, philology, physical anthropology, and social Darwinism. The objective language of scientific positivism served to disguise the power relations at work in these discourses.[22] Unsurprisingly, all the "sciences" managed to reach the same conclusion: the superiority of the (male of the) Caucasian race, especially by comparison with Africans. Science thus concurred with religion and culture in narrating the superior position of whiteness in the general scheme of things, and the standard against which all others were to be measured. Scientific discourse was thus obsessed with the "puzzle" of in-betweenness which threatened the axiom of the incommensurability of the races. Colonial discourse, generally, was preoccupied with explaining deviance, with characterizing the gradations of slipping away from the white norm (Young, 1995).

The ideological function of establishing whiteness as the measure of human development emerges only too clearly. Commenting on social evolutionary theory, a late Victorian version of the great chain of being, Brantlinger (1985) puts it succinctly: "Evolutionary thought seems almost calculated to legitimize imperialism. The theory that man evolved through distinct stages—from barbarism to civilization—led to a self-congratulatory anthropology that actively promoted the belief in the inferiority—indeed the bestiality—of the African" (p. 184).

Within imperialist discourse, race functioned as a surrogate class system; race and class terminology were virtually interchangeable, and unsusceptible to political change (Brantlinger, p.181). Obviously, not all white people benefited in the same way, depending on their particular relationship to the means of production. Still, the advantages of whiteness provided a mechanism by which working class whites could be rewarded for their loyalty to white elites, especially where whiteness was constituted according to the notion of free labor as opposed to slavery (see Roediger, 1991, 1994; Boulton, 1995).

Giddens (1979) identifies ideology as having three main functions: to represent sectional interests as universal; to deny or transmute contradictions; and to naturalize the present through reification. The ideology of "whiteness" served these functions extraordinarily well, naturalizing the advantage of white people in such a way that it seemed unrelated to black people's disadvantage (see Lipsitz, 1995). A facade of an organic situation could be created (Guillaumin, 1995) where the groups were perceived to be naturally complementary, the exploitive nature of the relationship disguised: black people became colonized because of their predisposition to be colonized (p. 163); white people occupied preferred positions because their superiority was endogenously determined.

The role that two concepts, in particular, played in the construction of this ideology should be noted. The first is the notion of the "human," which the earlier analysis of the chain of being already revealed to be a highly political category. Balibar (1990) makes the point pertinently:"[T]he human species is the key notion in relation to which racism has constituted itself and continues daily to constitute itself" (p. 289). Racism continually replays the scenario of "a humanity forever emerging from animality, and of a humanity eternally menaced by the grip of animality" (p. 291). Young (1992) pursues the implication of the contested nature of the "human":

the ontological category of "the human" and "human nature" [has] been inextricably associated with the violence of Western history. If the human is itself revealed as a conflictual concept it can no longer be presented as an undisturbed ethical end. (Young, p. 248)

Presenting itself as exactly that ethical end, however, humanism played an important role in narratives of modernism. The Enlightenment's highly rated Man was understood to have an unchanging nature, and to be a "product of himself and of his own activity in history" (Young, 1992, p. 245). The human being possessed certain essential qualities that remained eternal, and these were of course Western (bourgeois) qualities. The assumed universals were

predicated on the exclusion and marginalization of the "others," such as "woman" or "the native" . . . however exalted in its conception, [man was] invoked only in order to put the male before the female, or to classify other "races" as subhuman, and therefore not subject to the ethical prescriptions applicable to "humanity" at large. (Young, pp. 246–47)

As suggested by the above analysis, the somewhat decentered position of white women within the construction of whiteness is complex and ambivalent:

In some contexts, white women might indeed be associated with the idea that female nature is inherently uncivilized, primitive when compared to men, and lacking in self-control. In the context of imperialism or modern racism, the dominant ideology would place white women firmly in the civilized camp, in opposition to non-European women whose lack of social and political rights are to be read as a mark of cultural savagery. This means that white women can occupy both sides of a binary opposition, which surely accounts for much of the confusion and ambivalence to be found in the ideology of gender relations. (Ware, 1992, p. 237)

The benefits of whiteness came mainly through being associated with white men, who were "the ones who constructed white history" (Frye, 1983, p. 225). As both female and white, white women belonged to the group that white men needed to draw on for mates, if they were to perpetuate their privileged species. White women could therefore enjoy "secondhand feelings of superiority and supremacy," as well as the hope of becoming equal, of being able to participate firsthand within the structures of racial dominance (Frye, 1983, p.125). Yet, the very same mechanisms of definition that were used to elevate whiteness were utilized to elevate maleness as a natural category in opposition to women. Frye (1983) points out that white men's domination and control of white women are an essential part of their maintaining racial dominance. Whiteness needed to create docile bodies, both of its women, and of those it marked as excluded. Treacherous white women were (and are) considered a threat to the continuation of the superior race. For this reason, control of their women's sexuality was an important component of the white narrative (Nederveen Pieterse, 1992). As the most precious possession of the white man (Ware, 1992) protecting their imputed vulnerability therefore provided the pretext for instituting harsh measures against indigenous men, constructed as rapacious and insubordinate.

One of the consequences of this ambivalent position has been that some white women were in time able to recognize the correspondences between their position and that of subordinated races, a phenomenon that fed into the early abolitionist and feminist movements, as well as more recent resistance against abuses of civil rights (Segrest, 1994; Ware, 1992).

The second concept that needs closer scrutiny is the very idea of the natural. Guillaumin (1995) shows that the idea of "naturalness" is modern, and "written into the industrial-scientific society" (p. 138). The idea of using nature as a way of marking exploited groups arose in the eighteenth century (p. 140): "From the circumstantial association between economic relations and physical traits was born a new type of mark ("colour"), which had great success. Later developments turned it from the traditional status of a *symbol* to that of a *sign of a specific nature* of social actors" (Guillaumin, p. 140, emphasis in the original).

In this scheme,

> scholars started looking for a "naturalness" in classes and exploited groups . . . whatever the twists and turns of the particular argument, the natural mark is presumed to be the intrinsic *cause* of the place that a group occupies in social relationships. It is supposed to be the internal (therefore natural) "capacities" that determine social facts. (p.142, emphasis in the original)

The natural category therefore exists as if dissociated from social and economic relationships, as if determined by the traits of the people who constitute the group. Significantly, the system of domination is inscribed on the (marked) body of the dominated. The dominating position is unmarked, allowing freedom and greater possibilities, and simultaneously setting itself up as normal, positioned beyond any obligation to explain itself.

A great part of the ideological power that the narrative of whiteness acquired came from this idea of nature as it was formulated by modernism. In diverting attention from the real causes of social inequality, the ideology of whiteness produced what Mumby (1993) refers to as "cultural deformation." Symbolic practices were systematically deformed so that relations of domination and dependence were reproduced, and the processes of meaning making as articulated by dominant interests were largely uncritically accepted. Conceptions of alternative meaning systems were thus limited. Inequality between those understood to be white, and those classified as black or shades of brown, came to be simply "the way things are."

The levels of meaning in the phrase "master narrative" become clearer when viewed in this analytical framework. In addition to being aligned with modernism[23] and sexism, the term also indicates the hegemonic function of the narrative. In its ideological function the master narrative tries to arrest the continuous play of signification so that the particular positioning it favors is seen to be natural and permanent, rather than arbitrary and contingent (Hall, 1994), and attempts to offer stable, monological subject positions to those it interpellates (West, 1993). Providing the frame for relationships between people of European stock and others, the master narrative both signified and legitimated domination, serving to repress other possible articulations.

Ideologies, however, never exist singly, or in isolation, but always develop in relation to others (Pêcheux, 1982). A variety of ideological systems or logics are available in any social formation.[24] Both Brantlinger (1985) and Nederveen Pieterse (1990) point out that Africans certainly created their own counter discourses about colonization and the meaning of whiteness,[25] and certainly not all European people were interpellated into the master narrative to achieve the same fit. Depending on such things as specific practices, particular outcomes, and combinations with other discourses, differing articulations of the master discourses have developed in different contexts. Moreover, internal complexities in the discourse could be differently deployed in differing situations,[26] and have given rise to different resistances. Nevertheless, the broad contours and patternings of the master narrative have provided the hegemonic discourses in contradistinction to which other narratives accounting for the relations of European dominance over subordinated others would have to differentiate themselves. All subsequent narratives would, in some way or another, have to take this narrative into account—whether to reinforce, affirm, qualify, modify, contradict, resist, or deconstruct this system of meanings.

The above chapter has postulated that social identity, far from being related to originary, essential qualities that inhere in individuals or a group of people who are naturally bonded for whatever reason, is, in fact, constructed though discourse. The attempt of a dominant discourse to fix social identities is an exercise of power. The chapter traced the emergence, at the time of European global expansion, of a reconfiguration and "upgrading" of available discourses to create a pattern of sense making, a master narrative of whiteness. This master narrative justified and secured pride of place for people of European stock in relation to the people they encountered as they remodeled the rest of the world in their image. But domination did not come without a cost to the psyches of the oppressors.

The next chapter will comment on this master narrative in relation to South Africa, and analyze how the European settlers, through a particular confluence of political, historical, economic, and geographical factors, gave the master narrative a particular spin that still influences relations within the country as it renegotiates social identities in the process of reconstruction after Apartheid.

Chapter 2

∽

"White" South Africans

Cultural identities come from somewhere, have histories. But, like everything which is historical, they undergo constant transformation. Far from being eternally fixed in some essentialized past, they are subject to the continuous "play" of history, culture and power. Far from being grounded in mere "recovery" of the past, which is waiting to be found, and which when found, will secure our sense of ourselves into eternity, identities are the names we give to the different ways we are positioned by, and position ourselves within, the narratives of the past.

—Stuart Hall, *Cultural Identity and Diaspora*

According to the historian Fredrickson (1981), South Africa and the United States, more than the other multiracial societies resulting from the expansion of Europe between the sixteenth century and the twentieth, "have manifested over long periods of time a tendency to push the principle of differentiation by race to its logical outcome—a kind of *Herrenvolk* society in which people of color, however numerous or acculturated they may be, are treated as permanent aliens or outsiders" (pp. xi–xii).

Once the Nationalist government came to power in South Africa in 1948, however, South Africa certainly was the society most overtly organized around a legalized axis of "race." Goldberg (1993), for example, regards South Africa as "the limit case" of racist culture; Derrida (1985) calls Apartheid "racism's last word"; "the ultimate racism in the world" (p. 291). Williams and Chrisman (1994) mention that both Hannah Arendt and J. A. Hobson see South Africa as the fullest expression of imperialism's logic (p. 7). The

23

Nobel Prize winner Nadine Gordimer (1987) does not mince her words:

> An extraordinary obdurate crossbreed of Dutch, German, English, French in the South African white settler population produced a bluntness that unveiled everyone's refined racism: the flags of European civilization dropped, and there it was, unashamedly, the ugliest creation of man, and they baptized the thing in the Dutch Reformed Church, called it *apartheid*, coining the ultimate term for every manifestation, over the ages, in many countries, of race prejudice. Every country could see its semblances there; and most peoples. (p. 209)

As the above quotation states unflinchingly, the European narrative of a superior group of "white" people with special entitlement took hold with a particular strength and tenacity in South Africa, shaping the society legally, politically, economically, and culturally. The narrative has been articulated in complex ways, mutating along different lines for sections of the white population, and with changing circumstances through the country's history, and in different parts of the country. Fredrickson (1981) cautions against oversimplifying this complexity:

> South Africa . . . compels recognition that race relations are not so much a fixed pattern as a changing set of relationships that can only be understood within a broader historical context that is itself constantly evolving and thus altering the terms under which whites and nonwhites interact. (p. xvii)

A detailed exploration of the complex manner in which the narrative of white identity has played itself out in South African history is clearly beyond the scope of this book; this chapter provides a synoptic, and therefore inevitably very simplified, exposition of the constitutive role this narrative has had in shaping the society.

Despite the risks of generalizing, a fair observation can be made that two major factors have differentiated the particularities of South African whiteness. The first is the presence of a small group of people whose self-image and expectations were shaped by the general contours of the master narrative of whiteness, in an environment where they were vastly outnumbered by the indigenous

population, which they subjugated, but never decimated.[1] The
Bantu peoples, such as the Nguni (Xhosa and Zulu), the north and
south Sotho, the Venda, the Pedi, and the Tswana had a fairly sophisticated level of social and military organization, which initially
provided a measure of resistance. The African kingdoms were not,
however, able to form a united front against the colonial advance
(Unterhalter, 1995).

After conquest all retained their own languages, their cultures
that proved resilient and inventive in the face of oppression, as well
as a sense of their connection to the land through an irrepressible
collective memory. This meant that white people in South Africa
never achieved the comfortable assurance of their political, cultural,
and even physical survival in the land they colonized, as did whites
in other deep settler countries. However strong-armed their measures to entrench their dominant position, at some level of awareness white South Africans have always been reminded of its tenu-
ousness. The fear of being overrun, the fear of domination, the fear
of losing the purity that was supposed to guarantee their superior
position, the fear of cultural genocide through intermingling—these
anxieties were always present. While already at least partially con-
stituent of whiteness (see the previous chapter), these fears have
been fed by, and continually have fed into, external realities in mutually reinforcing, and certainly destructive, cycles. Whiteness in
South Africa has always, at least in some part, been constellated
around discourses of resistance against a constant threat; it was a
bulwark against what at some level was sensed to be the inevitable.
Holding on against the odds, holding back the peril, the anxiety at
the heart of whiteness in South Africa permeated the nation's psyche with a characteristic structure of feeling:[2]

> For most of its existence, the sense of the end of history, the
> coming of bloody and final conflict, has characterized South
> Africa's view of its own history. . . . It is a vision of a "rolling
> apocalypse" in which the predicted end is only just put off by
> another war, another proclamation, another bomb, by segre-
> gation, by Apartheid, by the end of Apartheid, by "one set-
> tler, one bullet," and now by elections. (Thornton, 1996,
> 157–58)

The second factor that has differentiated whiteness in South
Africa is that it has been shared, reluctantly most of the time, by two
major groups of European stock, each of which has always considered

the other group an unworthy custodian of the entitlement. Having been conquered at more than one stage in their history by the English, the Afrikaners regarded the English as imperialists who treated the Afrikaners with little more dignity or respect for their cultural integrity, than they did the indigenous black people. Given the absolutely central place that the distinction between themselves and the indigenous people held for Afrikaner identity, this was flagrantly insulting (Fredrickson, 1981). For the English, backed as they were by empire, their sense of superiority to the native inhabitants was utterly above question. They did not regard the more rural and often illiterate Afrikaner folk as of the same order of civilization. Like ethnic working class whites and partially racialized groups in America (Ignatiev, 1995; Roediger, 1991, 1994), Afrikaners had to "fight" for the status of first-class citizens: "What was termed the 'racial question' in early twentieth-century South Africa referred not to relations between Europeans and Africans but to the relationship between the Boers and the British. Relations with the Africans were termed the 'native question' (Nederveen Pieterse, 1992, p. 104).

Nederveen Pieterse illustrates this racialization of the Afrikaner by quoting Lord Kitchener's characterization of the Boers as "uncivilized Afrikaner savages with a thin white veneer" (p. 104). The texture of the Afrikaners' whiteness, then, was coarsened by discourses of indignation and rebellion toward the more confident whiteness of overlordship assumed by the English.

This is therefore an interesting configuration of whiteness, which one could characterize as an internal colonization within the white group. While they did, in varying degrees at different times, recognize a unity in whiteness, neither wanted to be white in the same way. Certainly, whiteness did not draw them into a common identity as early, nor as "seamlessly," as it did the various white ethnic groups in the United States, where this "internal colonization" did not occur.[3]

Nevertheless, while English and Afrikaans white South Africans have historically maintained ethnic distinctiveness (though this is now less pronounced), both groups have defined themselves primarily and more fundamentally in disassociation from the "nonwhite" racial groups. For example, similar epithets, such as the notion of the perpetual child, have been applied historically by Boers and British alike to the indigenous population (Nederveen Pieterse, p. 104). Although the manner in which this paternalism played itself out in relation to the "other" differed, the ideology of the patriarch bound them to Europe. On the other hand, the whole construction of "home" was fundamentally different for these two groups and integral to their respective identifications with Africa.

Some reading of the early history of the Cape settlement shows that the first Dutch inhabitants had never intended to settle at the Cape of Good Hope—the goal had been to establish a halfway station for the Dutch East India Company's ships sailing to the East. This beginning is ironical given that the question, "Who owns the land?" is a central signifier in the whole history of South Africa, to this day.

Immigration from Europe to the station was limited early on, and growth of the "white" population was slow. As few European women came to settle in the relatively arduous conditions at the Cape, there was a good deal of intermarriage between the Dutch settlers and the slaves the company imported from Madagascar, Indonesia, Malaysia, and West Africa (Fredrickson, 1981). Early Dutch attitudes at the Cape condoned interbreeding, as Dutch blood was regarded as "strong" enough to make good Dutch citizens of the offspring.

With the establishment of Free Burghers (Free Citizens) who were no longer employees of the company,[4] there was some movement into the interior by the Trekboers (migrant farmers) and further intermingling with the indigenous Khoikhoi people. The offspring of this miscegenation formed the main genetic pool of the colored people of the Cape, and the Griquas further north. The presence of entire population groups whose very existence blatantly challenges the notion of the "naturalness" of racial purity has always been a difficulty for proponents of racial separation in South Africa (see Guillaumin, 1995). An historical embarrassment, the implications of this interbreeding have been repressed within Afrikaner culture, though most eminent Afrikaans families are known to have some "impure" blood in their ancestry. Certainly this repression has been part of the split self in conservative "white" South African identity.[5]

The Free Burghers dissociated themselves from European control,[6] and started referring to themselves as "Afrikanders"—people from Africa. This group included not only Dutch settlers, but employees from all over Europe who had been recruited by the Dutch East India Company, and later the French Huguenots and German settlers (Unterhalter, 1995) who were assimilated into the Afrikaner culture. Dissociation from European control was by no means identification with the indigenous people, though, nor a renunciation of what they regarded as a superior cultural heritage. Rather, the self-identification with Africa reflected the attitude that the Burghers were legitimate occupants of the country (a belief that has remained central to white identity in South Africa). This legitimate occupancy included the right to wield power over both the indigenous people and the slaves the settlers took with them as they moved into the interior. Although, or perhaps because, their lifestyles came somewhat to resemble those of the indigenous people—mostly subsistent and close to the land, in some instances even nomadic—early Afrikaners held onto the markers of difference between their culture and those of "nonwhite" people with great vehemence.

As Fredricksen (1981) comments:

> It appears that South African masters remained acutely uncomfortable with slaves or other nonwhite dependents who practiced the same religion and thus partook of the same cultural heritage as themselves. Indeed, the kind of "homogeneity" between "white" and "Christian" or "black" and "heathen" that Morgan Godwyn found in late seventeenth century Virginia persisted in the discourse of Afrikaners until late in the nineteenth century. What is more, they made strenuous efforts to see that these linguistic correlations mirrored reality—by neglecting and sometimes vigorously discouraging the propagation of Christianity among their nonwhite dependents. Since they craved a cultural gap as well as a racial one, they preferred to allow color and religion to remain reinforcing aspects of differentness rather than making a clear decision, such as was made in the South, as to which was to have priority. The long delay in the legitimation of racial slavery may therefore have been one factor making the South African white-supremacist tradition more dependent on cultural pluralism than the American. (p. 85)

The above quotation indicates the close association of religion with whiteness for Afrikaners, an association that has proved very tenacious. Christianity was racialized (Fredricksen, 1981), but it was a very specific form of Calvinism that the Afrikaners espoused. Again, Fredricksen puts it well:

> [T]he frontier farmer already possessed a body of folk beliefs dispelling any doubts about what role God had prescribed

for the nonwhites in their midst. Its inspiration was an old testament Christianity of an attenuated Calvinistic origin that constituted a prime source of group identity. Because of its lack of sophistication, it would be misleading to describe this faith as Calvinistic in any sense that an American Puritan . . . would have acknowledged . . . in its popular form it was basically non-evangelical, and thus out of harmony with the proselytizing missionary Protestantism of the nineteenth century.

This simplified and literalistic version of Reformed Protestantism was partly an outgrowth of frontier life. Having trekked in many cases beyond the reach of established congregations, the Boers did most of their worshipping within the patriarchal family. Their only guide was the Bible itself, which they readily interpreted in the light of their own experience as a pastoral people wandering among the "heathen." (p. 170)

"Christian" and "heathen" came to function as categories denoting *racial* types (through the mechanisms of the Manichean allegory discussed in the previous chapter). This justified different treatment, which as Fredricksen points out, was "the right to apply force in an arbitrary way" (p. 171). Fredrickson continues:

It was no giant step from such beliefs to the notion that the Boers were a chosen people, analogous to the ancient Israelites, who had a special and exclusive relationship with God and a mandate to smite the heathen. (p. 171)

How literally the Boers did indeed identify with the destiny of the Israelites is contested by historians and social commentators. G. M. Ridge (1987) argues that they used discourses of Israel's experience to give form to their experience, resurrecting the myth after the event in a way that could sanctify self-interest:

Unlike their English neighbours, who were also "emigrants," they seem seldom to have thought of "home" as somewhere behind them. Instead they struggled for years to find a new home and a new unity as a people. They used Israelite metaphors to explore what they were doing. (p. 106)

In contrast to these clear-cut beliefs about "whiteness,"[7] British settler attitudes were more complex and ambivalent, and certainly more influenced by contemporary international thought as it changed over time. With their cultural and racial superiority as a people never in any doubt, the British adopted a more pragmatic and often equivocal attitude toward indigenous people. British cross-cultural experience in South Africa fed into the "science" of race, usually based on descriptions of the Khoi (referred to as "Hottentots") and San (referred to as "Bushmen") as icons of otherness (Dubow, 1995; Magubane, 1999; Nederveen Pieterse, 1992). The Cape was the "first outpost of European anthropology in Africa. A precursor of later colonial societies in Africa, the Cape was also a laboratory of European anxieties, where prejudices were indulged to their ultimate limit" (Nederveen Pieterse, p. 102). So, for example, a leading British anthropologist, Francis Galton, described an encounter with indigenous people on the coast:

> a row of seven dirty, squalid natives came to meet us. . . . They had Hottentot features, but were darker of colour, and a most ill-looking appearance; some had trousers, some coats of skin, and they clicked, and howled, and chattered, and behaved like baboons. (quoted in Nederveen Pieterse, 1992, p. 103)

The Scottish-born medical doctor, Robert Knox, wrote an anthropological study while serving as an army surgeon in South Africa from 1817 to 1820. His words, below, exemplify how the notions of superior and inferior races led to the intensification of wars against the Africans after the British took over the Cape in 1806:

> What signify these races to us? Who cares particularly for the Negro, or Hottentot, or the Kaffir? These latter have proved a very troublesome race, and the sooner they are put out of the way the better . . . Destined by the nature of their race to run, like other animals, a certain limited course of existence, it matters little how their extinction is brought about. (quoted in Magubane, 1999, p. 26)

The later formulation of such beliefs, social Darwinism, is evident in the opinion, expressed in 1903, of Lord Milner, the British high commissioner who was responsible for the reconstruction of South Africa after the Anglo-Boer war:

The white man must rule, because he is elevated by many, many steps above the black man; steps which it will take the latter centuries to climb, and which it is quite possible that the vast bulk of the population may never be able to climb at all. (quoted in Fredricksen, 1981, p. 195)

After the Ango-Boer war, South African scientists, as members of the intellectual community of the British commonwealth, and yet "in the field" in Africa, were regarded as having a special contribution to make to the science of race. South Africa was regarded as a "laboratory in racial and cultural relations"; an "international repository of data and focus of scientific research into problems of race" (Dubow, 1995). South African scientists working in the field of prehistory, particularly physical anthropology, "enjoyed an unrivalled international reputation as well as giving the international racial paradigm an indigenous focus" (Dubow, 1995). It is not particularly surprising that the famous discovery of the "missing link," *Australopithecus,* in 1924 by Raymond Dart, was one of South Africa's foremost intellectual achievements (Dubow, 1995).

With much closer ties to "back home," being "white" for the British settlers was having the right to maintain a European frame of reference in Africa. In many ways the British remained psychologically more alienated from the African continent than the Afrikaners. They kept a tighter hold on their European identities, and fought the anxiety of potential cultural disintegration (a danger presented by the African sun) through a process of gentrification (see Clingman, 1991; Goldberg, 1993). Their mission on the continent was to exert a civilizing influence on the natives, while exacting economic benefit in exchange for the favor. Of course, this calling could only be fully met if the "purity" of British blood was retained. The notion of the dangers of racial decline through hybridization was later "confirmed" by scientific "facts." J. M. Coetzee (1987), in his analysis of the work of the South African writer Sarah Gertrude Millin, describes the fall into the damnation of hybridity:

The hybrid is further damned in that the two bloods in his veins are debased bloods to begin with. The Adam of his line is likely to have been feeble of mind or ridden by senile lust, the Eve a woman from a "broken tribe" with no race pride left (GSC, p. ix). His roots therefore lie in degeneracy, which is passed down in the blood. . . . Slaves and tribes that have lost their social organization in the aftermath of conquest

pass on the germs of slavehood and feebleness to their offspring (GSC, pp. xii, 203). . . . [A]lcoholism, malnutrition,
and venereal disease leave their various taints in the blood
(AR, p. 67; GSC, p. ix). The man of mixed blood thus remembers through his blood the miserable history of his line as it
degenerates, falling away from an original purity. (p. 41)

The more international frame of reference of the British settlers, however, also exposed these settlers to counter discourses on
issues of "race." The European humanitarian movement and the an-
tislavery campaigns of abolitionists like William Wilberforce influenced the British rule of the early Cape colony. While pragmatic concerns of economics and empire never were ignored, and no clear
ideology of democracy as emerged in the United States was ever embraced (Fredricksen, 1981), a major factor in the British administra-
tion of the early colony became mediating between the Afrikaners
and their servants and slaves. With the abolition of slavery, many
already straitened Boers suffered genuine financial loss (Fredricksen, 1981). Taken together with their other grievances about the
lack of British government protection against African warring along
the frontier, the feelings of injustice experienced by the Boers led to
an exodus of Afrikaners into the interior in 1836, known as the
Great Trek. This was the beginning of the development of a "tribal"
identity of Afrikaner Christian nationalism, which was inextricably
interconnected with their particular expression of "whiteness." As a
Voortrekker[8] woman wrote:

It is not so much their [the slaves] freedom which drove us
to such lengths as their being placed on an equal footing
with Christians, contrary to the laws of God, and the natural distinction of race and colour, so that it was intolerable
for any decent Christian to bow down beneath such a yoke,
wherefore we rather withdrew in order thus to preserve our
doctrines in purity. (quoted in De Villiers, 1987, p. 101)

Afrikaner "freedom" came to be understood as freedom to exercise racial hegemony. The right to be "white" was yoked to the right-
lessness of "nonwhites." Being "civilized" in a savage, untamed country entailed the right to be masters of the heathens. The Boers never
attempted to enslave the Africans as chattel slaves; it was more a
case of creating conditions of unfair and unfree labor. For example,
Davidson (1991) quotes David Livingstone to the effect that the

Voortrekker commandants "lauded their humanity and justice" in making the "equitable regulation" of having Africans work for them in exchange for the right to live in the land (p. 269). Through a series of bitter wars with indigenous African people, notably the Zulus, the Afrikaners came to feel that they had "won" the legitimate right to occupy the land that had indisputably previously been inhabited by native people (De Villiers, 1987). However, the Boers believed, fallaciously, that most of the land they moved into had previously been unoccupied; that they had arrived at the same time as the Africans who were taken to be migrating south (Edgecombe, 1991, p. 125). They believed they had an equal claim to the territory. In part the belief that the land was "empty" could be the effect of the migrations caused by reconfigurations taking place within African nation-building (a process known as the Mfecane), but it also undoubtedly was part of the European construction of Africa as being devoid of legitimate occupants, barring game. The sense of having a special destiny as a chosen people in the land they were opening up for white settlement was confirmed when, after having made a covenant with God, they won the "Battle of Bloodriver" against the Zulus in the face of seemingly impossible odds. This incident remained a crucial component of Afrikaner identity, though obviously not homogeneously interpreted, especially not any more.[9]

When two independent Afrikaner republics (the Transvaal Republic and the Orange Free State republic) were established in the interior as a result of the Great Trek migration, racial exclusion was built into the constitutions. So, for example, the Constitution of the Orange Free State Sovereignty, which was similar to the constitution of the United States in many ways, guaranteed the freedom of the press and did not preclude women from voting, but excluded the Griquas from citizenship (Fredrickson, 1981).

The reasons for the Anglo-Boer wars that led to the British defeat of the independent Afrikaner territories are complex and beyond the scope of this discussion, but certainly British imperialism (especially as gold and diamonds had been discovered in these territories) was an overriding factor. The issue of racial exclusion was held to be a major motivation for British aggression, though the subsequent ignoring of African interests in the union mocks this. It was more probable that the Transvaal Republic's "Uitlander Law" (i. e., Foreigner's law—which bears a family resemblance to Proposition 187 in California) frustrated the British capitalists' desire to amass wealth as they deemed fit for themselves, in what had become Afrikaner territory. The British attack on the settler republics in 1899 had the effect of consolidating white ethnicities as settlers from other parts of Europe, who had been attracted by the gold and diamonds, were impelled to choose one side or the other. Even twelve thousand British subjects from the Cape Colony joined the Boer armies against the British in the Anglo-Boer war (Unterhalter, 1995).

After the war, the British under a liberal government were somewhat shamed by the international response to the suffering of the Boers, who had tried to stand up to an imperial power vastly more powerful than they. Afrikaner farms and homesteads had been destroyed in the British "scorched earth" policy, leaving the Boers without means of livelihood, the women and children having been interned in concentration camps.[10] In 1910, with the peace negotiations, the British reconstructed the country into a union of the former independent Afrikaner territories and the British colonies of the Cape and Natal. The united South Africa truly became a white settler state, politically self-governing. In a direct affront to South African black people who sent an eight-person delegation to London in 1909 to protest the draft South Africa Act, South Africans of color were completely excluded from representation in the union. By this time, notions of racial difference and European superiority had become ingrained. White power had already been widely institutionalized economically and politically (Unterhalter, 1995). In the peace negotiations, the overriding concern was to make the country "tolerable for whites" (Schutte, 1995) by "defending civilization against black conspiracies" (Davidson, 1994).

The ethnic differentiation between those who regarded themselves as Boers or British, as well as class, regional and political divergence, was deliberately assuaged to form what Basil Davidson (1994) has called a "solid unity of interest and intention" (p. 128). The British victors, Davidson comments, were "quick to reassure their defeated Afrikaner opponents that systematic discrimination against the black majority would . . . be written into the foundation of the Union of the South Africa" (p. 130). The new laws, introduced once the settler minority governed the united country were rigorous in creating a "whites only" rule. After the Afrikaner Nationalist Party parliamentary victory in 1948, the system was further entrenched by the policy of Apartheid, but the essentials had been enshrined in the Act of Union. The rationale for the harsh racist laws was tied up with need for cheap (really cheap) labor for the deep mines and the extensive farms (Davidson, 1994). As the mining centers expanded into boom towns, the demand for food made previously subsistence farmers turn to commercial farming. This initiated a major impetus to appropriate any remaining rural land from Africans, and ushered in the iniquitous Natives' Land Act of 1913, which allowed Africans to own a mere 7 percent of South African land.

In contrast to this officially legislated "white" solidarity under a racialized democracy, divisive ethnicities were ascribed to the "non-white races." This enabled the small white minority to rally around their color, while deemphasizing the vast numerical advantage of the majority black population. A mixed race grouping, on the one hand, and the people from India, the Middle East, and East Africa, on the other, came to be formalized into separate racial groupings called the Colored and Indian "races" respectively. Disparate African chieftaincies were set up, each to head an "ethnicized version of 'custom'" (Mamdani, 1999). These divisions were central to the way in which the others were ruled, to their access to land and to the labor market (Unterhalter, 1995, p. 221), and central to the maintenance of the Western whiteness of the minority: "It is through this dual institutional apparatus that power sought to enforce a dual political identity: A racial identity that united beneficiaries alongside an ethnic identity that fragmented victims. (Mamdani, 1999, p. 127)

The exclusion of blacks from the new political dispensation represented a major betrayal of black aspirations (De Villiers, 1987; Fredrickson, 1981), and led to the formation of the africanist South African Native National Congress in 1912—later to become the African National Congress (ANC). Increasingly, the South African political landscape was characterized by parliamentary white politics, opposed to extraparliamentary resistance politics. Their exclusion reinforces the point made earlier that whiteness for white South Africans meant entitlement to the land (and everything in it), against any odds. In 1913 the Land Act (mentioned above) was passed, which allocated 93 percent of the country's land to whites (Fredrickson, 1981). The Urban Areas Act of 1923 established "a regime of strict physical segregation and discrimination" (Davidson, 1994, p. 302). The fear of being "outvoted" by blacks, ever present in constitutional issues for whites, is also reflected in the 1930 decision to grant "universal suffrage" only to whites. The fear of losing privilege and wealth, the fear of political domination, the fear of the population demographics, the fear of chaos, the fear of an African future—to the extent that a more unified white identity started to coalesce in South Africa after union, it had these fears as nidus.[11]

The system set up by the British anticipated the Apartheid laws that were later to be introduced by the Afrikaner Nationalist government, but at this stage the system favored English-speaking South Africans. Davidson (1994) observes that, for the British, the dispensation

> fully realized their aims in conquering the Afrikaner republics: they had provided an "ideal structure" for the development of a specific capitalism fueled by British capital, which entered the country increasingly after 1920 and which ensured the English-speaking minority of a uniquely high standard of living while, at the same time, ensuring a uniquely high rate for British investors. (Davidson, p. 131)

The balance between the two white ethnic groups was to swing, however. The growing working class of Afrikaners in the aftermath of the Boer war, the great drought and depression, and the system by which farms were subdivided among sons, forced impoverished Afrikaners into the urban areas where they had to compete with African labor for unskilled jobs on the mines. The politically turbulent time that followed introduced a system of "civilized labor" where the white working class was protected through legislation, guaranteed that semiskilled and skilled labor would be reserved for whites. The working class was split, "blacks" and "whites" ensured of a different relationship to production.[12] Black labor was frozen into a preindustrial, precapital relationship, practically indentured, making South Africa's economy an anomaly in the industrial world (Hall, 1980). The belief that it was the task of government to ensure, absolutely, white privilege, had informed the Free Burghers' anger against colonial rulers in the frontier days at the Cape. The belief was now being recycled into the logic of Apartheid, the rigorous system of laws that was designed to guard white supremacy.

Again, the intricacies of the events between the two world wars that led to the rise of Afrikaner nationalism, and the consequent victory at the polls of the Nationalist Party in 1948, are beyond the scope of this chapter. Labor issues were a burning factor, as was the question of allegiance to Britain and its allies in the two world wars, and the "problem" of a rapidly increasing black presence in the urban areas.

Pervasive in all the issues, though, was the deep bitterness that still smoldered about the Boer War. Among the Afrikaners, the perception gained ground that General Smuts was unreliable as a protector of "white" privilege, particularly poor "white" privilege. Although a Boer general in the Anglo-Boer war, Smuts had adopted the "moderate" stance of advocating unity among white South Africans, rather than Afrikaner nationalism. Smuts led the country into alignment with the British Allies in both world wars. Motivated by pragmatism, and certainly not by nonracialism, on the question of the presence of black migrant workers, he accepted the recommendations of the Fagan report published in 1948. These included that black people should be accepted as permanent residents in urban areas; that segregation should be acknowledged as impractical, and more, rather than less, immigration from the "native reserves" should be allowed (Stadler, 1991). The leader of the Nationalist party, D. F. Malan, maintained that this would lead to natives being represented by natives in parliament, Indians by Indians—thus conjuring up the worst fear of conservative whites—the beginning of the steady decline of "white" interests in South Africa (De Villiers, 1987). In contrast to the specter of integration, the Nationalists advocated uncompromising adherence to the traditional policy of *baasskap* (mastership). In the words of the then Transvaal leader of the Nationalist Party, J. G. Strijdom:

> Our policy is that the Europeans must stand their ground and must remain *baas* in South Africa. If we reject the *herrenvolk* idea and the principle that the white man cannot remain *baas* if the franchise is to be extended to the non-Europeans, and if the non-Europeans are given representation and the vote and the non-Europeans are developed on the same basis as the Europeans, how can the Europeans remain *baas* . . . Our view is that in every sphere the Europeans must retain the right to rule the country and to keep it a white man's country. (quoted in Bunting, 1964, p. 129)

De Villiers (1987) comments:

> None of what followed, the sad history of Apartheid, can be understood unless the deep psychological scars and insecurities of the Afrikaner proletariat can be set against the actions of their nationalist politicians. Malan's skillful use of both British and black symbols explains his victory . . . Malan succeeded in persuading the Afrikaners that Smuts would swamp them in English and that the English would allow all whites to be swamped in turn by the inchoate black masses. (pp. 308–9)

At a more fundamental level, the scars and insecurities, the selfish expectations that made the Afrikaner proletariat buy into the Nationalist policy, indeed the very terms of the policy itself, were all only possible because of the particular way in which the master narrative of whiteness had been articulated in Afrikaner culture, and especially because of the manner in which that articulation had come into conflict with the British inflection of the same narrative:

> Apartheid did not come from thin air; it was grafted onto ideas that were already there, produced by 300 years of turbulent history. . . . Apartheid . . . [was] an ideology of protest [against the British] grafted onto received ideas. (De Villiers, 1987, p. 310)

Those received ideas were outlined in what Nederveen Pieterse (1990) calls the "pre-industrial, pre-history of Apartheid"—the familiar European clichés about black Africa, the images of Africans, the discourses about Europe's "others" and the appropriate "white" relationship to them; attitudes that were "shaped, imagined, and transmitted" in everyday culture already at the time of early settlement at the Cape (p. 102).

That Apartheid was a family member of other expressions of Western racisms, and slotted into Western global projects is something that needs to be stressed, not to provide excuses, but because the fullest expression reveals what more subtle articulations may disguise, even obfuscating complicity. Returns on investments in South Africa were generally higher than the world average. Davidson (1994) reports the Economic and Social Council of the United Nations findings that British investment in South Africa stood at an average of 21 percent in 1980 compared with 9 percent elsewhere, whereas American companies were earning 29 percent in this country compared with 18.4 percent elsewhere (p. 304). Goldberg (1993) has shown how Apartheid drew on (and distorted) Western political concepts such as plural democracy and Western systems of government (the British Westminster system). He also points out that the spatial characteristics of South African racism bear a family resemblance to the ways in which "race" affects social organization in other Western countries. Trinh (1989) draws attention to the use of Western liberalism in Apartheid discourse, and argues that the preservation of capitalism is closely tied to the preservation of white life. Goldberg (1993) makes a similar point about the present drive toward privatization in the country.

Schutte (1995) maintains that the various Apartheid laws can be seen as an expression of Afrikaner needs. So, for example, "the Bantustan [Independent Homelands] policies can be viewed as indicators and reflections of the relevance that cultural and political identity had for the ruling Afrikaners" (p. 22), whose brittle social identity had always been challenged. The creation of an Afrikaner-centric historiography, so pivotal to Afrikaner rule, reflects the need to establish the permanence of the Afrikaner's place in history. This faith bolstered the struggle for survival against forces that had always seemed to threaten to wipe them from the records of time. In manipulating these needs, Dr. Verwoerd, the grand architect of Apartheid, was the politician who most focused on whiteness as such. He presented the English as white, but not reliable (De Villiers, 1987). The emphasis was always on group identity, and the cultural complexity of the South African situation; the "white" group cast in contradistinction from the many African tribes.

The thoroughness with which the draconian Apartheid legislation ensured the separation of the racial groups, "protecting" the Afrikaner version of pure whiteness, its privilege and advantage, and fixing economic relations to provide a form of affirmative action for Afrikaners, at whatever cost to the other human beings involved, needs no elaboration. The establishment of "homelands," which would provide for citizenship of black people within small, economically unviable "independent" states, was a chilling exercise in social engineering. It sought to bring the ultimate vision of Apartheid into being: "an Afrikaner-run republic with . . . No more black South Africans" (*Illustrated History of South Africa: The Real Story*, 3rd ed., 1994).

Of course, the narratives of whiteness that informed these dominant constructions were not the only conceptions of what relations between those of European stock and those of non-European stock could be. Those who envisaged a more tolerant, liberal white society, those who envisaged a nonracial society, such as the African National Congress and the Communist Party, and those who envisaged an Africanist regime, such as the Pan African Congress, constantly challenged the narrative of white supremacy. What this white-centric account of the post-Union history of South Africa cannot do justice to is the extent of opposition in every form—strikes, boycotts, marches, riots, uprisings, sabotage. Alongside this "white" history, runs a parallel history of political mobilization, struggle, and protest, in turn met with ever more reactionary measures aimed at containing the mounting resistance and eradicating the leadership.

In response to the Suppression of Communism Act in 1950, and the banning of the African National Congress in 1960 and the incarceration of its leaders, the movement went underground. Many of the leaders went into exile, and organized an external wing of the movement to put into place a variety of resistance strategies. One of these, the policy of "armed struggle," was accepted as an inevitable and necessary means to counter the violence of the Apartheid regime and bring about meaningful change.

The growing isolation of the country's government from the international community, and the government's manipulation of the media to obfuscate the real consequences of their policies, increasingly screened whites from contrary interpretations of their society. The government worked hard at creating the impression of the normality of South African racial relations, trying to render the system innocent through stressing similarities between South Africa and "mainstream" Western societies. It compared the conditions of Africans in South Africa favorably with those in other African states (see Goldberg, 1993). Enabled by economic and political advantage, hundreds of everyday trivia reinforced the sense of white superiority in a self-fulfilling manner. Even work relations, the one arena in which whites and blacks encountered each other, were mostly alienated, with the possible exception of one deeply gendered anomaly. Black women working as domestic servants in white households frequently acted as de facto mothers to white children, giving rise to race / gender intersections that influenced identity, but which are far too complex to analyze in detail in this text. The peculiar logic of racism managed to explain any anomalies or contradictions in ways that blamed the victim, thus maintaining the white self-image of respectability.[13]

The white society was not unvaryingly duped, and some resistance to the Apartheid system from within the white community was always present, though increasingly repressed by the government. White opposition came largely from members of the English-speaking community who had never identified with Afrikaner nationalism and were more influenced by liberalism[14] (but who nevertheless, more often than not, enjoyed the comfortable "white" privilege Afrikaner "law and order" protected, without having to take the moral censure for the system of Apartheid). Some did take a principled stand. There were also Afrikaners who carried on the more pragmatic (though not actually antiracist) tradition of Smuts. Still others courageously took a truly oppositional route, often at great personal cost. Two outstanding examples of such courage are

Braam Fischer, who defended the Rivonia trialists in 1963 (including Nelson Mandela) and was later incarcerated himself, and Beyers Naudé, who set up the Christian Institute as an intellectual center against oppression, and spent many years under house arrest.[15]

As Thiele (1991) suggests, organizing along racial lines requires energy and resources. In the fall of Apartheid, we once again recognize the symptoms of *regime fatigue*. Maintaining a system aimed at the preservation of racial purity and privilege for whites in the African context simply had not been feasible (to say nothing of its morality). Apartheid collapsed under the strain of both internal and external pressure. A disastrous attempt at reform was engineered in 1984, through what was called the Tricameral Parliament. It accommodated whites, Indians, and Coloreds in separate legislative houses, but excluded black Africans. This precipitated escalating internal violence, and the country was plunged into a state of emergency. The civil war was becoming more visible with the presence of the armed forces in the townships, and negotiations seemed the only hope for peace. In a historic opening speech to Parliament in 1990, the new President F.W. de Klerk unbanned the ANC and all political prisoners, and the process of bringing back the exiled leaders began. A difficult, but successful, period of negotiation followed, which led to the democratic elections in 1994, the first elections in which all South Africans participated, and the inauguration of Nelson Mandela as the first black president.

South Africa was the last country in Africa to achieve majority rule. It also is home to a comparatively larger group of white citizens than any other African country, a group that had certainly not been prepared by their society's racial assumptions for their new circumstances. White South Africans would have to draw on the available repertoire of discourses (not necessarily only narratives of "whiteness"), and reconfigure and reinterpret these to create meaningful identities within drastically changed political circumstances.

In his ethnographic study of white South African consciousness on the eve of political change, Schutte (1995) found the paranoia so characteristic of South African whiteness (Goldberg, 1993; Trinh, 1989) to be pronounced. For many white South Africans there was a sense of being cornered, of having to adopt a defensive position toward the outside world as well as the black "enemy within" the country. The ability to preserve a European way of life and the right to cultural self-preservation were perceived as being immensely threatened.

Schutte observed that in the run-up to the 1994 elections
Africans were considered by whites to be "far behind," often innately
and irremediably so. Black interests were perceived to be a bottomless pit, a drain on whites. Discourse about "civilization," or the lack
of it, was still prevalent. Schutte encountered few whites who were
envisaging a blending of cultures in the future dispensation. Although this summary does not reflect the nuances between the
groups he studied, Schutte does comment on the underlying commonality he found in white consciousness. As political change was
approaching, Schutte's analysis suggests, white identity was becoming more reactive.

Ending their study of white Afrikaners in the early 1990s,
Goodwin and Schiff (1995) underscore the immensity of the change
in identity that white South Africans would need to negotiate:

> If, as we know, our race problems are not solved, then surely
> South Africa's aren't either. The abolition of slavery in the
> United States was only the beginning of the struggle; simi-
> larly, the abolition of statutory apartheid only begins South
> Africa's healing. . . . most whites have yet to relate to the
> black population in any deep and empathetic way. (p. 389)

The present study takes the exploration of white South African
identity further by looking at the narratives white South Africans
are creating now that the change has been a reality for a few years.

Writing in postelection South Africa, Dubow (1995) observes
that in South Africa old-style racialized discourse is "in a state of retreat as the demise of apartheid and the construction of a new social
order rapidly engenders a determined politics of reconciliation and a
desire to efface the past" (p. 291). Yet, as he observes

> racial discourse is as much about what is not said as what is
> openly articulated. And the careful veneer of non-racialism
> in public life is not necessarily reflected in private. At pre-
> sent the creation of a successful multi-racial society seems
> to demand that questions of the past are not too searching.
> This attitude is reinforced by a collective determination to
> forgive and forget. As historians, however, we have a duty to
> raise uncomfortable questions about the past, not least be-
> cause the legacy of apartheid is certain to outlast the im-
> print of its legislation. . . . An important part of that fasci-
> natingly ugly history is bound up with the complex ways by

which whites came to persuade themselves of their innate
superiority and God-given "right to govern." (p. 291)

This chapter has analyzed the particular ways in which whiteness was configured within the South African context to create that
"fascinatingly ugly history." In drawing on the master narrative, interpreting it and adapting it to the particular circumstances in
which they found themselves in the country, whites were able to
maintain their advantage as the dominating group that controlled
the political, material, and symbolic resources of the country for
three centuries. Yet, at all times, as the above chapter has shown,
the attitudes and behaviors, real and imagined, and even just the
presence of the large nonwhite majority, have defined the deepest
interior of white identity. The center was constituted around the
marginalized.

Scratching beneath the surface of the "conscious celebration of
unity and shared nationhood" which Dubow (1995) remarks upon,
the next chapters will analyze contemporary constructions of whiteness in South Africa, now that political circumstances no longer
support the master narrative, now that the margins have acquired
the power to unfix themselves.

Section Two

∾

Shades of Whitenesses

There's a lot of redefining going on, even identity crises.

—respondent, study questionnaire

We have to make choices from a range of different stories—stories about what the universe is like, about who the good guys are, about who *we* are—and we also have to make choices about how to make choices. The only thing we lack is the option of not having to make choices—although many of us try hard, and with some success, to conceal that from ourselves.

—Walter Truett Anderson, *Reality Isn't What It Used To Be*

Chapter 3

⤞

Things Bad Begun: Growing up "White"

Before the "world" was white; now the "world" I live in is a ·
black world and determined to a large extent by black people.

—respondent, study questionaire

Chapter two briefly outlined the particular spin that the master
narrative of whiteness acquired within the South African context,
from the time of European arrival at the Cape of Good Hope until
the elections in April 1994, when South Africa became the last state
in postcolonial Africa to achieve black majority rule. The following
chapters present the results of a close analysis of questionnaires
that a sample of fifty-nine white South Africans answered on their
perceptions of, and attitudes to, being white in the New South
Africa.

The questionnaires were sent to contacts in several different
parts of the country, who circulated it within their range of acquaintances, and in some cases "snowballed" it further afield. This method
managed to lasso diverse pockets of the population, achieving a good
range of responses that reflect many different positionalities within
the white community in South Africa. Geographically, respondents
were drawn from Cape Town, Johannesburg, Pretoria, Vereeniging,
Northern Province, Eastern Cape, Kwazulu-Natal, and Karoo. Differences in home language, English or Afrikaans, and in political orientation, accompanied this geographical spread. As well as reflecting
different provinces, the distribution included a diversity of urban
and rural white South Africans, as well as a wide range of occupa-
tions and incomes. The respondents varied in age from high school
pupils to one retired person. (For details, see the Appendix.)

The close relationship between the ways in which our imaginations are working on events, our sense of agency and of identity, and the narratives we construct is well theorized (see Riessman, 1993). The series of open-ended questions to which the participants responded were intended to solicit their interpretations of their position within the South African society, and of the significance of the recent political changes in the flow of their lives. The questions were able to elicit the general contours of what can legitimately be called the respondent's "story." The manner in which the person constructed causal connections, creating a sense of logical coherence between past, present, and future, as well as a significant turning point was implicit in the answers. Reflecting on the responses, a reader could identify who the respondent regarded as the main protagonists in this social drama, how the "other" was being constructed, and even, how well he or she was coping with the changes. Our narratives are largely rhetorical devices through which we attempt to persuade that we are good people, and as such, they are certainly exercises in impression management (Riessman, p. 11). Identifying how whites are wanting to see themselves, and how they want to be known, was one of the most important themes of my analysis.

Similarly, there is a close relationship between the narratives we tell and the cultural resources we draw on. When we attempt to understand ourselves, we draw on the repertoires of sense-making devices that our cultures furnish (Gergen, 1988, p. 96). The assumptions we make, what we regard as "natural," as valued activities and endpoints, as important to include or exclude, what we consider unthinkable—through these and other such taken-for-grantednesses, our culture speaks itself. The task of discourse analysis is to articulate the manner in which the individual's story is embedded within culturally shared interpretive repertoires (Wetherelll and Potter, 1998). As Gergen (1988) points out, it is through being tied to larger social stories that events gain significance (p. 95). My metanarratives, which the following chapters tell, are the attempt to explicate this connection. In grouping and interpreting the respondents' interpretations of their whiteness, my discussions therefore produce a new level of sense-making. This interpretation is informed by analysis also of unintended messages the respondent communicates about what are perceived to be appropriate relations between the different groupings within the country. As such, the metanarrative is an attempt to situate the ideological positioning of the narrative within the broader social context (Billig, 1988, p. 200). As Billig explains, ideological analysis involves discovering how explanations of one sort of social event fit into wider patterns of explaining social events.

Section one has outlined the broad ideological heritage related to the meaning of whiteness, and how this has been shaped within the social and historical context of South Africa. The next section places different attempts at sense-making in relation to this ideological tradition (see Billig, 1998). The responses, once typed up, were reread closely several times, and analyzed carefully to identify commonalities, themes, and trends that emerged in response to the issues raised in the questionnaire. A clear sense of coherent patternings and recurring organization emerged. Those with similar attitudes toward, and beliefs about, key issues were grouped together. The discursive shapes that emerged from each of these groupings, in terms of choice of vocabulary, recurring concerns, awareness of issues, and overall stance, constitute a narrative in each of the following chapters. In shaping out the contours of each narrative, responses to each of the questions were collated, as well as the contrasts between respondents noted. I was concerned to identify the coherent pattern, rather than give an account of any individual's view.

Because my goal was to capture different accounts of what it means to be white in the New South Africa, there was no attempt to gain quantifiable data regarding how widespread the support is for the respective narratives. One respondent who clearly positions him or herself differently on key aspects of his or her racialization is sufficient to indicate that this story is being told within the country. For most of the narratives, though, the comments of several respondents hung together in a consistent, multivoiced, pattern. Similarly, in almost all cases, all the comments of a particular respondent would fit neatly into the interpretive frame of only one narrative. There were a few exceptions, however, where a single comment would seem to fit into another narrative more appropriately than the rest of the comments by a particular respondent.

As my unit of analysis is the narrative, not the individual participant, I have trusted my judgment on this. Although different streams of sense-making within the responses were clear, there obviously were no "naturally" demarcated cut-off points between the narratives I describe. Again, I had to trust my judgment about when a big enough difference in degree in terms of orientation justified being regarded as another narrative, or just a variation within what should still be grouped together. Although I try to present some of this complexity, my discussion inevitably cannot do justice to all the nuances of the responses I grouped together in a narrative.

Before the individual narratives are discussed, however, the rest of this chapter outlines some general points that emerged about white South Africans' understanding of their racialization, especially of the respondents' accounts of their first awarenesses of being "white."

Whites in South Africa seem to be clear and unanimous about at least three things: (a) that the meaning of whiteness has indeed changed in recent times, though the nature, desirability, and extent of the change is interpreted differently; (b) that whites certainly were privileged in the old order, though attitudes to, and insight into, this privilege differ; and (c) that (to a varying extent) this privilege was part of the taken-for-granted life world of the old order, though a greater awareness of some of the implications dawned earlier and with clearer focus for some than for others, and with different responses.

These three points are what white South Africans would agree are the facts. The narratives that I will be addressing in the following chapters enable different ways of dealing with these perceived facts and legitimate different responses to them. A more detailed analysis of these approaches and responses will be given as each individual narrative is discussed. At this stage, however, some general discussion of the experience of being socialized into white South African society, based upon respondents' comments, will provide a useful point of entry for comprehending the social and personal sea changes the specific narratives are trying to negotiate.

The different discursive constructions identified in the manner described above tell diverse stories about the position of whites within, and their relationship to, the new order. Each narrative also clearly positions itself in relation to the other narratives that can shape subjectivity for whites, and does this primarily through defining a different relationship to the historical "others," black South Africans. In this way, the narratives range along a continuum from those that are most influenced by the master narrative, to those that undermine the most basic tenets of the master narrative. In other words, I would like to pause on the taken-for-granted privilege (c) above), before proceeding to the discussion of the individual narratives in subsequent chapters.

Commenting on early experiences that first made them aware of being white, two respondents recalled childhood moments of curiosity about physical difference. One of them wanted to touch the hair of a little black girl her own age. The other remembered being bathed by her nanny and drawing attention to the difference between their skin colors. Their simple observations of visible difference would soon be polarized by socialization into a world of "them" and "us." Many respondents experienced their socialization into whiteness as so all-pervasive and diffused that they could not recall any specific incidents, or tie it to any particular associations. They (mis)recognized the polarization as simply part of the generalized sense of the "way things are," along with everything that entailed. These people commented, for example, "I have just always known that I was white"; "I grew up with it"; "I have just always been aware that I was white and not black." The fact of one's whiteness had the bedrock certainty of "snow is cold, rain is wet."[1] A young farmer from the Eastern Cape imparts a sense of these matter-of-fact processes of childhood racialization.

* My whiteness didn't mean much—I always knew the black people I grew up with were different (color) to me. It just felt odd that we couldn't go to school together.

The comment above prefigures the major observations about the racialization into whiteness in the old South Africa that this chapter will explore. On the one hand there is the sense of the commonplace that accompanied "racial" learning, of the casualness that was internalized along with privilege; on the other hand there is a discomfort, an uneasiness, which had to be repressed in the process of socialization into the racist society.

While not necessarily able to recall any specific incident that marked their early initiation into racial socialization, several people were able to identify an area of South African society that they first recognized as racialized, but usually understood as "normal life."

* I have no recollection of a particular incident, rather a gradual realization of a separation in housing, education, etc. [research technician]

* I came to feel privileged through not having blacks on the beaches, buses, etc. [engineer]

- My playmates at home were not allowed to go to school with me. [college student]

A few respondents mention a growing realization that the way the country functioned on a daily basis was formally structured:

- White meant privileged, at least in relation to black and colored South Africans. This I realized once I knew what apartheid was. [secretary]

- It was the first time I realized that the laws governing blacks and whites were different. I was only ten years at the time. I accepted it without question. [medical technologist]

Unsurprisingly, for many respondents early awareness of racialization is associated with their black African nannies, other female domestic servants, gardeners, or farm laborers and their children. Through the way they were positioned vis-à-vis people who shared their daily lives, white children acquired a general sense of superiority. As one put it:

- I grew up in a house where "black" was viewed as being less human, less intelligent. [researcher]

They came to accept entitlement and privilege:

- I was brought up on a farm where the white people always had all the advantage, e. g., schools , buses, money, education. I always thought that because I am white I am entitled to these things, and because of their skin color, "they" are not. [secretary]

In these everyday ways their class expectations were formed. A surgeon summed up his childhood insight as amounting to "poor gardeners are all black." A professor recounts:

- I was aware of the char^2 in our house being "colored." It was significant because "workers" in my house were not the same skin color as "family" and "friends." My whiteness was a "sign" that I was not destined for "menial" tasks.

In other words, young white children understood that they would be the natural heirs to a superior life:

- I was brought up with a nanny and so it was more or less something I took for granted. In this situation I was aware mostly of the differences in living conditions. [artist]

This superior quality of life was also understood to be premised on exclusiveness and status:

- When I was a little boy on the farm, my only friend was a black boy. I went into our house, and when he also wanted to come into our house, my dad told him to stay outside. Then I realized I was white. I felt that my whiteness gave me status in life. [high school pupil]

Asymmetrically structured relationships, unequal styles of interacting, all were established as the norm. For many, being white provided the guarantee of agency in relation to passivity, of being the dominators in situations of interaction, of getting their own way:

- I grew up on the Platteland[3] and we played with the little black boys, but somehow there was an understanding that we were the masters. I think that the fact that we took the initiative in most of the games we played gave us the feeling that we were superior. I think that I interpreted my whiteness as a leader amongst my little black friends. [lecturer]

In these and many other subtle and not-so-subtle ways, the lesson that one treated "blacks" and "whites" differently was imbibed from the social milieu as unconsciously and un*self*consciously as catching measles or mumps from the surrounding air:

- At some point I became aware that there were both black and white people. My parents always had black servants. There was nothing significant about this, just the fact/reality of the way things were. I grew up thinking that everything associated with whiteness was better. Black was definitely "less than" and to be related to with distancing or in a condescending way. [youth worker]

Sadly, the behavior of the "others" themselves seemed to corroborate what the children were learning about the "way things were." A respondent reports having felt justified in his sense of superiority by an early conversation:

- It was a colored farm worker who told me that he was a "hotnot"[4] and will always work for white people. I felt superior to him. [high school pupil]

As well as communicating "proper" ways of interacting, society passed on messages about the appropriate emotions to experience interracially. The following anecdote, also told by a high school pupil, communicates the combination of fear and self-congratulation that typifies white colonial settler identity:

- At the age of about six, my father worked at a state hospital in a rural area. The majority of the population was black and it served as a real eye opener to me because we were but a handful of white people amidst the masses. In a way it was pretty scary. It made me feel superior despite the fact that we were the minority because we were the ones with the education. I felt that without the white people to help organize them, they would be lost, and chaos would be the order of the day.

The social construction of "white" emotions is further illustrated in the following examples related by three women respondents. They remember being taught, as young white girls, the fear that drives segregation and the need to live defensively and suspiciously. They imbibed a horror of familiarity, especially of physical contact with "nonwhites."

- My nanny had me on her back, and whilst baby-sitting, took me during the evening to chat with other blacks. My parents were distressed at this. I was 4–5 years old. I learnt that some things were taboo for whites. There was a sense of not being safe in black settings. [researcher]

- I was molested as a 5-year-old by a garden boy and the horror and outrage of my parents made an enormous impact on me. "Whites" were not supposed to be in a position where this could happen. It was my fault for "hanging around" the gardener. [secretary]

- I was scared of black people because my mother was scared. [college student]

In such an environment of generalized, free-floating danger, the need for safety becomes paramount. One young respondent romanticizes her parents' paranoia:

- I was pleased to know that I was a white child and that I had such wonderful parents, who wanted the best for me by telling me about the blacks. [high school pupil]

On the one hand, then, whiteness attracted danger, because it was the target of envy. On the other hand, however, it provided protection from many of the unpleasant things that young whites saw happening to "others." A university lecturer, who does not give details of the incident, reports witnessing a scene that filled him "with shock, horror and compassion for the victim." It was his whiteness, he realized, that made him "safe from similar physical violence against my person." Nevertheless, this protection was dependent on precarious social arrangements that could disintegrate at any point; the protection could turn out to be what was actually delusional. Another respondent draws attention to this sense of insecurity:

- I was comfortable in that I was in a high status position, but aware that without such "protection" my whiteness was very fragile. [professor]

Of course, there were counter discourses present in the country. Although subjugated, they did provide different systems of sense-making that relativized the taken-for-granted world for those who were exposed to their influence. An example of virtuoso microopposition by a domestic servant is hinted at in the anecdote referred to earlier of the little girl being bathed by her nanny. The respondent observes that she has remembered the incident because "we agreed that her color was prettier." For children who were exposed to counter discourses, however, the impossible contradictions between what "ought" to be and what was took a heavy psychological toll. One woman, who relates that she "grew up in a political home," remembers:

- When I was seven I started having nightmares about hungry black waifs—full of guilt and fear. The dream occurred quite often. I felt responsible, impotent, guilty, and also under threat. [teacher]

Many of the white children growing up in Apartheid South Africa experienced incidents that disturbed them, unsettling the easy surface of the "way things are," and leaving psychological impressions that have lasted.[5] These incidents have provided, and still provide, the seed ground for reevaluating the assumptions inculcated by the culture of their childhood, and the points of take for counter discourses about whiteness. Experiences that troubled young white children ranged from those that stirred a sense of embarrassment to those that aroused alarm and distress. One woman described her girlhood discomfort at being treated with a deference she could sense was inappropriate:

- I wondered why, when as a child of nine years, an old black man made way for me on a pavement [sidewalk] and looked downward as not to see me. [development organization employee]

Another woman recounts a similar feeling of fraudulence. She was unable to process the conflict between the way she was being treated and the rule that one should respect one's elders. She describes the awkwardness of being singled out for special treatment:

- I was embarrassed at being more courteously treated than an elderly black man, and that I should be privileged in the eyes of the other white man. [consultant]

A scientist describes a distasteful incident from his childhood that shocked him at the time and left a lasting impression:

- On a school bus, there were school kids spitting at a black man. I remember this because I felt revulsion and annoyance. I thought that one should not treat anyone in this way.

Others were jolted into an awareness of what whiteness could mean through witnessing violence that happened to "others":

- I saw a black boy being beaten up. He was a servant, and had allegedly stolen. [photographer]

- I remember the brutality of seeing a black man being beaten up by the post office officials at the age of ±6 years. It seemed white people could assault black people and no one stops them. What did the black man do? He seemed harmless. White people can treat black people brutally. Black people don't retaliate. [therapist]

Finally, a few respondents were made conscious of their whiteness through actual political discourse. These people pinpointed events that had caused national controversy during their childhood years. So, for example, a Capetonian woman recounts:

- At the age of 12/13 years I became aware of the efforts of the Apartheid government to disenfranchise the "colored" people of S.A. The incident was of major media interest and created a lot of opposition in S.A. political/legal circles. It seemed ridiculous and highly immoral that we whites could seek to deprive others of their legal rights. [computer analyst]

The experiences of people who came to South Africa as immigrants at a later stage in life were different. Most of these people commented on becoming aware of the system of Apartheid, per se, and how this struck them, rather than early experiences of being racialized:

- I have only lived in this country since 1982. We were driving into Soweto in 1983 and we were told to leave the township by the police. I was embarrassed, not knowing which side of the cage we were. [professor]

- At the age of 27 I arrived in S.A. emigrating from a European country—looking for a job I paged through adds in newspapers. Most of them contained the advert "European lady . . . to do. . . ." I realized how the Apartheid policy was implemented in practice. [administrative assistant]

- I recall two months after arriving in S.A., eight months pregnant, missing a bus, then not being able to take the next bus—it was for blacks only—the stupidity of color segregation. I disliked being different. [sales person]

An American immigrant, who recalls his early racialization in Alabama at the time of the desegregation of the schools, relates an interesting exception. "As white kids," he comments, "there was great pressure to band together against a new black teacher. I interpreted my whiteness as superiority, cliquishness." These recollections of the respondents of their early understandings of the racialized nature of their life world illustrates that most white South Africans grew up in a context in which, for the most part, the superiority of whiteness was not problematized, let alone the notion of "race." Whatever their individual experiences or responses, it was the Apartheid version of the master narrative of whiteness that underwrote their material and psychological existence. The master narrative provided the dominant frame for sense making, in effect even defining the terms for oppositional identities. The next chapters will outline what can be seen to be the collapse and fragmentation of this master narrative, and the emergence of alternative and competing narratives to describe, explain, and produce whiteness in the changing South Africa, given that the political structures no longer support the master narrative. Some of these narratives try to retain as much of the master narrative intact as possible; some draw on discursive repertoires that were subjugated in the old order; some on narratives that have been present in South Africa for centuries; some draw on new discursive resources.

Chapter four outlines the construction of whiteness that assumes a basically unchanged power relationship between "whites" and "nonwhites." This narrative is called *Still Colonial After All These Years*. The narrative, *This Shouldn't Happen to A White,* is the subject of chapter five, and it is told by those who feel that they are being victimized by a reversal of the "normal" state of affairs. There are white South Africans who accept the change in power as irreversible and are trying to find practical and even creative ways to remain white in the New South Africa. They tell the story, *Don't Think White, It's All Right*. This narrative is discussed in chapter six. White South Africans who feel they did not internalize the enculturation of racialized South African society tell the tale detailed in chapter seven, called, *A Whiter Shade Of White*. Finally there are white South Africans who are moving away from their whiteness in different ways, and they are the narrators of the story, *Under African Skies, or, White But Not Quite*.

There are now many shades of "whitenesses" legally available to white South Africans; all but one, the previously legally endorsed master narrative. The center did not hold.

Chapter 4

༷

Narrative One:
Still Colonial after All These Years.

There are many things the blacks will have to learn.

—respondent, study questionnaire

Although the situation in the country has changed dramatically, some whites are telling the same old story about whiteness, as if the master narrative is still appropriate for orientating them to their new circumstances. The colonialist narrative is told with varying degrees of animosity or goodwill toward the "others"—by some who are pitting their wills against change as well as by some who would regard themselves as genuinely committed to change. The defining characteristic of this narrative, however, is that the person still constructs whiteness around the belief that whites are in a position to define themselves and the "other" more or less unilaterally, and that intervention needs to take place on "white" terms, for the "good" of the "blacks." Power is perceived to reside in the hands of whites, who should still largely dictate the content and pace of change. I will discuss two main versions of this narrative, *The Hardliner Colonial* and *The Altruistic Colonial*.

The Hardliner Colonial

Our identities are as the sparrow to the elephant.

—respondent, study questionnaire

The tellers of this hardline colonialist narrative seem to have emerged from an ethnocentric childhood with little regard for human dignity. Current circumstances provide the cement to harden this ethnocentrism into outright xenophobic rejection of the "other," based on a firm belief in the innate superiority of the "white" race. An analysis of the responses of a businessman from Gauteng[1] illustrates this mindset. He says:

- My whiteness was never a real issue. Generally white was more superior intellectually. Today I am more convinced than ever of this. [businessman]

This person regards "minimal missionary work to uplift blacks" as what he is contributing to societal transformation. His interaction with African peers in the workplace over the last nine years has led him to the insight that he is "there to promote, uplift and encourage the blacks who can and want to learn." This humanitarian undertaking is, however, hindered by "their lack of commitment in wanting to be uplifted, and their inability to maintain higher standards." In the future, he hopes "to continue for the positive, without having to lower standards to accommodate blacks." Beneficently, he will "acknowledge and recognize blacks that have committed to, attained, and maintained higher standards." This endeavor to bring "blacks" up to the level of whiteness is apparently foreclosed; the cultures, he confides, are "historically entrenched and completely incompatible." Alluding to a biblical text, he regards the difference between his identity and that of black South Africans as biologically fixed, comparable to the difference between "the sparrow and the elephant."

The respondent's own racialization is accepted as an unqualified good:

- Whiteness has EVERYTHING to do with my culture and identity.

Blatantly self-advancing in his thinking, he laments the loss of advantage in the new order:

- Your whiteness is no longer your friend, granting favoritism, but a barrier.

Whereas a nod is made to the deleterious effects of Apartheid on black South Africans ("they were definitely MORE affected"), the

major effect of Apartheid was to provide nurturing ground for the
innate spitefulness and vengeful nature of the "others." "Blacks," he
says, "want to get back at whites—at almost any cost." Although he
is "not concerned" about how black people regard his whiteness, the
words he imagines to be going around in their minds are "You will
soon wish you were black."

The reader can identify the master narrative, fired in the
Apartheid kiln, in almost every aspect of this account: the unilateral
weighing of costs and benefits; the paternalism and self-congratulation; the emphasis on "standards," "civilization," and "intellect,"
which equate with "whiteness"; the repressed guilt in the phrase
"they want to get back at whites"; the way in which "others" are defined (with biblical sanction) so that they are held in a double bind
that promotes the interests, but which also reveals the underlying
paranoia, and the thinly disguised drive to power, of "whiteness."
The logic twists and turns to support the ideology of white superiority and preferred entitlement in the face of contradictory evidence
and changed circumstances. Whiteness still *ought* to be able to perform the function of social control.

Other respondents bring out other aspects typical of the old
colonial narrative. The following assessment, given by an accoun-
tant, is also steeped in paternalism, evoking the familiar colonial
trope of perpetual children:

- I have a farming interest, and therefore work with unskilled labor. They expect me to care for them. I see my
  whiteness as being a caretaker. [accountant]

Yet another familiar trope, that of the white rescuer, particularly as
a function of superior development and reason, informs this man's
observation that:

- Being white means that I am part of the culture that
  has developed SA socially and economically and has
  created an orderly way of life which appears to be what
  the blacks want—perhaps the presence of whites will
  help the attainment of blacks' goals without too much
  disruption.

Finally, the usual tactic of dividing subordinates into "good blacks"
and "bad blacks" emerges in this apology for conservative racism:

- There is a major difference in "blacks/nonwhites" in towns/cities and on farms. In towns people want the same objectives (basically) but on farms you have a lot of peasants who only want to drink and have no responsibilities and who have no basic moral standards—these people are commonly called "kaffirs"[2] by the people who work with them. Unfortunately most farmers (boers)[3] only associate with these peasants and therefore their perception of "black" people is distorted. [accountant]

The comments of a schoolboy from a rural area reveal the extent to which he is determined to hold on to the controlling master narrative into which he has been interpellated. His words reveal the impossible contradictions he experiences: he insists on the view of whiteness that has been passed on to him, while the world around him has changed. Un(self)consciously he embraces the brutality licensed by an environment that did not challenge, and in fact condoned, racial violence. He reminisces:

- In front of our house is a little playing park with seesaws and swings. It was of course only for white children. When the black children came to play in this park, we would chase them away by throwing stones after them and shooting slingshots. I was white and my friends too. So we were used to the fact that "they," the "blacks," never trespassed in our park, and that we had ours and they had theirs. I was also used to it that I was the boss and "they" were the slave or the underdog. Back then, everybody knew his or her place, today the "blacks" and whites are mixed and confusion is caused. You don't know if it is right or wrong. For example, in the old days "blacks" used to sit in the back of the car, today they are sitting up front, and is it right or is it wrong? [schoolboy]

The "natural" hierarchical order of Baasskap[4] that had been maintained by the system in the "old days," and legitimated through the Apartheid segregationist version of pluralism ("we had ours and they had theirs") has been upset. The present confusion serves to justify the old order. Now the promised land has been lost:

- To be white now means almost a sort of outcast.

The error on the part of the whites, it seems, was misplaced leniency:

- They are used to be given what they want and that is where we the whites done wrong. We are used to give.

Bleak as this picture is, it can be managed if blacks make the necessary adjustments, like not desiring unreasonable reciprocity in expectations and behavior:

- The "blacks" want to be like us, they want to be treated like us. They want to push us around like the old people[5] did to them and still is doing.

"Blacks" will need to do the emotional work if the new order is to work:

- There are many things the "blacks" will have to learn. They must realize that they can't expect the whites to do what they want, because the whites are used to the old ways, the ways they were learned and brought up with.

They also need to acquire some moral worthiness, like "whites," and not cause upheaval:

- Being white always meant to me that you must work for your money and bread, but some "blacks" still expect everything to be given to them by striking, etc.

This young man copes with being in a multiracial school by compartmentalizing his life:

- I have a few black friends in school, but it is only in the school time and on the sport field that we are friends. After school and sport they go to their old friends, and I with my friends.

What these friendships have taught him about his whiteness is that "blacks" can, in fact, learn the necessary tolerance that coexistence is going to require. "They understand sometimes why I react to an event the way I do," he explains. "They know I have been brought up in that way, and it is almost second nature."

A clue as to why this young person needs to hold onto the narrative of white superiority with such intransigence lies in the double bind caused by his parenting. Growing up in an authoritarian society, where accepting and obeying parents is an absolute norm, he would be a traitor to them if he did not uphold their teaching. The old narrative remains the given to which the future must adjust. The vehemence with which this tale is told indicates that this narrative, old as it is, is being asserted with renewed vigor in reaction to new, "liberal" narratives about whiteness. Being loyal to these conservative teachings creates a confusing world of contradictions for the young scholar, requiring feats of rationalization that can only be described as psychological gymnastics. The narrative is out of kilter with the realities he faces.

- You are born and your parents bring you up in the way of the old South Africa. The past is being held against you.

The confusion in the above narrative provides a segue into the other version of the *Still Colonial after All These Years* narrative, the *Altruistic Colonial*.

The Altruistic Colonial

> Their consciousness has lifted.
>
> —respondent, study questionnaire

The words quoted above are those of a man with a Ph.D., self-employed in the field of social transformation, and active on the committees of several nongovernmental organizations. His commitment and genuine intentions toward the New South Africa are beyond question. His response is interesting in that he draws on the old colonial narrative yet also aligns himself with narratives that promote integration. The result is a construction that reflects a struggle to reinvent a future in the name of the old.

This respondent lived in Europe until the age of twelve, and saw black people only occasionally. He reports his early learning, and present understanding, about whiteness as follows:

- I read adventure stories about explorers meeting savages. I recognized there were utterly different, lesser human beings, enlightened (to some extent) by contact with whites. White people were the only "real" people. Today I regard myself as a member of the human race of Caucasian origin with a European cultural tradition and civilization. The associated "worldview" has become dominant in the world, partly for better, partly for worse. I am very conscious of the cultural roots and identity of a white person and would never be anything else, but I am growing in understanding and appreciation of the other streams of humanity. [consultant]

He continues:

- I have had innumerable advantages not shared by other population groups. However, my experience has probably not been that different from the experience of whites in Europe or America. I don't believe "blacks" could have absorbed the educational and life experiences I had because of a radically different orientation in the cultural being. This difference takes much more time and shift in consciousness to be bridged.

As the above quotation shows, the narrator of this tale identifies with the supranational whiteness associated with European heritage. An imagination formed by the cultural "textbooks" of colonialism, the adventure story,[6] contributes to the sense of having been culturally advantaged by superior traditions. The influence of Enlightenment humanistic discourse and social evolutionism is evident. Contrary to the *Hardliner*'s tale, the *Altruistic Colonial*'s tale draws on "pure" European colonial discourse, less inflected by Apartheid. In fact, the humanistic tale is told in deliberate opposition to the cynicism and selfishness of the *Hardliner*. Although the narrative harks back to an earlier era, there is recognition that whiteness is undergoing a shift in South Africa:

- Our culture, although still dominant, is not exclusive, and we have to be more careful and sensitive in our interactions.

He feels he has grown through increased exposure to "the emergence of competent articulate blacks" and he welcomes the change, which he feels is "accelerating":

• It is better so. . . . As the streams commingle and share one society we learn to grow together in understanding.

What is significant, though, is his protective stance toward a universalizing European culture, and his faith that European diffusionism will provide the desired influence on the future and benefit "blacks," provided they are receptive to its efficacy. This is true despite some paradoxical insights in recent years. Contradictory internal strains within this narrative are suggested by the following juxtaposition of phrases:

• I feel good about my heritage and free from personal guilt.

• My whiteness is not all there is, and its culture is seriously flawed.

• There is a fear in me that what is of value in my culture will be lost and trampled underfoot and my true worth will not be recognized.

Similar internal contradictions also pervade this respondent's sense of the future. He anticipates becoming "more at ease in a different social milieu; also more defensive of my own values." Assessments of the feelings of "others" pull in different directions, too. He assumes that his cultural tradition is always the desired one. It is "a source of envy, a wish to emulate." "Others" regard it with

• a potential for unreasoning desire to see it suffer and put down. Also much goodwill and recognition of need for "us" in their emergence. Envy and resentment below the surface.

The asymmetry brought about by the inherent value of the different cultural traditions affects all aspects of the new society. It affects what one brings to interactions, he observes:

• There still tends to be a feeling of patronage and duty toward others with less opportunities/abilities.

Moreover, the nature of adaptation that occurs through interaction is also of a different kind:

- They have altered to the extent that their consciousness has lifted, and mine has adapted and learnt.

The asymmetry in the contribution to be made to reconstruction is also evident:

- We are immensely important in developing less advantaged groups, both economically and in adapting to life in a modern society. I have a role in helping create a precedent of successful integration in South Africa for this country and humanity.

The colonial mission within history has changed its formulation somewhat, but remains clearly recognizable. Idealistic to the last, this narrative sets South Africa up as having an important role to play in the world as proving site for furthering the progress of humankind.

Told with greater or lesser integrity towards all South Africans, the narrative of *Still Colonial after All These Years* holds on to a sense of the importance of whiteness as it has been passed down the generations. Power is, and should be, in the hands of whites to influence change along European, "white" ways for the good of the future for all. The next narrative also clings to whiteness as the ideal, but sees it as having been disempowered, with catastrophic implications. This is a story about whiteness besieged, insulted, and victimized by present circumstances, which have robbed it of its power to control, and even influence, the future. The present, this narrative insists, is the complete antithesis of "normal" expectations; the world is turned upside down and inside out. This narrative is called, *This Shouldn't Happen to a White.*

Chapter 5

༄

Narrative Two:
This Shouldn't Happen to A White

A couple of years ago, white was the color to be. Now it's no
more so. Now the color to be is black if you want to survive.

—respondent, study questionnaire

The people who are constructing, and in turn are being constructed by this narrative, inhabit a world of clear-cut dichotomies.
The colonial binaries that structured the master narrative still provide the scaffolding for reality, but some have been illegitimately reversed. The social edifice now wobbles precariously upon a new and
unreliable structural base. Faith in white superiority (though not always openly acknowledged) is unshaken. The problem is that a new
environment, hostile and unfairly inimical to the interests of those
most deserving of benefit, has been foisted upon the country. Whiteness has become more keenly felt; it is sharply visible in unprecedented ways. A young person from the rural Karoo area confides
that an unpleasant turn has occurred in the salience of "race" to the
lives of South Africans:

- A few years ago being white did not have a serious effect
  on my life, but it is beginning to affect my life now. [high
  school pupil]

In this narrative, there is no doubt about when the change in
the fortunes of whites occurred; it can be pinpointed with great
accuracy:

- The day of the election [school teacher]

- It changed, because our government became black [marketer]

- Our lives changed when Nelson Mandela became president [high school pupil]

Having closely identified with the culturally transmitted versions of history carefully manipulated by Apartheid propaganda, most tellers of this tale lack appreciation of the broader political and historical processes that shaped the recent events in their country. At a personal level, their obedience to the prescribed norms of racial separation precluded meaningful engagement with the events that shaped the lives of "others," and prevented any personal insight from mediating the misinformed collective story they inherited. The inversion of the fortunes of whiteness is therefore as abrupt and traumatic as nonsensical. In the words of a secretary from Gauteng:

- We have lost our rights very suddenly and we were powerless to stop it. [secretary]

The turnabout was not only sudden, but also absolute; it is therefore usually articulated in terms of exact opposites:

- I feel that being white is now to be oppressed. The racism is inverted. [high school pupil]

- Whiteness means a formerly privileged, presently endangered, position. [engineer]

- A race that is much discriminated against nowadays. [school teacher]

In some versions of this story, the (out of) proportions of the reversal are quite catastrophic. The extreme outrage of a young Afrikaans woman reflects the unconscious acknowledgment that "race" was a construction never intended to be used against whites:

- In the days before the election, it was a privilege to be white for the people around you had respect for you. Nowadays you are dirt itself. Nowadays it is said, try something white and you are dead. Yes, now we are dirt itself, and we have no say in the economy. Now it's keep quiet or we take your home or kill your family. We (blacks) are rulers and you must call us Boss from now on. [high school pupil]

The extent to which narrators of this tale recognize the effects of the past on their "others," and the compass of their own earlier privilege varies greatly. One respondent, a university lecturer from the Northern Province,[1] disclaims loudly:

- The discrimination against black was appalling, dehumanizing and criminal. Such brutalization has resulted in our very violent society. [lecturer]

At the same time this narrator ascribes the present state of "racialism and discrimination aimed at whites" to "a poorly educated, highly indoctrinated populace"; that is, to the ignorance and gullibility of the black population. Evidently, brutal as the past was, a reasonable, well-informed population would have supported the perpetuation of white domination against their own interests. Brutalization, dehumanization, and criminal injury do not warrant measures for ensuring present fairness, let alone future redress or compensation.

More usually, though, there is a tendency to underplay the full impact of the past. "They were denied certain rights," admits the marketer from Gauteng, "and therefore had to work harder at achieving something in life." The superficiality of this (lack of) understanding amounts to a denial of how options for advancement were legally foreclosed to black South Africans in the past. Detracting from past injustice and suffering accentuates the purported unfairness of the present situation:

- SOME black people were held back by SOME people, but on the other hand, many did achieve great heights— why? Now we are discriminated against. They are always saying that people who were "previously disadvantaged" must now be advantaged. [school teacher]

Closely allied to the tendency to discount past suffering is the denial of any systemic, structural, or economic advantage for whites enduring into the present:

- Being black in S. A. were difficult for generations, but they have all the opportunities now that we had for generations. [secretary]

What advantage whites gained in the past is invariably attributed to their personal enterprise, skill, and diligence:

- I do not consider myself as "white," but as a person who has made the best use of the opportunities that arose. [engineer]

- Blacks want to have what we have, but in a shorter time, and without the skills and the knowledge that took years to obtain. [secretary]

- They think that everything gets served on a silver platter and that white people didn't work hard in order to achieve what they have achieved. Nonwhites are being treated with a "poor hard-done-by" attitude and literally being handed job opportunities, as an example, on a silver platter. [horticulturist, recent European immigrant]

In the present circumstances, this worth(iness) is being overlooked or ignored. As the school teacher comments—it all makes her "very cross." Overwhelmingly, there is a sense of regret, even openly acknowledged bitterness, at the deeply felt loss of the old order. Whereas the previous system was legitimated by white superiority, the present system is sustained and advanced illegitimately and unreasonably:

- Although most of the whites are good qualified and trained for their jobs, they are replaced with blacks with NO experience and a preference to strike every second week, and NO willingness to learn. [secretary]

If anything, the foolhardiness of the change and the intimations of impending calamity *confirm* innate white superiority. Any hope of a solution in terms of "whitening" blacks is futile. A young farmer from a traditionally English-speaking rural area explains:

- They cannot live up to the higher standards that whites are used to. How do you change a person's culture? [farmer]

All these narrators agree, unequivocally, that whites are now being victimized. Reasonable expectations of "normal" entitlement are being flouted:

- In recent times it became a battle to live a normal life. [high school pupil]

- It is a hard life. To be white nowadays means you must give up everything that you have worked hard for. [high school pupil]

- Whites are being expected to shoulder more and more financial burdens as well as the fact that white opinions and concerns are essentially ignored or deemed racist. [medical technologist]

It is overwhelmingly in the world of work and economics that the present abuse is experienced:[2] financial injury is added to the insult of the indignity of the current situation through policies such as land reform. The young farmer speaks about what affects him most closely:

- Taking land away from one and giving it to another just causes further tension. [farmer]

Overwhelmingly, affirmative action is the lightning rod that catches feelings of grievance:

- If you are a white male your chances of getting work is minimal. Some firms aren't even allowed to take in white people anymore. [high school pupil]

- Affirmative action has implemented reversed discrimination especially towards YOUNG job seeking white South Africans. [marketer]

- Affirmative action handicaps our whites looking for a job. [secretary]

- White people are still being looked upon as being wealthy and thus available for handouts, and if one considers affirmative action the white again has to sacrifice. In this case his or her position (i.e., earning a good income) for a nonwhite. [horticulturist]

In stating her case regarding perceived white disinheritance, this recent immigrant from western Europe reveals the extent to which whiteness takes economic privilege as simple entitlement. It is unreasonable to expect white benefits to be shared:

- White means one pays much more taxes, white means that if I don't pay my rates or electricity the services are disconnected almost immediately. However, how often do we hear of some township (nonwhite) that is millions to thousands in arrears and still they have water and electricity. Look how the standards of well-being of the white person in South Africa has dropped when compared with five, ten, twenty years ago. The white person pays more taxes, does not get cheap or economic housing, the government revenue is spent on housing instead of a decent network of public transport, thus most families need two vehicles and thus most families must have a double income. Funds are not spent on schooling, thus since good schooling is important to most whites, private tuition is the only option, an expensive option. [horticulturist]

For some, the victimization is so extreme that it amounts to persecution, even terror. "Whites," another high school pupil tells us, "are a target for them to steal, rape, anything to get back at whites."[3] The medical technologist cited earlier believes that the changes in her life are attributable to "a desire in the black community to destroy anything built up by whites for the wrongs of the past." It is really a desire for revenge that informs government policy:

- I attribute present changes to revenge for whatever happened in the past disguised as redistribution and equal opportunity. [farmer]

Implicit in all these comments is the acknowledgment that it would be quite logical to expect revenge. Feelings of guilt are never far below the surface ire, and sometimes are almost expressed. The farmer comes close to admitting the niggling hunch that revenge may even be deserved:

- White is now perceived as an object of revenge. We (black people) will try to do to them (white people) what they did to us. A lot of changes can be justified, but if the changes are perceived as punishment or revenge, then I would not like the changes to continue. [farmer]

The tellers of this tale refuse to acknowledge any debt. They try to minimize the cost to themselves, to discourage and restrict change, and to maintain as much continuity as they can with the old order:

- They are trying to change the injustices of the past too fast or at any cost. [engineer]

- I would like to see affirmative action take a more natural infiltration into the system. [marketer]

Present changes to the societal structures are forced, even violent:

- There is no need for the forcefulness with which the mistakes of the past are trying to be corrected. [marketer]

None of the respondents who tell this story report being involved in societal reconstruction, which is unsurprising, given their perception of what the political change has meant to their lives. Adamantly opposed to furthering the present direction of change ("NO! Why?"), many gesture toward liberalism; all are open-minded. The tellers of this tale demonstrate how one can accumulate virtue within psychological bastions secured by denial and defense.

- There is no difference between races only people. There is no future for racists. [engineer]

- Some [blacks] really have a problem—not being white. *I* don't mind them not being white. [school teacher]

They regard themselves as moderate ("I would not mind having a FRIENDSHIP with a mind stimulating black" [marketer]), peace-loving, Christian folk:

- My feelings may change to resentment, but I hope not, because I love the Lord and He loves us all. That is all that counts. I am simply hoping to live in peace. [school teacher]

Benign, according to their own self-assessment, they see themselves as misunderstood by the rest of the world. The immigrant quoted previously opines:

- I feel it is high time that the people worldwide acknowledge that this is not a color problem but a clash of different mentalities. In this world we will never be the same and the sooner the white accepts the nonwhite for what he really is and vice versa and lets everybody get on with living the way God wants us to live the better! (Since God is the creator he has all the answers on how to live). [horticulturalist]

There is even a claim of total racial innocence:

- I am rather puzzled. White? Black? Not White? Not Black? So what? The color of a person's skin has as much significance as his/her eyes. [lecturer]
- White is a skin color. It's one's attitude and outlook on life that is important. [medical technologist]

Nevertheless, what is presented, perhaps experienced, as racially innocent is more accurately understood as psychologically infantile. Those who subscribe to *This Shouldn't Happen to A White* have not humanized the archetypal projections of the master narrative. Some simply refuse to think about how "others" may experience their whiteness:

- It is not something that I think of. [school teacher]
- I do not think it matters. [engineer]
- Their perceptions of me being white is a PERCEPTION and therefore does not make me want to understand or waste my time thinking about being white. I just try to be a full person. [marketer]

For this businessman from Gauteng thus aspiring to fulfil his humanity, to cultivate a friendship with a black person would be straining against the normal flow of things, artificial. On both a personal, as well as a national level, change should happen "naturally," by "natural contact," a kind of effortless osmosis that would gradually relieve whites of the disproportionate burden they have borne. He explains that endogenous processes within their community should drive the advancement of the black population:

- I would like to see a more independent nation and they will still want to be taken care of and not work on merit. I would like them to help themselves. [marketer]

With normally expected social constraints inoperative in the New South Africa, social problems are becoming frequent. "Blacks" are encroaching, wanting an inappropriate familiarity. The school-teacher complains about the violation of social distance:

- They cannot keep it at the level of a business friendship. I will respect[4] them so long as they know that I wouldn't let them interfere with my life, for they are of a different color. If they respect me for who I am, I will respect them. [school teacher]

It is a small step for the unwanted familiarity to swell into full-fledged, racially-motivated sexual taunts:

- It has always irritated me that nonwhite men will wolf whistle at white women. What is significant is that they don't do it to women of their own color! [horticulturist]

Given the pressures caused by unnatural integration, the structural changes being brought about by the new government are dangerous; they incite racial stress. Ultimately they will also prove to be self-defeating, because integration cannot be thrust upon people against their wills:

- Forcing people to get on, e.g., sudden multiracial schools, causes further tension. [farmer]

Better material would be needed for meaningful integration. The minds of black people are filled with hate, envy, and loathing:

- They regard us as oppressors that got rich of them working for us. Walking in the streets you hear these allegations all the time. [high school pupil]
- Some regard us with envy, others with hatred. [surgeon]
- They think my whiteness is a sign of privilege, something to be despised. [medical technologist]

Whereas the thoughts of black people are transparent to whites, the tellers of *This Shouldn't Happen to a White* are in agreement that any possible perceptions that black people may have of whites can have little to teach whites. The lecturer, despite claiming to have been "CLOSE family friends for at least fifteen years" with black South Africans as a consequence of his professional career, sports links and extramural studies, sums up his learning about his whiteness in these interactions as "none." "White" self-understanding arises endogenously and is self-contained, accurate, and uncontaminated by "their" perceptions, which are anyway misrecognitions:

• Interacting with others does not affect my understanding of being white at all. It has changed my understanding of what white means to them. [surgeon]

Such misrecognition of the innate superiority of whiteness is cause for righteous indignation:

• My perception of whiteness has not changed through black acquaintances—not that I know of. I never think of the fact that I am white, unless someone provokes me. [school teacher]

• I realized that they think whiteness is a sign of privilege when a black colleague refused to accept that I had also been through a tough time financially. She refused to accept that what I had achieved was through hard work, study, and perseverance. . . . Such relationships have not altered my understanding of my whiteness. [medical technologist]

The narrative of *This Shouldn't Happen to a White* draws on discursive repertoires of injury, disability, warfare, confinement, displacement, and exile. The pervasive tone is outraged, aggressive, blaming. Showing little awareness of moral complexity, contemporary issues remain ordered by the Manichean allegory; they are still simply black or white. A fundamental competitiveness infuses this narrative, which tellingly dwells mostly on perceived economic consequences of the political change. The events of this world, the narrative suggests, can only be resolved through absolute gain or absolute loss; resources need to be fought for, and one can only be firmly on top or utterly pulverized at the bottom. Losing is terrible and awful. This being so, now that whites are at the "bottom" the narrative encourages an intense undertaking of "me-too-ism," which equates their present circumstances with the suffering of "others" in the past. But whites also still have to carry the old burdens that accompany whiteness in Africa.

"The attitude of the black community is they demand of the white community to supply them with First World privileges and technology, but at the same time condemning the whites for their whiteness," the horticulturist solicits sympathy for the double-bind of being white in the New South Africa.

The dice are loaded by setting up the issues in absolute, catastrophizing terms, such as fighting for survival and fending off the prospect of losing all one's rights[5]. The narrative does not encourage rational reflection on the range of options available to white South Africans. The future is unmitigatingly gloomy in the hands of people who cannot but foul it up:

- South Africa is on a treadmill—going nowhere and therefore achieving nothing. [medical technologist]

- Despite the political cant, ours will never be a truly democratic society. The tyranny of the majority will devour individual genius, while mediocrity will be entrenched by a shaky constitution. [lecturer]

- The life of a white in the new South Africa will be hell, for since the blacks have taken over the whole land, we have been set back and it is on the road to hell. [high school pupil]

The calamity needs to be checked. The disintegration of normality is symbolic of an entire world order going awry. "If it goes on like this," one Afrikaans schoolboy warns, "the world will get into a more difficult spot than it is now."

The tale speaks of growing alienation, of spiraling aggression. Premised as it is on "either-or," the narrative seems to offer only two options: withdraw or fight. The most complete withdrawal is a choice open to the most privileged: emigration. For those who remain, withdrawal entails narrowing one's life into a smaller realm of simple self-interest, minimal desires, and anomie:

- [The injustice] has prompted many whites to start a business in the private sector and maintain their self-respect.[6] [horticulturist]

- We are uncertain of the future. I am simply hoping to live in peace. [school teacher]

- On certain conditions, I will accept them and try to help, but that's going to be hard!! [secretary]

- I am becoming increasingly cynical about the human condition in general. [lecturer]

Others, again, experience this new topsy-turvy world as taunting them, and they plan to meet the challenge:

- I think my attitudes will harden and as is already happening I will become more racist. [medical technologist]

- On the moment my feelings against blacks are not very good. If they keep trying to rule our lives, it will get worse. [high school pupil]

When told by Afrikaners, this tale draws on narratives deeply embedded in the white Afrikaner psyche in the course of a history through which they came to regard themselves as a perpetually persecuted ethnic group in a land that was promised to them. English-speaking white South Africans draw on Afro-pessimistic narratives that reach far into their colonial history and memories of empire that remind them that their fate does not have to be linked to this land, this continent.

"How does the chant, 'one settler, one bullet' grab you? Revenge is sweet, isn't it?" the irate young farmer demands. *This Shouldn't Happen to a White* has the potential to "talk" those who speak it and are spoken by it into the mindset and passions of backlash. Much depends on the size of the exaggerations and distortions that a rioting collective imaginary can maintain; the extent to which the real unsettlement of social transition provides evidence for those scanning for proof of their aggrievement; and how many whites support the spiraling cycles of paranoia. It is conceivable that people who allow their minds to be shaped in this way may begin to engage in collective private violence, such as was known in the south of the United States. This phenomenon has been relatively absent from South African society.[7] Nevertheless, the overall climate of reconciliation (at best) and pragmatism (at least) that prevails in the country does not bode well for their cause, and the chances are good that they will become increasingly marginalized in their narrowing, sulky world.

Luckily, even in the face of present despondency, the old narrative can still console. There is always the mere fact of one's whiteness to sustain one. A high school pupil from the Karoo has the last word in this tale. She reassures herself:

- Nowadays discrimination is against whites and no more against blacks very much, but I am still glad to be white, simply because we are much more civilized than the black culture (they believe in witchcraft, etc.).

Although the next narrative also still draws on some of the logic of the Manichean allegory, the binaries are not precast in concrete, and some flexibility begins to be possible. In this narrative, the position of whites is seen to have been relativized and their role diminished, rather than totally reversed. Although the narrators of this tale see themselves as having lost the power to control the destiny of the country unilaterally, and recognize that the priorities in the country have changed and are no longer set by people who think "white," they envisage options for themselves. They are beginning to map out a modus vivendi. I call this narrative *Don't Think White, It's All Right,* and it is the subject of the next chapter.

Chapter 6

༕

Narrative Three:
Don't Think White, It's All Right

Being white means coming to terms with being a minority
member of our society. Accepting that is most important in
dealing with the change.

—respondent, study questionnaire

The white South Africans who feel psychologically comfortable
dwelling in the discursive milieu of this narrative accept the fact
that whiteness has been relativized (though most say marginalized)
within the New South Africa. While still drawing on some of the discursive repertoires from the "old order," there is a realization that
the tools of the master narrative will not build a sound home in a future organized from fundamentally different ground rules.[1]
Whereas the bearers of the tale, *This Shouldn't Happen to a White*
reject the changes in their circumstances, the spinners of *Don't
Think White, It's All Right* are working on accepting the present,
though not without a good measure of griping and complaining.
Whereas *This Shouldn't Happen to a White* is told in absolutes and
extremes, *Don't Think White, It's All Right* is marked by a vocabulary of greater tentativeness, often ambivalence, definitely greater
open-endedness. The task at hand needs to be taken on. The tale
certainly contains elements of disharmony; yet the tone tends somewhat toward a qualified optimism. Generally, the tellers communicate a sense of personal validation and faith in their heritage. That
provides the necessary stoicism in the face of an uncertain future.

For these people, being white is integral to their identity, even
as they go into an uncertain future. The degree of equanimity they

feel about the process of adjustment, the level of acceptance of their new status, as well as the extent of their commitment to reconstruction vary considerably. Nevertheless, these people see whites becoming one strand within the future "rainbow" society; a strand that should be maintained with greater or lesser integrity. *Don't Think White, It's All Right* can be regarded as the "multicultural" narrative for the New South African society.

Whereas these respondents also relate their change of fortune as some kind of reversal, the terms of the inversion are not seen to be quite as dire. The present situation of white people is not simply and unrealistically equated with that of "blacks" in the Apartheid era, as was the case in the previous narrative. The tone of the following assessments of the New South Africa is clearly different from that of the previous narrative:

- There is reverse discrimination, though a white person has alternatives, which blacks never had. [insurance broker]

- Being white definitely had many advantages in the old South Africa. Being black then also had many disadvantages. Today, however, your skin color is no guarantee for getting a job, for instance. The whites are not the only ones in high positions and whites are not seen as the oppressors anymore. [high school pupil]

With automatic privilege a thing of the past, one has to earn one's way ahead. This is not impossible, nor unreasonable:

- Being white in the Old South Africa was a privilege. One certainly had many advantages, while other South Africans had to struggle against Apartheid. In the new South Africa they have to learn to cope with their new freedom. In the new South Africa being white means that you must work even harder to achieve your goals. So, being white or black has certainly affected both parties. [high school pupil]

Generally, this narrative recounts that what has happened in the country is just in principle, although it is certainly uncomfortable for whites, and not always equitable in execution. "It was a fair election," a schoolgirl says.

"No one wants war," a marketer from Johannesburg weighs up the situation. There are few alternatives in the New South Africa, so one might as well be realistic. He continues:

- Extreme racists aren't going to get us anywhere, except in the international media headlines. One has to become more tolerant of other people's way of life. If you reject or dislike these, you will isolate yourself within a smaller community. If one is prepared to work to get ahead in life, one has to accept that you will meet and be around different people. [marketer]

Dissatisfaction with affirmative action, complaints about the burden of taxation, concern about perceived spiraling crime and lowering standards—these are all as integral to this narrative as the previous narrative. Unsurprisingly, white men, particularly, feel targeted. A professor from Cape Town sees this new "inequity" as a hangover from Apartheid thinking:

- There is a polarization, especially in economic terms, of an "us" and "them" mentality. If the coin comes up heads, then the other side is down. I find this disappointing. Hopefully we can move away from this Apartheid coin! [professor]

Usually the April 1994 elections are still seen as the pivotal point of change, but not necessarily the direct cause of the social upheaval. The changes taking place in their lives are attributable to broader social movements and longer term historical processes, such as:

- Inevitable political transformation with resultant power changes. [researcher]
- Gradual emergence of black power. [dentist]
- The new political dispensation and new political attitudes. [teacher]

One Afrikaans school pupil points out that breaking the grip of the old order was an express necessity for the beginning of a more hopeful future. "We needed the elections in 1994 and the new government. If not for that, nothing would have changed," she writes.

The strain that runs through all the variations of this narrative, however, is that these respondents regard their whiteness, whether construed in terms of culture, ethnicity, or race, as important to their present identity and for negotiating their future in the changing circumstances in which they find themselves. This fact is owned openly and honestly. There is a difference, however, in the extent to which this identification is entrenched, and to which it is perceived as threatened. For the sake of analysis, therefore, I have divided this narrative into two "streams." The "stronger" version is called *Whites Are Doing It for Themselves;* the "weaker" version is called *We Can Work It Out.*

Version One: Whites Are Doing It for Themselves

The center of gravity of my whiteness is my culture.

—respondent, study questionnaire

Those who talk this talk feel a very strong connection to their ethnic and cultural traditions. Some now feel this more than ever before. They see the way ahead requiring a steadfast grip on their heritage, for personal and collective survival. *Whites Are Doing It for Themselves* shares much of the discourse of *This Shouldn't Happen to a White,* but entertains less indulgent attitudes of victimization. Determination to maintain an identity as "intact" as possible is more the watchword for both English and Afrikaans speakers in South Africa who voice the sentiments of *doing it themselves.*

"As a white person, I see myself as an Afrikaner in heart and soul" a pupil from the Karoo asserts. Her comments show how being Afrikaans (not just white) is the highest priority for those Afrikaners who are *doing it for themselves.* Deep patriotism to Afrikaner ethnicity, seen as an indigenous white South African ethnicity, anchors the future. The young women's comments bear this out:

* I love my country, no matter what happens. I am proud to be "white," but not in a taunting way. [high school pupil]

An academic from Pretoria puts it like this:

* What is important to me is the fact that I am an Afrikaner, and that I would like to remain an Afrikaner. I

would like to see the rights of small groups (Afrikaner) entrenched in the constitution. Whiteness is greatly integral to my culture and identity. The Afrikaner or Boerevolk[2] is known to be a white volk, as whiteness and the Boerevolk are almost synonymous. One of the characteristics of the Boerevolk is whiteness. [researcher]

Unapologetically asserting the right to be white in the New South Africa, based on a historical claim of belonging on the land and a belief in the inherent value of whiteness, Afrikanerhood must be maintained in the future. The agreement on this point is evident, as are the tropes from the master narrative, which sustain the faith:

- I am not going to feel sorry because I am white. [high school pupil]

- I think that deep down, most blacks would like to be white. In some way, they envy whites for their whiteness. Bearing this in mind, I am glad to be white, and should I be physically reborn, I would like to be white again. [lecturer]

- I cannot speak for the blacks, but being white has most definitely affected my personality, my beliefs, my education, my wealth, etc. Perhaps, being white affected my life in a positive way, while being black affected many blacks negatively. White people tend to care more about their surroundings and keeping it clean than blacks do. [insurance broker]

Whiteness is an unproblematized fact, but so are the changes in the social position of whites a fact. This means that the road ahead may be tough:

- I don't feel bad about it. It is a fact. Blacks are now governing the country and they are now playing the tune. Many white people feel themselves threatened in the New South Africa. The fact that large numbers of professionals are leaving the country is enough proof of the statement. [lecturer]

- White isn't the elite race anymore. White people are realizing that they have to share their country. I think it was a change for the better. At the moment it is not going very well with our economy, but Rome wasn't built in a day. [high school pupil]

The value of white expertise to the future is strongly asserted. White Afrikaners are seen as having a legitimate and meaningful contribution to make. They bring the experience and will that has accompanied a long history of commitment to the land; their loyalties have never flirted outside the country's borders. A lecturer from the Northern Province maintains:

- I think it will be a great mistake to try to eliminate white initiative, entrepreneurship, professionalism, and know-how from the South African economy. [lecturer]

The lingering influence of the master narrative is abundantly evident in this narrative. Conviction of the innate and enviable worth of whites still provides the most significant handle for getting a grip on things as the Afrikaner culture lurches into unmapped terrain. Enterprise, order, leadership: these are white gifts to the developmentally, perhaps evolutionarily, challenged. Part of the "white" role is to prevent the country from becoming increasingly "third world." Yet, unlike *This Shouldn't Happen to a White,* which adopts an indignant, rebellious stance to the perceived undervaluing of innate white worth, this narrative proceeds a tad more cooperatively. It is more amenable to offering this expertise and talent to the overall project of reconstruction. An important proviso to this contribution, however, is that Afrikaners must perceive the interests of their minority group to be taken seriously. The lecturer from the University of the North cautions about an issue that lies close to the heart of his people:

- I think that the government's land reform initiatives should go very slowly. This is a very sensitive issue that should be governed with the greatest care and mutual respect. [lecturer]

Again, the similarity to, yet also the distinctiveness from, *This Shouldn't Happen to a White* is apparent. Whereas it is a thinly disguised secret whose interests are primarily in need of care and will be served by the slower pace of reform, there is a greater willingness to work toward mutually acceptable solutions.

Another parallel between these two narratives lies in the tendency to focus on the dangers of being white and the threat to physical safety. The perception of an increasing crime rate in the country alarms deeply-held notions about the perils of being white in Africa, perils that may spiral out of control without a white government to contain black hatred and predisposition toward criminality. The same lecturer emphasizes this:

- There are many, especially the radicals, who hate white people and would like to see them removed from the face of the earth. Among the latter is a large criminal group who murder even among their own people (blacks). Of course this is nothing new. Ever since I grew up those blacks who hate the whites did so, before blacks took over the government. The frequent attacks and murders of white persons by blacks [is disturbing]. Three weeks ago an old man of ninety (white) was murdered by two blacks just five houses away from where I stay. [lecturer]

Although the major energy in this narrative is directed toward the assertion of group self-worth and self-preservation, it recognizes (unlike the previous narrative) that this self-preservation needs to happen within a larger framework, that of the "overarching good":

- The change in the structure of South Africa asks for great adjustment from both white and black. The black people have to get used to all their new rights and freedom. The white people as the oppressors have to get used to it that equal rights are here to stay. [researcher]

- The changes have to continue for better or for worse. South Africa needs to be accepted abroad for the economy's sake. [high school pupil]

There is no point in blowing against the wind—the new social order is emerging, and may yet be quite practicable:

- The fact is that whites and blacks have now come to know one another on the ground in politics, have socialized at universities, in business, etc. [lecturer]

In summary, the terms of the story are clear for the Afrikaners telling this tale. They want to be able to go on being white Afrikaners. They will adapt and make necessary adjustments, but they want their concerns, interests, welfare, and safety to be taken seriously. This narrative, then, usually is told with a twist in the tail. A bottom line sets conditional limits on cooperation. If need be, they can resist:

- If the harassment of whites continues, my attitude toward radical/criminal blacks would become more negative, and this may affect my overall feeling toward blacks in general. If things change for the better, I have no problem with working and living in a country governed by blacks. [lecturer]

- Things are so unpredictable. White people are paying half their salaries to the state and it is getting worse with prices of everything going sky high. If there is not going to be a radical change in this country's economic policy, then I'm not going to be happy about working here. [high school pupil]

Constructions among Afrikaners that serve to legitimate white emigration from the country have been very rare in South African history since the first settlement of the Dutch in the Cape Colony, but the implications of the above quotations are unmistakable. If they cannot *do it for themselves* in a way that feels appropriate and satisfactory, these Afrikaners will make their presence felt, or make other arrangements.

"I'm only comfortable with blacks and coloreds who also like Shakespeare, Brahms, Van Gogh, privacy and punctuality." With these words, an English teacher establishes the tone of the English version of *Whites Are Doing It for Themselves*. As opposed to stressing roots within South Africa, the English-speaking version of *Whites Are Doing for Themselves* reasserts the importance of ethnic origins in Europe, most particularly the British Isles. All the following speakers draw on a long tradition of liberal whiteness in the Cape Town area:

- Whiteness is largely associated with European culture. My cultural identity appears much stronger than my national identity. Monty Python and the King Singers are White/English. [dentist]

- My culture is Eurocentric. My value system is embedded in European Protestant ethics. I think being "white" is a historical fact. My understanding of it has not changed. I value my roots, ethics, values. [researcher]

- I see myself as Eurocentric in a multiracial, African country. [teacher]

The refrain of reversed fortunes, of feeling undervalued and marginalized, is repeated in this version of the narrative, as in the others discussed so far. A self-reflective respondent adds an interesting dimension to this refrain by drawing attention to his sense of having lost credibility. This dentist says:

- White means that one is a has-been, discredited, untrusted. Whiteness was privilege, power, and advantage. Those features have no credibility now, and along with them being discarded, so whiteness is also a discard. [dentist]

Even while emphasizing the importance of their Europeanness, some of these respondents recognize that growing up with a monologic cultural identity in a multicultural society has been retarding social skills. A Capetonian woman ascribes her interpersonal difficulty to the effects of Apartheid:

- Growing up in the Apartheid system has closed communication between different ethnic groups. [I have developed] few skills in chatting to people of other groups. I have a sense of not being comfortable in the setting of mixing—although willing and eager to do so. [researcher]

An interesting trend among these responses is that cross-racial contact, even friendships over many years ("my first nonwhite friend was in 1963," the teacher tells us), seems to reaffirm the value of European identification. This teacher, who previously worked in one of the Apartheid homelands, felicitates herself on the greater mobility to which a European tradition provides a passport, compared with the more parochial span of African culture:

- It [a cross-racial friendship] made me realize I was much less bound to a specific community and geographical area than my friend. My understanding of "blackness" grew. [teacher]

The self-reflective dentist referred to earlier, pinpoints his own self-confessed chauvinism:

- The closest I have come to an "affectionate" relationship has been with Indian women. Such areas as religion and customs were obstacles/differences that were hard to ignore. These relationships highlighted a sense of chauvinism about being English and European. I was not able to take much from them of life/customs. [dentist]

This respondent also performs some interesting self-censorship of the European essentialism that tends to inform this narrative:

- I do not feel that my gain was provided by their loss. My gain was in emerging in a culture which has become dominant vis. literacy, trading, technology, materialistic. Dominant by oppression? Maybe!! [dentist]

European essentialism is particularly evident in the tendency to stress "European" values, values that are now seen to be somewhat under threat:

- Western values are also being challenged for more African ethnic values. Things that are important to me are not considered issues of importance, e.g., environmental preservation, cleanliness, punctuality. [researcher]

As they move into an uncertain future where whiteness is perceived to be under threat, their European heritage and the dependable, "endogenous" European qualities gain greater importance. These attributes also suggest criteria for lines of resistance in the New South Africa:

- Whites' entrepreneurial spirit will be stimulated. [teacher]

- I make a stand for quality and merit. The same rules should be applied for everyone. [dentist]

The fact of the matter is that identification with a world beyond the boundaries of South Africa enables English-speaking South Africans to engage in a different kind of psychological withdrawal. The professor of dentistry exemplifies this disengagement:

- I look to overseas to develop a reputation as a scientist and teacher—not to move away but to be acknowledged. The climate does not feel supportive here, and I think it will become less so. But we're a damaged society and the wounds and scars are deep. [dentist]

When all is said and done, what is required may not be a change of heart so much as a change of strategy:

- It is difficult to change one's attitudes toward others, but if you keep these attitudes to yourself, it will benefit the country; i.e., cooperate for the good of all. [marketer]

It is noticeable that whereas *This Shouldn't Happen to a White* tends to dwell almost exclusively on the material and economic consequences for whites of the recently initiated political changes, *Whites Are Doing It for Themselves* focuses to a greater extent on the cultural. The English version of the narrative tends to have an indisputable subtext of cultural chauvinism, sometimes consciously recognized, more often not. Like *Still Colonial after All These Years,* an unapologetic claim to an identity based on a continuation of European-centered heritage is adamantly asserted. Little reflection is given to the extent to which the heritage thus hallowed has contributed to bringing about the current situation. Eurocentrism is unproblematically accepted: believed to have been a trustworthy compass in the past, it is relied upon to provide the bearings for the future. In contrast to *Still Colonial after All These Years,* however, the goal is to establish a more modest power base for these values within a country where power is acquiring an African epicenter.

The "weaker" version of *Don't Think White, It's All Right,* which will be described next, is marked by a great deal of pragmatism, as opposed to the cultural intensity of the stronger version, *Whites Are Doing It for Themselves,* just discussed. This less strident version, as mentioned earlier, is dubbed *We Can Work It Out.*

We Can Work It Out

As I spend more time with them, I see that people of different races can live together without discriminating against each other.

—respondent, study questionnaire

The narrators who are intending to *work it out* also take whiteness as an integral part of their identity. They neither equivocate about their whiteness by redefining it, nor do they deny it; rather, they postulate equality between "races." No group should have to lose its identity or be dominated. A person "listening" to this narrative becomes aware of the fact that these narrators are doing their homework to "get the story right." Not yet expert, but learning, they are beginning to dissociate themselves from some of their childhood lessons, drawing on other discursive repertoires, and finding sensemaking frameworks that will be more rational for their present circumstances. It is no longer only "the blacks" that have a lot to learn:

- To be white in S.A. now means much less than it did in the past. S.A. is now shared by all its people. Democracy helped this shift in many whites' understanding. [professor]

The influence of the discursive repertoires of liberal humanism becomes more prominent than in the narratives discussed previously:

- Being white forms an important part of my culture and identity. Although I think that it forms an important part of my culture, I still think that all races ought to be equal. [high school pupil]

- Being white means being totally equal to being black. [researcher]

- I have a very good girlfriend with whom I grew up [on a farm]. To me this relationship showed me how thin the top layer of your skin is. Under it we are all the same. [high school pupil]

- Everyone is gray now, if you like. [marketer]

- For some blacks my whiteness may be a problem. For most of them it is not, because they accept me as a human being and not for being "white." [high school pupil]

The individualistic discourses of liberal humanism are not new in South Africa, but previously were applied selectively to the "internal affairs" of the white group. Separated pluralism governed the official take on what was appropriate for the relations between groups within the country, and provided the intellectual legitimization for

Apartheid. What is new here, then, is that liberal humanism is being applied by whites in reference to the entire population, without fear of being branded "subversives." As elements of liberalism have been increasingly adopted within the politics of the African National Congress,[3] and inform the negotiated constitution, the infiltration of this discourse into narratives of whiteness in South Africa indicates an attempt to be more in alignment with the new dispensation. In this research sample, most of the respondents telling this narrative were young Afrikaners.

The more rational tone of this narrative no longer construes racial equality as equivalent to victimization of whites. Similarly, loss of guarantee does not amount to simple and universal "reverse discrimination":

- Being white now does not mean such a great deal as it had in the past, because now everyone is equal. Today, your skin color is no guarantee for getting a job. [high school pupil]

Relativization, this narrative indicates, does not summarily entail destruction. The past is not inevitably reversed; there are other possible scenarios, other options. Above all pragmatic, this narrative seeks out those possibilities through a cooperative attitude, all the time hoping not to give up too much white identity in the process:

- Being white means coming to terms with being a minority member of the society. Accepting it is most important in dealing with change. It is unstoppable, and it is better to work with it and try to influence the direction of change. [professor]

Several respondents articulated positive feelings about the political change in the country, and usually reported feelings of relief, a sense of personal liberation, and enhanced self-esteem:

- Being white in South Africa in the present time is not only a time of freedom for the blacks, at last, but also for many white South Africans who didn't agree with the doings of the old regime. [high school pupil]

- I feel relief in the freedom I and "they" now have. [insurance broker]

- The unification through sport feels great. At least we can celebrate national victories as a nation. Everyone wins. [marketer]

Several wanted the present trends to continue ("Because I think it is very fair," one of the high school pupils considers), although some of the familiar provisos still feature:

- As long as they don't tax me more. [professor]
- Yes, but away from the bitterness, and towards reconciliation. [artist]

Strikingly, the respondents who use this narrative framework are more inclined to talk in terms of relational constructs, stressing mutuality and openness. While "us" and "them" still clearly structures most of the thinking, the "other" is less a demon drawn from the collective imaginary, and more a person. And, they comment, they learn from relating to "others":

- I become more aware of the fact that they accept me as a human being as I spend more time with them. [high school pupil]
- It has altered my understanding of how other people saw my whiteness. [researcher]
- Interacting with black acquaintances has made me feel less important. Humbler. [artist]
- I am a bit more aware of cultural differences. [professor]

They sense a different type of interaction evolving:

- My understanding of my whiteness is being changed by the representations of the media, and by the changing nature of the attitudes of the "colored" people toward myself. [artist]

Several respondents, like the person quoted immediately above, report that the changes in media representations are also shaping new awarenesses of "self" and "others." Respondents in this group tend to have more substance that is specific on which to ground their comments about the "other" than they had access to in the previous regime, when the media were heavily censored. This applies to both positive and negative perceptions:

- [I am learning from] dialogue with various role-players and the reporting on the media, but habitual habits in me and others hinder my growth in understanding. [teacher]

- The representations of the media have made me more aware of what "blacks" think. I suspect some of them have a reluctant feeling that they should forgive me because of the example that Mandela has set them. [marketer]

- In the national negotiating forum the militant trade unions appear to me antiwhite. [professor]

Although not actually advocating it, some strands of this narrative recognize that *working it out* may entail some cultural and racial blending. It is not unthinkable, and for some may even be quite sensible:

- I see the cultural differences becoming less distinct. At the moment there is Westernization (largely) of the black person and Africanization (slightly) of the white person. [artist]

"Listening" to this narrative shows that the lexicon in *We Can Work It Out* has moved a considerable distance from *This Shouldn't Happen to a White*. It is more moderate, more reflective of a sense of proportion. The telltale vocabulary of colonial racism still shows up, for example, in discourse about "development" ("I find that with black people of the same development," the researcher says, "the cultural difference is not so pronounced"; "Understanding is of course easier if one is on the same level intellectually," the insurance broker concurs). And the fears have not magically gone away ("If there is simply a redistribution of poverty, the polarization will increase," the professor predicts). Nevertheless, the vocabulary of blame is somewhat replaced by talk about taking personal responsibility for one's future, talk about accepting personal accountability, about exerting oneself:

- If *I* don't make an issue about my "whiteness," I find it doesn't bother them. [high school pupil]

- [Cross-racial friendships] work if everyone tries very hard to understand one another. [high school pupil]

- Everyone must learn to take responsibility, and to accept the many changes that are taking place. [artist]

- Where possible, in my contact with people, I try to make people aware of their racist remarks and viewpoints. [researcher]

In other words, by contrast with the previously analyzed narratives, this narrative allows forays into observing the "self," as opposed to simple projection onto the "other." Questions of personal morality and ethics start emerging. Comments about the mental states peculiar to white consciousness, about new awareness, become more frequent. The tricky issue of how far personal responsibility extends raises its head. As the truth about the past emerges, so do jarring questions of collusion with the white supremacist regime (committed with greater or lesser consciousness) and contentions of unfair benefit from the regime. With these issues becoming part of current debates, feelings of guilt inevitably surface. Acknowledgment of collective accountability has consequences for personal self-image, and lays the possibility open that claims for restitutive action may be legitimate. The tendency in this narrative is to snatch at the plentiful rationalizations that dismiss "white guilt" as a pointless, unconstructive, and pathological emotion. "White people have a guilt complex about what happened in the Apartheid era," the researcher explains.

This guilt avoidance places limits on the introspection that most of those *working it out* perform; a comfort zone, both emotional and economic can be protected behind metaphorical and actual walls. The marketer is representative of the conviction that the elections formally equalized society and that this exempts whites from further compromise. He is comfortable with the statement, "I feel less guilty now and less sorry for other races."

It is tempting to fantasize about an easy way out, a way that will blot out the claims the past has on the present and will keep all these things distant and impersonal. Such a desire is apparent in the following comment by the researcher:

- It is a pity that people can't live together in peace. It will also be a bonus if all can be forgiven and we can start anew, although this is impossible. [researcher]

The researcher's comment also illustrates that the fantasy of avoiding personal sacrifice is dependent on the willingness, yet again, of "others" to accept their past injury with grace and equanimity.

There are tellers of this tale, however, who face the issues of collective responsibility less defensively, and insist on tougher personal accountability:

- Being white means that one has to come to terms with the possibility that some form of expiation is required on one's part; and also the fact that one is no longer more privileged and may conceivably be less so in the future. [artist]

On the whole, those who use this narrative find that as a consequence of understanding the present in new ways, one begins to frame the past differently:

- It feels strange to have a government that does not have the white people's prosperity at heart, but wants to change everything to the advantage of the other people. It makes me more aware of the fact that I grew up with racist ideas. [researcher]

The "problem" whites are addressing also starts acquiring a different face. What exactly is it that one is losing, that one is giving up? What is it that one stands to gain? Along with this reframing, the sense of connectedness that a white supremacist social government explicitly tried to outlaw, is given space to emerge:

- I feel a general sadness at how unnecessary all the suffering under Apartheid was and how much suffering the future will still bring. [salesperson]

To summarize, the two versions of *Don't Think White, It's All Right* analyzed above indicate that there are discourses circulating within the New South Africa which, while not encouraging abandoning of white identity, do envision possibilities of new forms of subjectivity within more inclusive structures. Whereas the stronger, more defensive, version, *Whites Are Doing It for Themselves,* indicates a greater desire for retaining cultural boundaries, *We Can Work It Out* shows more pragmatism and personal flexibility, as well as evidence of some developing appreciation of the ethical implications of white identity.

The next narrative to be analyzed disavows implication within the structures of racialization that have characterized South Africa's troubled past. It avoids the pain of acknowledging the personal ramifications of South African socialization. It is the narrative of *A Whiter Shade of White*.

Chapter 7

༄

Narrative Four: A Whiter Shade of White

I don't think I am white. I like to consider myself a person
without color.

—respondent, study questionnaire

Given the uncomfortable feelings that may accompany being
white in the New South Africa, it is not surprising that several respondents do not want to own up to being white. These people en-
tertain a construction of whiteness that frankly disclaims any implication in whiteness, or avoids any real reflection about the
issue. Denial is the overriding factor. There are several interesting
permutations of this narrative. Some of the versions are discursive
constructions that straightforwardly evade issues of privilege and
power, shielding assumptions of white entitlement from scrutiny.
Other versions vent resistance to the way whiteness has been constructed in recent South African history. Raconteurs of this narrative dissociate themselves from the white groups who are held responsible for the country's dismal racial record, while yet
screening out attention to personal involvement in structures of
whiteness.

People of greatly divergent political persuasions tell versions of
this story; all the permutations require rationalization. Sometimes
the different permutations employ distinctive appeals to avoid own-
ing the label "white"; at other times they may use the same appeals,
but with different subtexts. In the present time of flux in the country, when social identities are unfixed, decentered, and social signifiers are contested by competing interests, the same rhetorical appeals can be used in competing ways. Consequently, some clues into

background and context are often needed in order to interpret more accurately what is being asserted.

This chapter identifies some of the major appeals used to construct a narrative of a whiteness that purports to have eluded enmeshment with "race" and the concomitant white privilege.

Appeals to An Overarching Identity

The appeal to an identity within a larger, more inclusive grouping is not new in white South African identity politics as a way of indicating that one has overcome partisan loyalties, and that one supports a "greater good." To lay stress on being "South African" was to emphasize that one was not identifying primarily as an Afrikaner or as an English speaking South African. As such, the self-label "South African" had connotations within "white" society of being moderate and reasonable—having put the Boer War behind one in the interests of creating a unified citizenship. A deliberate attempt at building a nation that would rise above the historically entrenched power struggle between the English and the Afrikaners, the term remained equivocal about which ethnic group was governing, and in whose interests. Consequently, its success at containing internal tensions within the white population varied at different points in the history of this century. Black South Africans, of course, were excluded from this nation-building project.

Today the title is being used again to build a new encompassing, overarching South African identity.[1] White South Africans certainly try to to show a more inclusive frame of mind that now incorporates black South Africans. Yet, as in the past, a person claiming the designation can be evasive about his or her own sectional advantage. Internal contradictions within society are obfuscated. One can see, therefore, that the woman respondent who explicitly denies that black people have suffered any systematic, sustained disadvantage, but at the same time writes, "To some extent I am really just a South African," is trying to have it both ways: to be accredited with being broadminded while yet keeping a racist mindset. Her ignore-ance of the impact of "race" is highlighted in her ingenuous disclaimer with which she concludes: "Being white has never bothered me."

The teacher whose words are quoted in chapter three may differ in the degree of her posturing and level of piousness (the open-mindedness is undertaken in His name), but very little in intention and genuine goodwill from the woman quoted below who openly rejects a racially inclusive South African identity:

- I am not a South African, but a WHITE South African, because their culture and identity was never the same and never will be. Maybe in three hundred years things will change.[2] [secretary]

An alternative overarching identification that those whose talk is *whiter than white* now claim, is the appellation, "African." As before, it is the context provided by the rest of the response that indicates when this label is being used as whitewash. Some white South Africans are using this label in all integrity to indicate an important shift in subjectivity, of identifying with the current nation-building project which redefines South Africa within the context of Africa. Yet the ambivalence provided by the overarching nature of the appeal enables fuzziness about partisan interests. It can render a base of privilege unassailable through adopting an alias of correct national identity.

The insistence on being "of Africa," an act of dissociation from European roots, has been important in Afrikaner identity since the earliest times of white settlement. The self-identification with the land also indicated a strong claim of *entitlement* to the land in contestation to black African claims of prior settlement.[3] A respondent derides the ability of black Africans to govern the country with anything but chaotic tyranny. Yet he also claims:

- I do not think being white has much to do with my identity. I regard myself as an African, and want to be judged in such terms.

It is apparent that he is making much more of a statement about his intractable rights as an Afrikaner, than about any shift in consciousness toward inclusiveness, or away from "whiteness." He does not mean to imply any identification with the issues facing indigenous Africans. The terminology has shifted, but not the sentiment.

Both the examples discussed above are perhaps more likely to be used in this equivocal way by Afrikaners, who have always prided themselves on their patriotism, in contrast to the apparently less committed English South Africans. But there are English-speaking South Africans who are "white" enough to have become quite translucent. For various reasons, they look over their shoulders when issues of "race" and "racism" are mentioned. The next sections of this chapter discuss the appeals they use to avert attention from their collusion in whiteness.

Appeals to Nonapplicability

As far as many English-speaking white South Africans are concerned, they did not institute or support Apartheid;[4] indeed they may have actively opposed it. They therefore do not feel that they were implicated in racism. The tendency to conflate racism with Apartheid, and therefore to feel absolved from deeper soul-searching, is quite strongly represented in the sample. Some of these respondents appeal specifically to "leave of absence." The logic of this comment by an administrative assistant of Polish background draws on this appeal:

- I spent most of my life, especially my formative years, outside of SA and as a result do not feel my life has been significantly affected by whiteness, i.e., the color of the skin as a distinction didn't apply. I was discriminated against for my belonging to a minority group. [administrative assistant]

Being "white" in Europe, one gathers, had no racial overtones. This respondent declares herself to be in favor of the political changes, but harbors the by now familiar disgruntlement about perceived escalating reverse discrimination. She neatly evades a question about *her* changes in understanding with observations about how *other* people need to develop and change. The familiar strategy maintains the focus of discussion on the "other":

- It is difficult to expect drastic changes in people's mentality over the period of two years. [administrative assistant]

Her own attitude has always been impeccable:

- My attitude will always be one of equality for everyone. [administrative assistant]

In a similar evasive appeal to absence, a computer analyst claims that whiteness has "no significance in any terms" for her identity. She wrote a note attached to her response:

- I don't relate, somehow to these questions. Whiteness has never been an issue for me. Perhaps it's relevant that during my school days I lived in the United States. [computer analyst]

She does concede, though, that:

- Yes, white is a culture, apart from others, and yes, it is changing dramatically in SA. People seem to have loosened their previous barriers and seem more open to "letting each other in"—perhaps not only racial barriers, but general openness. [computer analyst]

The respondent's discourse of obligation, guilt, and duty divulges a preoccupation with the need to be morally irreprehensible, a common thread which runs through the narrative of *Whiter than White*.

- We did carry a huge moral and psychological burden even though many of us ACTIVELY opposed Apartheid. Always the question: "Should we not be doing more to oppose?" . . .
- We've got rid of the moral millstone of Apartheid. . . .

Such is the fear of being perceived to be aligned with what is morally reproachable that even to talk about "race" could implicate one in racism. The topic is a no-no:

- Whites can never know how blacks were affected by Apartheid. [computer analyst]

A medical scientist, who spent her childhood in England and welcomes the political changes, claims, "I do not think in terms of color." Close friendships as longstanding as twenty years, "haven't altered [her] understanding of whiteness." Nor, she attests, is her understanding of what it means to be white in South Africa currently undergoing any change. Impermeable, the whiteness of those who never have recognized it turns out to be strangely color fast.

Yet another respondent discloses that she has had cross-racial friendships in England since 1978, and in South Africa since her return in 1990. To the South African ear it is clear that she is a returned exile, and that she took a moral stand against Apartheid. She indicates that she has sorted out "race" by observing that the questions posed to her are "all too simplistic" and by prefacing her responses with such phrases as, "lots of things" and "of course." This is an interesting example of a respondent exercising her own power in the context of research. But the point here is that her replies show that she feels she has "arrived" at an endpoint of nonracialism. Having sacrificed so much for the ideal of nonracialism, she reacts to any reference to "race" as a betrayal of her ideological commitment. It also hints at the possibility that the pinnacle may, in fact, have been a foothill.

The difficult struggle with questions of how racialization entangles social injustice can not be totally unknotted through insisting that "race" does not exist. The expectation that in the New South Africa those whites who were opposed to Apartheid would receive special recognition morphs into the inkling that yet more sacrifice may have to be made. The very assumptions that provided a sense of self-worth may need to be reexamined. Adopting a lecturing tone, she indicates her knowledge of what is politically acceptable:

- To be white in a black context is the same in the dynamics that impinge on one as to be black in a white context. . . . Whiteness and blackness are less important than how each individual is personally, e.g., communication and relationship with black people succeed or fail for the same reasons as with white. [business consultant]

The color blindness this respondent wishes to emphasize obscures a great deal of the nuance of interracial contact in South Africa; real differences are too easily glossed over. The accumulative advantages of being designated "white" and the impediments of being marked "black" in a world still infused with a racist colonial heritage preclude the easy reversal of positions she implies. The stance does not acknowledge the complexity of communicating and relating within the context created by South Africa's historical legacy, and by genuine differences in ethnicity and culture. The "black" world is not taken seriously; certainly not on its own terms. Ironically, (in this case) color blindness also diminishes the bitter history of black struggle.

Whereas people who have been outside the country at crucial stages may quite easily deny implication in whiteness through viewing it as an indigenous South African problem, those who were permanently in the country have a more difficult task to split themselves off from the problem. The narrative of *Whiter Shade of White* does not let these people down, though, and provides other "outs" through appeals to cultural blamelessness. One way is to stress one's English ethnicity *within* the country.

Appeals to Politically Correct Ethnicity

A respondent from Cape Town, who provides a good example of this appeal, divulges his sense of his Englishness as racially unmarked:

- Whiteness has no part in my identity or culture. [scientist]

His account shows how, from his earliest awareness, racialized upbringing was associated with Afrikaners. He recounts witnessing Afrikaans children bullying black children:

- On a school bus, Afrikaans school kids were spitting at a black man. I remembered because I felt revulsion and annoyance at the kids. [scientist]

Whiteness, racism, Apartheid and Afrikanerdom are all conflated. The appeal is constructed through contradistinction from the other "others" in the lives of English-speaking South Africans, the Afrikaners, who are seen as the "real" racists, and from "their" politics, Apartheid. Part of the need to deny whiteness is to avert being regarded as "white" in the same way as those "other" whites. The revulsion at the nastiness of the children serves to smudge the commonality of white privilege that he shares with them, and pushes an awareness of his own racialization further out of reach:

- I did not think of [the incident] in terms of my whiteness but rather that one should not treat anyone in this way. . . . I do not consider myself in racial terms, and for as long as I can remember, I have abhorred the system of Apartheid. I find it difficult to answer race related questions. [scientist]

The strength of this protestation of racial blindness is directly related to the respondent's level of discomfort in talking about racial difference. He strives for color-blindness:

- I believe I now treat all people the same, though the circumstances of one's upbringing do affect how you react to other races. At some point I had to alter the way I dealt with blacks—I believe we all have to do this at some time. [scientist]

Ironically, the denial of difference protects this discomfort; keeps it intact, as he cannot engage with difference in a way that encourages knowledge of self or other. The internalized sense of (English) whiteness as the norm remains deeply buried, and continues unchallenged; it is as if difference from this norm is in and of itself insulting to those so positioned:

- The term "whiteness" tends to evoke annoyance—possibly due to a certain awareness of being different to other South Africans, though I have striven to treat all people the same. [scientist]

More than anything else, the response reflects a desire to have reached (or never to have left?) "den"—to have worked one's way clear of implication; to have achieved a safe space beyond the quagmire of "race" and all its potential for entrapment:

- I find it difficult to answer questions of this nature, because I feel I have "purified" my system of any racial tendencies I may have had due to circumstances. This "purification" process has been going on much longer than any political change. [scientist]

The crescendo of denial becomes quite deafening:

- I just am. I don't view myself in color or racial terms. . . . I don't need my whiteness for my identity—I am who I am; I just happen to be white. . . . I am who I am—I can't change that. . . . As I said before, I don't think in terms of my whiteness. [scientist]

The summation of his defensiveness and denial is a sad indictment of lack of insight into his social positioning:

- My being white is not an issue in my life! [scientist]

Appeals to A Transcendent Self

"I am who I am; I just happen to be white." These words of the previous respondent indicate that in formulating his position he draws on the discursive repertoire of modern humanism as a resource for establishing innocence. This type of individualism is often used very conveniently in positioning the person outside history and social context. More than any other, this seems to be the discourse used by white South Africans to exempt themselves from the burden of carrying "race." Often it underwrites or complements other appeals.

The implication is that one "really" consists of an individual "essence," the "true self" that transcends the (fortunate or unfortunate) accident of one's "outer" appearance or social position:

- I never thought to interpret such a thing! I don't regard it as part of my identity. I just am. [retiree]

Concentrating attention on the incidental nature of physical skin color ignores the orchestrated nature of racialization:

- White is just a skin color [photographer]

Similarly, editing out the collective nature of the racial project scores out the effects of systemic advantage and disadvantage. "I can't remember ever being aware of the fact that I am white in the racial sense," a lawyer brushes off the suggestion of implication in broader social fault lines. She continues:

- I work in a nonracial environment and am not aware of being regarded as white per se. It does not affect me personally, but in the main white privilege based on race irrespective of merit is disappearing, especially in government service. I do not perceive my whiteness in any particular way so I can't say it is changing or not. [lawyer]

As with all the appeals discussed in this chapter, the language of liberal humanism is sometimes used by people who are genuinely battling with issues of racial identity, looking for ways of thinking about society that avoid the damaging constructions of the past. It is also used, however, by those who find it a handy "cop-out." The *whiter than white* response employs the belief that, as individuals, we are "all fundamentally the same inside" or "it's who we are inside that matters" or "what we are depends on what we make of ourselves" to avoid weighing up the implications of real economic and social differences, and encountering the feelings of guilt that can accompany privilege. Social position is the consequence of personal attributes, attitudes, and aptitudes rather than factors like "race."

Appeals to essential, internal selves with endogenous qualities that presumably would have emerged much the same under different circumstances, claim a certain moral high ground. Superficially, the position appears nondiscriminatory. It makes a stand for personal merit and competencies, nondiscrimination in the workplace, and nonracial policy. As a group within the total white population who believe they always were free of racial consciousness, the people who subscribe to this creed now feel entitled to couch objections to the new order on the same nonracial grounds: affirmative action is reverse discrimination; racial restitution is an inequitable form of punishment; the past must be put behind the nation, and all should be treated as individuals. Because each individual is the author, or at least sole custodian, of his or her own identity, it also absolves one from grappling with questions of collective responsibility and the concomitant difficult ethical issues regarding the appropriateness of restitution for what was done in one's name. As the scientist says:

- I am who I am—I can't change that. [scientist]

Discourse about selves that transcend circumstances can, of course, also draw on dominant religious discourses:

- God made us all equal. If we have equal rights, we have equal chances. [secretary]

With the aid of such logical slippage, whiteness remains defended in the most unequal society in the world—neatly intertwined with moral rectitude.

Appeals to External Forces

The fourth appeal used to establish racial innocence is a denial of the possibility of personal agency. The claim is that as one was interpellated into the system by factors beyond one's control, one does not carry personal accountability. One respondent, for example, explains:

- I was a puppet of circumstance—I did not "milk" the system because I was white. The main effect of being "white" (once I was adult and could understand the system) was a sense of guilt at being privileged. Since the change of government, this feeling has abated somewhat. [medical scientist]

Another respondent, a photographer, also manifests this process of externalizing. He points away from himself toward abstractions:

- Factors outside my control have affected my life. [photographer]

Being white, he believes, has not affected his life as much as being black has affected the lives of "other" South Africans. The familiar ignore-ance of how both ends of the racial scales were needed to construct and maintain a racialized system sustains his stance of innocuousness. Privilege has shielded his life and emotions:

- I never developed the racial hatred the "other" South Africans did. [photographer]

Considering that one's whiteness is in the hands of powers other than oneself, it probably makes sense to entrust the rest of the country's lot to them too. Hope is placed outside of the realm of personal agency, in fate, time, divinity:

- It will be interesting to see how things will unfold. [medical scientist]

- Praying for a bright future seems important to me, there seems to be a growing faith in the future of South Africa. [photographer]

A major trend among these storytellers is that they are pleased to leave the past behind. They feel relief at being part of a democracy; the burden of guilt lessens as the country undergoes reformation and officially moves away from ethnicity-based politics. The applause is rousing:

- For the first time I can feel patriotic about my country. [research technician]

- There is huge relief at being part of an open/nonracial society. It's good to be "like everyone else" in terms of patriotism, legal rights, opportunities, etc. [computer analyst]

- I feel more relaxed about being "white." [administrative assistant]

- I welcome the political and social changes. [medical scientist]

- I feel very proud to be part of a democracy. [photographer]

- I believe we are in a time of great change for the better. As whites we may become marginalized somewhat, but if reason can prevail, we can all go on to become a united country with a great future. This country is unlike any other African country where the white colonialists simply left the country, having trained no one (of the locals) on how to run the country. Obviously as a white, I hope reverse discrimination can be held in check, and in the job situation (at least) the best person gets the job. [scientist]

At one level, the focus on the present and the future may be positive and constructive.

- One is aware of the obligation we all have to rebuild and develop our country in so many ways. As a white person, I have the same duty as anyone else to rebuild and promote SA. [computer analyst]

Yet, more commonly, a desire to close the discussion on the past is one strand within a general pattern of denial. The appeal to let sleeping dogs lie hides the crucial issue of which dogs are still holding onto the bones. It is an evasion of the extent to which the past

permeates the present, of how the legacy of social injustice continues into the future. It is a refusal to acknowledge that sustaining
"normal" white life perpetuates the disadvantages of others. Com-
placency, even indifference, is passed off as liberality:

- I don't think there is anything significant about being
  white in South Africa at the present time. [lawyer]

With the exception of those who use the *Appeal to Overarching
Identity*, which reveals the usual colonial projections about the
"other," narrators of this tale tend to be quite blank on the issue of
how the "other" perceives their "whiteness." This, too, is presented as
the morally correct thing to do—refusing to speak for the "other."
The fact remains, however, that this narrative is mum about what
the respondents perceive to be going on in the minds of the "other."
The responses indicate a general cautiousness to commit to a risky
statement that may indict them. But more importantly, they indicate that the narrators may not be able to ground statements about
the "other" in learning gleaned from relational interaction. The innocence that their "hands-off" approach safeguards, yet again,
seems to be insulated by ignore-ance:

- I don't know! I don't think "they" regard us any differ-
  ently generally. [medical scientist]
- Cannot comment. [scientist]
- One cannot make a generalization. [administrative
  assistant]
- No idea. [photographer]
- I cannot speak for others. [business consultant]

It seems fair to surmise that the absence of substantive knowledge
in these responses corroborates the observation that *A Whiter
Shade of White* is a narrative about denial: engaging in thinking
about one's own racialization is blindly terrifying. *A Whiter Shade
of White* confuses problematizing whiteness with evading it. As a
narrative that protects the innocence of whites, either through
splitting off the racial aspects of the narrator's experience and social positionality, or by repressing racial partisanship through sub-
merging it within an overarching identity, this narrative cushions a
low tolerance for personal culpability. If, as discussed in a previous

chapter, white identity is fragile as a consequence of its dependence on the "other" that carries its shadow projections, then this *Whiter than White* identity, involved in layers of projections and denials, speaks of great fragility indeed.

Chapter 8

∾

Narrative Five: Under African Skies (or White, but Not Quite)

The old elitist white society is breaking down and starting to merge with black and colored society due to increased exposure and interaction.

—respondent, study questionnaire

The narrative that is the subject of this chapter differs from the other narratives already discussed in stating roundly that whiteness as it served beneficiaries in the past belongs right there, in the past. Unlike other narratives discussed in previous chapters, this narrative does not retain the familiar old discourses of whiteness as templates for the future. Rather, it looks to creating and defining new subjectivities by drawing on other discursive and cultural repertoires to supplement or replace previous white identity. The different strains of the narrative vary in the degree to which the narrators feel personally empowered to perform this mutation of identity, as well as the direction of change to which they aspire. Unlike the *Whiter Shade of White* narrative, this narrative does not deny personal implication in social processes of racialization. The narrative is characterized by both *letting go* and *taking on*. To a varying degree the narrators tend to be aware of the need to let go of old selves, and to take on the responsibility of who they are going to become as they transform along with the changes in the country. This is the narrative that bespeaks those who are prepared to live closer to the edge, where "edge" does not signify an abyss, but the transition where the familiar and unfamiliar meet.

115

There are three quite divergent versions of this complex narrative; each of which will be discussed in turn. The first, *I Just Don't Know What to Do, Being White,* is told by those who see what they need to do, but don't quite risk the plunge. The second version, *I Don't Wanna Be White No More* is told by those who wish to do a fairly straightforward cultural exchange. The final version, *Hybridization, That's the Name of the Game,* refuses a precast frame for renegotiating white identity. This version insists that a new self must be negotiated in the indefinite spaces between the past and the future, the old and the new, the European and the African, the white and the black.

I Just Don't Know What to Do, Being White

> Black people MUST take center stage.
>
> —respondent, study questionnaire

I Don't Know What to Do, Being White is marked by feelings of ambivalence and duality. There is an awareness of complexities, of the way in which one and the same thing can be both positive and negative. Like the rabbit duck, past events and future possibilities show first one face and then the other to the vocalizers of this tale.

Most of the narrators seem to experience a split between the intellectual and emotional grasp of the larger political and structural changes occurring, and their sense of their own place within these changes. Like the tellers of the *Whiter Shade of White* narrative, they support the changes within the country, but unlike the tellers of the *Whiter Shade of White* narrative, they don't claim unequivocal feelings. Similarly, whereas those who tell a *Whiter Shade of White* feel they have arrived, either having sorted it all out before the elections or not having needed to sort anything out in the first place, those who *Don't Know What to Do, Being White* experience themselves facing new beginnings that they don't always quite know how to negotiate.

Whiteness in this tale acknowledges the historical experience of racialization within the country. Unfortunate, but almost certainly unavoidable, it is personal baggage a person will have to deal with as the future unfolds. It is a complex heritage from the past:

- My whiteness means that I am educated, articulate, Western, liberal (mostly). But it also means that I can be prejudiced and bigoted. It is more integral than my South Africanness as it is longer-lived and more entrenched. In SA society, "race" has been all-pervasive. It is *impossible* for me, as a 38-year-old, to deny its influence. I can modify/adapt my perception, but it remains influential. [In recent times] whiteness has come to be associated with the "old" "undemocratic" order. Perhaps, in general, with white marginalization. [academic development officer]

- My whiteness is a position of artificial privilege which is being challenged strongly by an emerging black consciousness. As I see it, whiteness now carries the stigma of Apartheid much as in Nazi Germany with "Arians." [secretary]

Whiteness, in other words, is a complex social identity; it positions the bearer within complex social constructions that have real material and psychological consequences. The narrators of this story tend to show a grasp of the overall political, historical, and structural processes that shape identities, perceptions, and life opportunities within the country. Because they tend to identify positively with the changes at these levels, they can muster a sense of perspective on the way in which the changes impinge on them personally. There is an awareness of a balance between loss and gain, an acquiescence that restructuring is going to pinch somewhere, and that there is no reason why that somewhere shouldn't be you. Given the legacy of inequality, it may even make sense that it is you:

- What is taking place is the *justified* transformation of a society which is predominantly black African. Black people MUST take center stage. [academic development officer]

- I feel more liberated, better informed, and aware, but less privileged and more vulnerable. However, the economic advantage still remains, and the better living conditions. But then, transformation takes time. There is an inevitable inertness in bringing about change. [oral pathologist]

In other words, whereas some of the other narratives have used appeals to overarching identity to declare the right to continued gratification in the New South Africa, those who tell this narrative see their fortunes as integrally related to larger processes that have to work out in ways that may actually be quite indifferent to their individual desires. The discomfort is not projected onto "others" perceived to be in the grip of a free-floating spite, who are "out to get you." Not only is it futile to try to insist history into a particular direction because it is uncomfortable for one personally ("the world continually changes," a secretarial student comments, philosophically), but upheaval is also easier to endure if one endorses the general direction of the historical trend as fundamentally just. Thus, what marks this narrative most distinctly is the split between the political and personal, and the fact that narrators consciously understand this split. For some this bifurcation is more painful than for others:

- At a "political" level, I am very happy. Very pleased that SA has begun a process of change toward, I hope, normalcy! Interpersonally, I feel marginal, insecure and isolated. [academic development officer]

- I realize that I lived a very sheltered and privileged life. I feel unable to cope with the radical changes that are taking place in SA. I feel guilty about that and try to make amends in my small circle of interaction with people of color. [secretary]

One respondent explains that his interactions with "other" South Africans, mostly in the professional realm, make him aware of the fact that he is still privileged, still advantaged. This response is quite different from the earlier narratives discussed, where so often people only affirm their pique through projections that bounce back at them. For a lecturer from a Western Cape university interracial interaction "has put everything in clearer perspective." This doesn't mean that it is easy. He continues:

- Often I feel excluded when it comes to elections to committees, etc., and it is difficult to get professional support from nonwhite colleagues. [oral pathologist]

He adds, honestly:

- I still have better relationships with white colleagues. [oral pathologist]

His comprehension at an intellectual level does not preclude feelings of alienation and isolation as he witnesses a social reformation that he supports, but that he feels essentially is not his own.

Another respondent, a woman well into her middle years, feels that her "very entrenched upbringing" prepared her poorly for the new approaches she needs:

- I have been exposed only to Western culture although I have dabbled in Eastern philosophies and religions. I know very little about black customs and culture. [secretary]

She reports feeling apprehensive and unsure of herself, and that she sometimes feels angry because she cannot understand the reactions of "others." And, as she says, she "can't undo the past." She feels morally convinced, but personally unaccomplished. This self-perception of ineptitude reinforces feelings of separation and alienation, and the process remains anxiety-laden. For her, consolation comes in the way in which her children are able to take the change in their stride. Vicariously she can partake in the evolution of the new society:

- Children interact far more easily—I see it in one of my sons particularly. To watch the ease with which my children interact with their peers is VERY encouraging. [secretary]

The consequence is a reversal in role-modeling; young people are left to lead the way when their parents in effect abdicate from addressing the relationship between the personal and the political in their own lives.

An interesting response from the academic development officer who has "several black African *colleagues*" and one "colored *friend*" shows his sense of personal "excess" beyond cultural stereotypes and projections. He feels modifications in his understanding of whiteness are encouraged by meeting people face to face, and by "people like Nelson Mandela." He believes that "others" see his whiteness as an indication that he is "an expert, superior," but also "a sign of being an oppressor." He continues:

- When these "other" South Africans are my friends, these labels disappear. [academic development officer]

His interactions with "nonwhites" motivate him, spur him on:

- I want to work hard to break down the stereotypes. I want them to see the "complex" me, not the label. [academic development officer]

His "whiteness," he adds, "is very nuanced by different contexts, people, experiences, and very difficult to generalize about." As a person who must be engaging in interactions with a great deal of honesty and awareness, he has a developed appreciation of subtlety and personal versatility that, while not negating the fears of personal marginalization, continues to feed his faith in the process to which he is committed. As he repeats:

- The positive shift is very important. [academic development officer]

I Just Don't Know What to Do, Being White teaches that even for many who are taking on the renegotiation of their subjectivities with a fundamentally positive orientation, convinced of the necessity of what is happening in the country and to themselves, and reasonably unafflicted by feelings of victimization and persecution, it is not a process that guarantees warm, fuzzy feelings.

A willingness to take on the implications of one's racialization into "whiteness," and to cooperate in dismantling the structural privilege it entailed, can be painful and lonely. It can simply reinforce the feelings of growing irrelevance that the other narratives strive so hard to counteract. For some this task is just too daunting. But for others, the pain is part of the growth. Feelings of inadequacy and alienation are inevitable, but are not the last word. No one said it would be easy.

"Pain" is the operative word in the next version of the *Under African Skies* narrative, *I Don't Wanna Be White no More*. As the name suggests, this tale charms those who speak it into the hope of a complete new beginning; a beginning where the pain of confronting one's whiteness will go away.

I Don't Wanna Be White No More

I will always strive to be an African, born and bred in South Africa.

—respondent, study questionnaire

Ironically, *I Don't Wanna Be White No More* has something in common with *This Shouldn't Happen to a White,* despite the fact that they are on opposite ends of the spectrum of white subjectivity. Both recognize that the tide has turned for whites and that, as an earlier respondent put it "black is the color to be." Moreover, and equally ironically, both narratives are told by people who are so in the grip of whiteness that they cannot dissociate themselves from it. Whereas the narrators of *This Shouldn't Happen to a White* are so "white" that they have not even begun to develop any of the self-reflectivity that would make them conscious of feelings of guilt, the narrators of *I Don't Wanna Be White no More* are overidentified with white guilt, and seek to escape from what would be an unbearable consciousness. This *secret* overidentification with the sins of being white is then externalized into a *public* overidentification with everything that is black. The way to avoid the pain of acknowledging what it has meant to be white is to escape into being black.

In fairness to these narrators, this overidentification is accompanied by varying degrees of romanticism and/or groundedness. The quotation at the beginning of this section was written by a young woman whose interracial contacts with a "brown boyfriend, his family and many friends through work" have been made "all within the last three to four years." By contrast, there are others who tell this tale who have been deeply involved in the struggle for black liberation, at great personal cost, and are conscious of this identification as an act of personal atonement for what has been perpetuated in the name of their whiteness. The contours of this narrative are adumbrated by the comments of two women respondents; they can be called the Romantic *Don't Wannabe* and the Dedicated *Don't Wannabe.*

"In the New South Africa black and brown are in," an excited youth worker and office administrator enthuses. Her romantic version of *I Don't Wannabe White No More* is a tale of discovery, tinged with opportunism. Suddenly, there is the world of the "other," no longer *verboten,* that beckons for exploration. The narrative beguiles its adherents into believing that, in addition to providing excitement, embracing this "other" world will mean not to have to deal with the "creepy-crawlies" that accompany being white. Its gaze set beyond the transient world of the phenomenal, the tale grasps eternal "essences." Therefore, although whiteness has meant "privileges in terms of education," it also means:

- Lacking in heart, color, texture, and the raw experience of loving. A kind of poverty we've brought upon ourselves because of the exclusion of black and brown in our lives. Who is better off now is hard to say—it all depends on what we hold as valuable. [office administrator]

Drawing on the ideological discourses of Afrocentricity,[1] the narrative inverts the values of the colonial racial binaries. Being closer to the "natural" and "instinctual" becomes the desired, opposing the "rational," "heartless" and attenuated world of whiteness:

- Whiteness is boring—superficial and very thin in comparison with the black/brown spirit—rhythm, joy, love, kindness, simplicity—and everything that counts a great deal. [office administrator]

It is congruent, therefore, that this tale is populated with new heroes, the black freedom fighters from the time of struggle. The respondent has formed her new understanding about whiteness through "reading one of Steve Biko's books—Human Rights Activist."[2] In her judgment, black South Africans view whiteness as "some sort of goal to attain, or as help which is intelligent and will know what to do and how to pay for it" but her message to them is:

- We created a monster with our bright ideas. If you could see some of the poverty in the white culture, you wouldn't want it! [office administrator]

In a celebratory tone, this romantic story looks forward to:

- more connection with all the people in the country— more openness—more heart—more interest. The intimacy to know and to be known. [office administrator]

The euphoria of the anticipated happy-ever-after ending is quite giddying:

- I think South Africa is a rudder of the huge ship of prejudice that exists in the world. If we can do it, I sense everything will shift the world round. [office administrator]

The Romantic *Don't Wannabe* is high, in love with the possibilities the New South Africa offers for new identities. The more grounded version of *I Don't Wanna Be White no More* also finds value in identifying with African society. "I desire to be an African in the true sense of the word," the second respondent affirms. She also comments on the vitality she experiences in "other" communities:

- In many ways life in white suburbia is claustrophobic, but in the oppressed communities life is alive, noisy, and happy (without romanticizing poverty, which goes without saying.) People share and help in times of family needs, e.g., if a family home burns down, the entire street is out helping with everything. [project coordinator, nongovernmental organization]

As can be seen from the above quotation, this narrator, too, valorizes the historical "other," but is truly involved in the struggles of the people she speaks about, and lives by the ideology she has embraced:

- The NGO [Non-Governmental Organization] I work for has worked toward development and transformation since thirty years ago. Our organization covers a large spectrum of people in poor communities of all races and also categories, i. e., Educare (children and workers), senior citizens, blind, disabled (adults and children), shelters and havens for outcasts and homeless. . . . Today I don't see color, but at least five years ago I felt guilty and felt responsible for the oppression of SO many people, men, women, and children. I also felt that I had to earn respect, and although one has to, this was different. [project coordinator, nongovernmental organization]

Her commitment on "black" issues, and the responses she has received from the people to whom she has dedicated her energy, provide her with the affirmation she craves, reassuring her and countering the feelings of personal deficit that have plagued her as a consequence of being white:

- I have nothing to hide and people know that. I have cried and laughed in many situations bearing the pain and joy of people. I feel accepted and real. I have never met with such openness and willingness to share and be friends. . . . People's willingness to share personal pains empowers me and drives me to make those changes happen wherever I am—in church, my family, my work. It gives me hope and even a glimpse of "New SA." . . . I have met many profoundly humble, proud, and loving people, the people whom the Apartheid government oppressed and killed for so many years. The people I meet today are not different from the people I longed to meet in my early years. [project coordinator, nongovernmental organization]

Her identification with political struggle has been long. And it has not been a romantic road to have traveled:

- I've never witnessed a "necklacing" or violent attacks where people have been brutally murdered—but I have experienced fear of teargas and rubber bullets in numerous marches and also the detention of my husband in the early years of my marriage. [project coordinator, nongovernmental organization]

Her commitment has not wavered, however, and her desire to be part of the world of the historical "other" is beyond question. In her version of *I Don't Wanna Be White no More,* the appeal to "Africanness" is not a mystification of sectional interest into an overarching identity, nor a claim of entitlement to the territory, as in some of the earlier narratives. It is quite specifically a swop, a preference for bearing the suffering of the oppressed rather than the guilt of the oppressor:

- I desire to be an "African" in the true sense of the word. My white culture has not been dominant at all. I will always strive to be an African, born and bred in South Africa. [project coordinator, nongovernmental organization]

Yet "Africanness" is something a white person has to earn. In order to deepen her understanding of the dynamics in which she is immersed, she is determined to read more South African history, to contest the Eurocentric versions that were taught in the white schools. Needless to say, the subjectivity of a "blackened" white is not one that places her in harmonious accord with the rest of the white population, who clearly regard her as a "race traitor." She comments:

- I do not feel threatened. The only problem I come up against is other white persons' jealousy and bitterness. [project coordinator, nongovernmental organization]

Given the perspective of the narrative, it is not surprising that the narrator welcomes the change in government and political dynamics warmly:

- The elections were incredible. We owe the changes to President Mandela and National Unity. President Mandela has united so much of the population with his profound spirit of hope and reconciliation. People are forced to look at each other in new, but scary ways. [project coordinator, nongovernmental organization]

It is also congruent that she evaluates the changes in the country in terms of their effects on the historically disadvantaged group, not on whites:

- I am positive. I am generally a positive, liberated thinker and welcome change especially if that change brings dignity to a people that have been treated like animals. But so far the changes have only been minimal. [project coordinator, nongovernmental organization]

Immersed in the realities of black township life, this woman's observations directly contradict the view advanced by *This Shouldn't Happen to a White* that the country has been thrown into complete reversal:

- Things have changed, but only marginally. The question is how do we fill ALL the gaps of deprivation. The task is enormous and friendships need to create a ripple effect. This is going to take time to build a nation of wholeness. It is also a question of trust and the hope that depends on how economically stable families are. [project coordinator, nongovernmental organization]

Far from being romantic about national reconciliation, this narrator is realistic about the fragility of the reconstruction process. She stresses the need for an inclusive, grassroots process and for interpersonal relationships. "It needs to have support through consultation," she warns. As can be seen from all of the above analysis, her own understanding of what "others" think is the result of extensive and close contact. For this reason, the behavior of "others" is not mysterious, arising out of strange, natural proclivities for crime, violence, and a hateful disposition, but are understandable reactions to poor socio-economic conditions. She is too close to the ground to be glib about the future and what it may hold for whites. While she acknowledges her fear however, she is not gripped by irrationality:

- To be white is not always to be filled with hope and joy, as not much has really happened to alleviate the suffering of most of our population. Although the state departments are changing, the pace is not fast enough. The pressure of poverty could lead to serious opposition, even a struggle. If that were to happen, being white would be of major consequence. I hope that no compromises with a "price" will be necessary. [project coordinator, nongovernmental organization]

This particular version of *I Don't Wanna Be White no More* is committed to micropolitics. It is a narrative about finding self-esteem through living "cleanly" and energetically in alignment with beliefs about human dignity and justice. But it is also a narrative about reducing the complexity of living with whiteness by taking on another racial identity. The feelings of impossible tension are alleviated by an act of racial and cultural self-negation. In all likelihood drawing on discourses of Christianity for legitimization, it is a story about taking on the "other's" struggle, and making it one's own. Unlike the Romantic *Don't Wannabe* who does not want to take on any guilt at all, the Dedicated *Don't Wannabe* is a story about being burdened with the full responsibility, and acting out all the guilt of one's entire "race":

- At times I am angry and even cry out for the people's lives to change. At times like these I feel hopeless when all I can offer is love, encouragement, and understanding. [project coordinator, nongovernmental organization]

In the narrator's words:

- This is far bigger than an individual can cope with. [project coordinator, nongovernmental organization]

Other than for the schoolchildren and students who completed the questionnaire, this narrator reported the lowest income: below R30 000 a year.

If this tale of *I Don't Wanna Be White no More* sees the self as having to fight the struggle of the "other," the final version of *Under African Skies* is a story about bringing the struggle home. "Race," along with its consequences, is something everyone is affected by, and needs to address. Yet the problem is not exteriorized; it is understood to be a problem for personal confrontation. Unlike *I Don't Know What to Do, Being White,* this narrative combines a sense of the structural and political implications of "race" with a committed personal engagement in dealing with it. Narrators interpellated into this story are moving beyond the safe home of their whiteness. This is a tale that negotiates the space, sometimes a psychologically perilous space, between collective cultural identities, courageously trusting in the emergent and uniquely syncretized identity forming in that liminal space. For these people the New South Africa is a personal expression of themselves, not only (though certainly also) a political reality. The unconscious contradictions that crisscross most of the other narratives are raised into consciousness and result in a greater awareness of personal and cultural complexity. This is the final narrative to which we now turn, and it is called *Hybridization, That's the Name of the Game.*

Hybridization, That's The Name of The Game

Now that we are here, I want to be a White African.

—respondent, study questionnaire

The beginning of this narrative often features fairly vivid memories of how whiteness dawned upon the narrator's consciousness:

- I remember when I was in primary school living on a farm outside Nelspruit. It was the different food the servant received, and her complaints to us children about it. It's a very distinct memory. I was probably ten years of age. She asked us why she was always expected to eat "old" bread. I felt it was wrong but could not give her an answer. Yet I did not have the courage to ask/challenge my parents. That open questioning was not part of the

child/parent relationship. So this grievance remains un-
resolved and therefore a vivid memory. I seem to recall it
also worried my younger sister but we never discussed it,
and definitely would never have dared to challenge our
father. Nor were we close enough to our mother to raise it
as an issue. [mathematical statistician]

By contrast, another anecdote recounts very deliberate tutelage into
whiteness, and incidentally also points to the role of white men in
policing the institution of whiteness:

- I emigrated from Israel to SA at the age of 35, and was in-
  structed by my South African husband to keep my distance
  from anyone who was not "white." Being white seemed to
  mean being separate and afraid. [physiotherapist]

Yet another narrator accessed his whiteness through having to deal
with areas of marginalization in his own life where he has encountered personal injury and insult.

- I have no memories of a specific incident. My memories
  focus more on when I first became aware that I was Jewish, and, later, when I became aware that I was gay.
  [marketing executive]

A woman who had emigrated from Czechoslovakia to South Africa
at an early age recollects her sense of belonging to a preferred marginalization:

- I could get a good education as I was not discriminated
  against because I was black. I felt discriminated against
  because I was "foreign" and my family was different: both
  my parents worked. [psychologist]

An acute understanding of whiteness as a social position associated
with privilege is pervasive in this narrative and, as the following
comments show, is accompanied by empathy for how this whiteness
impacted on "others":

- My associations with white—unearned privilege, unearned power, dominance. [director, management consultant company]

- I have had advantages as a white of "easy" access to education, as have my wife and sons, and to a rewarding career. In short: advantages and opportunities, privileges denied to the majority. [statistician]

In other words, no one who tells this tale would like to perpetuate whiteness as she or he has inherited it from the past; the opportunity to do things differently in the future is welcomed, rather than resented. It follows therefore that although the individual strains of this narrative are quite diverse, one thing is absolutely consistent throughout the sample: the narrators are unanimous in their support of the changes taking place. They experience great relief and pride. ("To heal our country, Yes!" a young secretarial student encourages.) That this support is not just lip service is corroborated by the fact that most of the respondents are involved in some sort of activity to make a contribution to the new society, in some cases running workshops that are directly related to consciousness raising and transformation.

For several of these respondents the commitment to intervene in the way "race" has been constructed within the country is facilitated by a fairly sophisticated grasp of whiteness as a deliberate mechanism of social advantage, rather than an ineluctable biological given. Some comments illustrate this "academic" understanding:

- I see whiteness as a "political" term, i.e., one that is useful in defining groups of people in terms of economic states and sociocultural backgrounds. It's a term laden with historical values. [marketing executive]

- Whiteness is a largely historically, socially constructed entity. I personally find such terms as white and "black," etc., and all the concomitant baggage which they carry to be unfortunate generalizations, which distort the world. In the Apartheid era white was propagated by the government and its many supporters as synonymous with clever, strong, superior, etc. This has changed. The mainstream (government, its supporters, the media) now is at best neutral and sometimes associates white with oppression, cruelty, etc. [lecturer]

Both the above quotations are the words of university graduates. Strikingly, the intuition that whiteness has been a deliberate ideological project, rather than just "found" in nature, is implicit in this comment by a young Capetonian who had just recently left school:

- I think of whiteness as a shame. White people take advantage and put "nonwhites" in a "bad light." It is hard to think about what we have done. [secretarial student]

Evidently then, although the most sophisticated understandings of whiteness in the sample are found in this group, "book knowledge" is not a prerequisite for telling this story, which seems to have a great deal to do with disposition and prior orientation. One respondent who is evidently "hybridizing" her identity, even offered this "commonsensical" definition of whiteness:

- I would interpret white as that of a person who has white parents. Although there are many "nonwhites" whose skin color is lighter than my own. [university student]

More commonly, though, this narrative evinces a fairly complex approach to the issue of racialization. "Race" is not denied but acknowledged as a shaping influence through historical and structural processes. Experientially, we all have acquired "race":

- Whiteness has been important in my life in that it has shaped the expectations that we have of ourselves and for ourselves, i.e., we are expected to be successful and financially secure, well-educated. [physiotherapist]

But at same time many of these respondents have a conviction of their "excess"—the extent to which they have been shaped, but yet not completely defined, by the social processes of racialization. This is not a narrative that emerges straight from the collective Imaginary, such as *Still Colonial after All These Years* and *This Shouldn't Happen to a White,* but it is also not one that claims to be entirely outside of, and free from, cultural influences, such as *A Whiter Shade Of White:*

- My "whiteness" is integral to my identity in that in SA it shaped reality—I don't like parts of that reality and felt a lot of shame. Now I feel pride. My sense of identity goes beyond "whiteness." [director, management consulting company]

- I don't see whiteness per se as integral to my identity—
  it's a proxy for a lot of other cultural and economic and
  other factors, e.g., middle class, Western in forms, formally educated. [lecturer]

- My identity is tied up with "whiteness," but other things
  like my family life, Christian activities, and my close
  friendships are more immediate. [research technician]

Nor do the ideological aspects of "race" escape some of the astute
chroniclers of this tale, who recognize that it is something we are indoctrinated into believing:

- The Apartheid system tried to make me think about
  "white" in a certain way and about "black" in another way.
  I strive to define my own reality and I try to avoid being
  hamstrung by other people's "projections." [lecturer]

Whatever whiteness may have meant in the past, this narrative
perks up in tone when it considers what may develop now that
whiteness has lost its power to dominate. It is easier to like oneself
once one is no longer automatically associated with, or implicated
in, what one detests. Whereas the narratives that retain the affinity
with the master narrative license congruence with the past, but incite dissonance with the present and the future, the tellers of this
tale prefer the present and anticipate the future, however complex
that may turn out to be:

- For me, the change in what it means to be white is a shift
  from shame to pride in the country and culture. For many
  others I meet, it appears to mean less empowerment, disadvantage through affirmative action, and anxiety producing. [director, management consultant company]

- Whiteness is now less powerful and controlling. It is also
  less derogatory now. I think people are starting to look
  beyond these hard and fast categories and to focus more
  on the individual. It's linked to the breaking down of barriers which leads to different exposures. [management
  consultant]

- For the first time I can feel patriotic about my country
  [research technician]

This particular judgment on how whiteness in South Africa is changing reveals something of the nature of the interpersonal relations the respondents are achieving. The generally positive appraisal of rapprochement and the expectation of a mutually built future stand in stark contrast to some of the earlier narratives where revenge and hostility seem to be the overriding expectation:

- My perception tells me that now a white person is more acceptable to other groups. I feel deep relief. [physiotherapist]

- At the time of independence white seemed to mean the old, the past, the evil, the lucky, those that had it easy. Now there seems to be a move from this to more acceptance of both shared experiences. Now, diversity is seen to be richness. [management consultant]

- There is a definite shift in the right direction with the cultures mixing more, socially, etc. [secretarial student]

- I feel good about the changes. More healthy. Free of a lot of guilt. But also quite anxious about my children's future—will they lack opportunities because of their whiteness? [lecturer]

The tone of the narrative is far from uniformly radiant, though. The refrain of fears about economic hardship, crime, and long-term insecurity recurs in this narrative, too:

- I anticipate that to maintain or improve my (own and family's) standard of living, I will need to generate increasingly higher levels of income. Perhaps this entails becoming less reliant on the state for income. [lecturer]

- At the moment survival at work has to be my top priority. [mathematical statistician]

In addition to those fears that this narrative shares with all the other narratives, there is also a conviction that the country has a long way to go in bringing actions in line with the discourse of reconciliation:

- It has begun to change in many ways although we still tend to carry many of the previous associations with us.

There has been quite a dramatic change in status, especially for white males. [psychologist]

- We are more aware that we have to give. Many whites
  are not open-minded to this. It's all talk in certain parts
  of the country where people still don't want to socialize.
  [secretarial student]

- I feel sad that SA is still such a race/color obsessed society (and that the world at large is so obsessed with the
  same). [lecturer]

A notable feature of this narrative is the honesty with which the
narrators chronicle the past. In the first place, they don't attempt to
belittle the effects of Apartheid on the "black" population, or to
match it with some parallel experience. But then neither do they
manifest ignore-ance about the effects of the past on themselves. Indeed, one of the things they specifically draw attention to is the collective cultural ignore-ance to which they were heirs. Cognizance of
belonging to a collective that has much to account for pushes to consciousness:

- It was possible to grow up in South Africa and be totally
  disconnected from the way the majority lived and coped,
  and to create a separate reality. The effects on me as a
  white woman relate more to being linked to an atrocious
  system through color and therefore association, and the
  emotional and mental consequences of that have affected
  me. Black South Africans suffered more, though, in every
  way. [director, management consultants]

- I have been affected in that I inherited all the notions of
  being more developed and superior that went with the
  previous Apartheid system. Also, there was a tremen-
  dous load of guilt and responsibility for the oppression
  that caused me first to choose a career in "black" education. [lecturer]

For these respondents, one must first know one's whiteness, reach
into it, feel its texture, before it will let one go. Facing the truth about
the past, distressing though it may be, is a necessary part of moving
beyond whiteness. This honesty about the past includes the willingness to admit to the inevitable feelings of grief that accompany

change, even change one has looked forward to. It also includes a desire to *learn* about the past in order to get beyond the systematic denial legislated by Apartheid. The discovery helps to explain the past
both of the "other" and of the "self":

- I am learning a great deal through the greater openness
  of expression—reading newspapers, and listening to
  other media, meeting with people other than white. We
  now hear about what people are thinking and are told
  about their past experiences. I feel sad about the past,
  but positive to be moving on to "shared" experiences. It
  also helps to understand a HUGE amount about my own
  background that I was unaware of. [consultant]

People's attitudes and behaviors become more comprehensible as
"hitherto repressed/unspoken grievances have emerged" [lecturer].
An appreciation of long-term historical processes puts the present
and future into perspective:

- Black pride and nationalism is no longer stamped out as
  it was before. I understand what is happening and have
  no problems with the rise of black culture. I still feel
  white culture has a lot to give to the future. [secretary]

An undertaking to confront the past honestly requires the courage
not to evade the unpleasant feelings that accompany a more informed knowledge of what really happened, of how one's good life
was built upon the accumulated suffering and deprivation of others
over many generations. An admission of personal culpability
through conscious collusion, and more often, through acts of omis-
sion, negligence, or passivity, cannot be averted:

- The white group has inflicted the Apartheid regime with
  its horrors and indignities by terrorizing millions of people.
  I feel guilty for not actively fighting it. [physiotherapist]

- I know one has to fight the eternal sense of guilt of being
  part of something one did not really believe in, but was
  passive to some extent in responding to. [consultant]

Without this personal honesty about the past, the narrative insists, it
is impossible to build future relationships with integrity and trust:

- I realize that many white people are claiming ignorance of anything before 2 February 1990, when De Klerk unbanned the ANC. Blacks began remarking about the "new skins" white South Africans were offering to one and all. Whites try to ingratiate themselves by claiming to have always been nonracial, to have never voted for the National Party, to have always had black friends, etc. [mathematical statistician]

Some of the people who relate this story have been intimately involved with "black" politics of struggle over a considerable time or have had long-standing interracial friendships. These are those who have been committed to renewing South Africa for a long time:

- It was at university fifteen years ago that I first really began to empathize and realize the human consequences of Apartheid through some black students I met at a religious conference. [lecturer]

- Some of my friendships go back to the late seventies, mostly coming from my wife's involvement with the Black Sash in Pretoria, and their advice office. Our friend was a translator. Before the emergencies of the 1980s I was successful in getting him released from the security police. During the struggle we had a number of close friends, and were aware of the changes in their circumstances, sometimes giving shelter when required. [mathematical statistician]

Others, again, have been on a very steep learning curve during the last three to four years. Unlike some of the narrators of earlier narratives who are stalling meaningful interaction, these respondents are not waiting for associations with "others" to come their way, but have started with the relationships that are at hand. They are immersing themselves in the new order. A few have been truly living at the interface between the cultures:

- I have developed one close cross-racial friendship, a large number of strong cross-racial working relationships, and spent most of last year living in a cross-racial household. [marketing executive]

- When I taught in an independent school in Lebowa[3] I found that as I became part of the culture of the school, I began to think of myself in terms of the majority members of that community. [lecturer]

Generally, there is an acceptance that as white South Africans are in a new situation, new approaches, new attitudes, new expectations are required. According to this story, however, the sense of greater legitimacy is satisfying. A person knows that one is not going to be overrewarded, merely as a consequence of one's birth:

- Everyone works hard and can no longer expect that fortune will come to you by default. [psychologist]

As the narrative prods the narrators further into seeking out uncharted ways, toward creating new subjectivities for which there are few[4] role models for whites in the history of this country or the rest of the world, they inevitably move further and further away from the master narrative of whiteness. Every successful encounter they experience along the way further undermines the "authority" of that narrative, destabilizing the way the binaries were fixed, suggesting that it is possible that "white" may still be done in "other" ways. This narrative draws on the discourses present in the country that stress the need to discover authentic South African solutions through synergistic thinking, utilizing all the resources South Africans can muster collectively.

The most notable aspect of the New South African whiteness as recounted by this narrative is the stress it lays on personal growth and learning. In some strains learning specifically about "race" and culture is a very high priority:

- Deepening understanding around race and culture and diversity are very important to me. [director, management consultant company]

- Through my increased exposure to black culture and more racial mixing, I am becoming more aware of cultural differences. [secretary]

As the young secretarial student points out, personal growth comes only with personal exertion and accepting mutual accountability for relationships:

- You are not automatically respected. You have to earn your respect with the majority of the people. [secretarial student]

Nothing is achieved unless the damage of the past is acknowledged:

- Relationships with my black friends take longer to build as they have to learn to trust that I am genuine. [psychologist]

Paradoxically, this insistence on acting within one's sphere of influence combines with a greater awareness of the structural and systemic aspects of "race." This narrative could be regarded as the racial counterpart of the ecologists' slogan "Think globally, act locally." The importance attached to interpersonal, intercultural contact is unmistakable in all the accounts. These narrators are forming nodes of connectedness within the new society:

- I have many business and social acquaintances, but I have mostly one-on-one friendships. We earn the friendship on both sides. [secretarial student]

- Because my friends and I talk frankly, I get an idea of their lives. Many aspects are very different from my life. But we get closer all the time. [physiotherapist]

Far from one-sidedly defining the "other," these narrators are earnest about listening to the voice of the "other," and using what they learn to develop more nuanced interactions:

- I check things more often than I used to in regard to my understanding, the reality, what messages I am receiving. [consultant]

- Knowing that there is a whole range of perceptions about my whiteness heightens my sensitivity—in some gatherings I might feel more cautious around being white. [director, management consulting company]

- I try to be sensitive to others' perceptions of whiteness and obviously when interacting with someone who makes a major issue of whiteness I proceed with caution. [lecturer]

"In my work," the psychologist explains, "I build trust relationships with clients. I am very aware of being white and how the other person sees me and how it will affect our relationship. If I sense tension, I am open about it and discuss it with my client."

The kind of sensitizing described above enables people who are choosing to construct their selfhoods by this narrative to recognize that only if they frankly acknowledge the effects of "race" are they better able to move "through" it:

- Once people know one, they are less interested in skin color and more in quality of character, I find. [marketing executive]

- I have developed relationships on different levels of intimacy. Some are intimate and others not so intimate. [lecturer]

Shunning the old dictatorial, unilateral ways, the emphasis here is on a dialogic approach to relationship, to both self and other. Openness is a prime value:

- My understanding about the feelings of frustration "others" feel has been an iterative process over many years. None of these ideas arose in a vacuum. . . . It is difficult to measure the pace of change. But I do think that the more the issues around race are openly discussed and debated, the greater the shifts in understanding will be. [marketing executive]

A dialogic approach means leaving behind the inflated self-image confabulated as part of the colonial master narrative. It means stepping off the "pure" side of the binary pedestal artificially fixed by the Manichean allegory, and entering the untidy cultural space in-between, which is where, as Brantlinger (1990) points out, the genuinely human exists. The "self" can be humanized; the projected shadow can be integrated. *Hybridization, That's the Name of the Game.* Some of the respondents indicated that they are, indeed, taking seriously the way their whiteness is seen by "others," and trying to learn about themselves from "their" perceptions:

- I have about six friends, all women, who are either black or brown, women I regard as good friends, not merely acquaintances. One is a ten-year friendship, the others about three to five years. These relationships continue to help me uncover layers of prejudice in myself. Honest relationship and honest communication helps this growth in me. [director, management consulting company]

- We now hear what people are thinking and are told about their past experiences. It helps me to understand a great deal about my own background that I was unaware of. [consultant]

Dialogue also means recognizing the extent to which the narcissistic self-perception of whiteness was based on lies, relinquishing white certainties. It entails taking the "others'" understanding of history seriously, allowing oneself to be moved by their experience, taking to heart how the actions of one's own collective have impacted upon the lives of other collectives:

- For about eight years now I have had many cross-racial relationships, ranging from acquaintances to friends. They have made me increasingly sensitive to the cruelty of white SA's colonial and Apartheid history in terms of their effect on people who were not "white." [lecturer]

The point emerges only too clearly: "self" and "other" are co-created. Getting the "self" into perspective inevitably means looking at the "other" through different lenses; hearing the voice of the "other" inevitably reconstitutes the "self." The greater humility of the dialogic approach advanced by the *Hybridization* narrative enables a more accurate, less illusory apprehension of different realities:

- The fact that whites were/are viewed with suspicion/curiosity/hate/tolerance dawned on me when I was a child. I find this variety of perceptions still exists. [director, management consulting company]

- Two years ago I spent six weeks in the USA with twenty-four fellow South Africans—all educated graduates. Until then I was unaware of the depth of anger, resentment, and bitterness "blacks" (African, Indian, and colored) feel toward whites. [lecturer]

- In real terms, very little has changed for the average nonwhite South African, so white is still synonymous with privilege. I am aware that there is still a lot of frustration and anger. [marketing executive]

- I think a lot of white people are now experiencing some of the feelings that black people experienced under Apartheid. In some ways it is fair that "we" have to struggle for jobs so we can experience some of what black people experienced. [psychologist]

There are even those who are overcoming the ultimate bogy of Apartheid whiteness, the fear of physical contact with the "other." The intimate learning one respondent reports arising from an interracial relationship neatly illustrates why the social taboo sought to prevent this potentially profound dialogic experience:

- I had an affair with a black woman through whom I became aware of the depth of pain and bitterness resulting from the Apartheid system. [lecturer]

Undemonizing the "other" makes it possible for whites to honor black people, to acknowledge their moral courage—a kind of acknowledgment that was extraordinarily rare in white South Africa only a few years ago. Far from attributing large-scale spitefulness to their fellow South Africans, these respondents are conscious of how much forgiveness and restraint black South Africans have mustered. Yet these attributes cannot be assumed to be bottomless:

- I feel gratitude for being treated in a nonvengeful way. [physiotherapist]

- Seeing the balanced way in which many African leaders speak on TV makes me very hopeful. [consultant]

- Whites have not changed enough to make me hopeful. [mathematical statistician]

All the same, "others" have their bogys, too. Dealing with the distortions of the collective imagination also requires confronting the stereotypes "others" have held in relation to whites. A student who has been studying at a historically black university explains a prejudice she has encountered:

- Black persons regard one as privileged and wealthy. If one happens not to be wealthy, but white, I have been told: well your parents were stupid not to use Apartheid to their advantage. My friendships have changed my friends' perceptions of my whiteness and other "whites." [candidate attorney]

The proviso, at all times, however, is honesty:

- I feel lumped with their stereotype ideas of whites, which I feel are sometimes unfair to me, though I truly can own some of their perceptions of me as a "white." [candidate attorney]

A particularly important aspect of this narrative, and one that distinguishes it incisively from *I Don't Wanna Be White no More,* is its insistence that the narrators remain centered in the experience that they need to confront. *Hybridizing* does not mean stepping into another's process to avoid one's own. Deconstructing whiteness is not synonymous with becoming black.[5] It does not mean taking on "their" issues, pretending to be in the same position as people who have been oppressed by Apartheid, an imposture that many black South Africans find insulting and negating of their experience. Whites have always had options not available to black South Africans. Being part of the struggle by choice was vastly different from fighting for one's survival due to being trapped in Apartheid's racism. Petulance about not being rewarded for past contribution to the cause only betrays that an element of paternalism must have informed the choice in the first place. A respondent from Pretoria understands this difference in positionality:

- I and my family were involved in the struggle, but we were not in the front line of the struggle. Though we were better informed than the majority of whites, unlike blacks we could withdraw when the going got rough. While I was a resource, it was not my struggle. Without black commitment my contribution cut little ice. For most whites the struggle was a nuisance at best, an irritation at worst. [mathematical statistician]

The process of working through the psychological and emotional consequences of having been oppressed is not equivalent to the process of raising to consciousness the effects of having been the oppressor. Recognizing the fears, uncovering the drive to power, acknowledging and dealing with the guilt, grieving for lost opportunities and one's own damaged humanity, learning to engage seriously with the life world of the "other," taking responsibility for developing a new subjectivity—these are the tasks of deconstructing one's own "whiteness." These are in no way isomorphic with the processes of overcoming internalized oppression. The narrative of *Hybridization* shows that it is those who discern this difference that will bring the most helpful attitudes for contributing to a joint future.

At a more practical level, not denying the historical positioning of whiteness in relation to resources enables *hybridizing* whites to use its advantage pragmatically. It can be harnessed to contribute to the development of assets among those who have suffered deprivation. A woman who has moved into the Muslim Quarter of Cape Town has grasped this point adroitly. Most of her friends are from this community and she is involved in the activities of the neighborhood. Her observation is that:

- White means being versed in the ways of institutions, i.e., banks, etc. I think my colored friends often wonder at first why I am with them and not other whites. Later they are happy to let me use my whiteness for our mutual benefit. [physiotherapist]

If power is what lay at the heart of constructing whiteness in the first place, then issues of power are central to deconstructing it. Accepting a more equal, or certainly different, power base for one's identity than pertained in the past is fundamental to *hybridized* whiteness. Noticeably, those who tell this tale do not refer to the position of whites as being "marginalized," which suggests a position of extreme social impotence. For these narrators, losing dominance does not simply equate with personal defeat, though it certainly is the end of the story of whiteness as the Master used to tell it. Whiteness no longer entails social control of others. Maturity informs the following words, again those of the Jewish woman who is living in the Muslim Quarter of Cape Town:

- As a white woman I am identified with one of the smaller ethnic/cultural groups of the South African population. I accept that most of the forty million South Africans are not white and we may find each other equally "strange." My culture is not the "norm." [physiotherapist]

It is not a maturity determined by age, though. A young student expresses the following desire:

- I want to grow to be comfortable with all races regardless of whether I'm in the "majority" or not. [secretarial student]

Sorting out questions of power within personal interracial encounters in postapartheid South Africa is not going to be straightforward, though. The marketing executive confesses that although he finds interracial contact outside of work fairly comfortable, he has "struggled within working relationships to deal with the power relationships of being 'white' and being 'black.'" Whereas formal power structures may have changed, internalized estimations of personal power have not necessarily done the same. Different, intersecting, and contradictory codes and structures pertain to power. Dealing with this "heteroglossia" can be confusing. Another respondent cites the deeply internalized sense of disempowerment among black people as a cause for concern:

- I encounter black people who imply that white people have all the ideas to guide blacks toward the solutions, that a white presence will "make it work." So there is still a tendency to ask whites what to do, a dependency on whites. To me, this shows that the meaning of white has not changed all that much. [marketing executive]

As the above discussion suggests, whites are still better placed to do many things at this stage. Their positioning in global history since the period of colonization can be turned into a resource, utilized for the benefit of all "racial" groups, rather than furthering the sectional interests it originally served.[6] This standpoint is premised upon the hopeful belief that things in the country can work out to the mutual benefit of diverse groups. There is wisdom, this narrator implies, in "starting from where you are" and giving something back:

- South Africa has a great head start on the rest of Africa because we have developed "Western" systems of transport, industry, and others. There is irony in this. Now that we are here, I want to be a white African. [physiotherapist]

Certainly, for many of the narrators of this tale, there is a conviction (desire?) that whites will have something of value to offer a new syncretic order:

- While we cannot be sure about what the future holds, and what our place will be in South Africa, I feel that we do have a place here, but not in the old elitist way. That is breaking down. We are developing a more equal society. [consultant]

The country is complex, the variables many, the moral issues inconclusive. This is not a tale that offers closure; the promises are few. Some narrators of the *Hybridization* tale are cautious about confusing desire with reality. The issue of white legitimacy and future relevance is far from a preconcluded issue, and may become more acute in time. A woman who is actively involved in antiracism activism in Cape Town shares some of her feelings of insecurity about her role, her mindfulness that she is potentially dispensable:

- I am an optimistic person—hope and faith live with me a lot. However, lately there have been bouts of doubt and fear about the future of this country and my place in it— I am learning to be OK with it all and use those bouts as times of honest appraisal about myself and my attitude, the facts and the possibilities. [director, management consulting company]

Feelings of guilt and shame, hunches of illegitimacy—the psychological baggage that *hybridizing* white South Africans carry with them is not going to be light. If the only discourse of whiteness from the past to identify with and draw on were the master narrative, these people will have little to sustain a positive self-image into the future. While this narrative desires a fuller, more nuanced identity that opens itself to African influence, following the route of *I Don't Wanna Be White no More* through appropriating black experience does not offer creative syncretism; it is cultural suicide. Yet there are also traditions of resistant whiteness in South Africa. Previously subjugated by the dominant narrative, these now offer cultural resources for *hybridizing* whites as models and as sources of affirmation. The person who earlier described his own social activism has found that excavating the contradictions from the past, people and moments that could have tipped the balance of history, dis-covers much to take with him into the future:

- My interest in Cape Colony history comes from reading about Sol Plaatje, and his commitment to English law and justice as he experienced it in the Cape Colony. I identify with those democrats, especially those white South Africans who have promoted democratic nonracial principles in the formative years of the country (William Porter, Saul Soloman, J. X. Merriman, J. W. Sauer, J. Rose Innes . . . the mission schools and Fort Hare, for example). . . . These people pressed for the extension of democracy to the entire population. My focus is on identifying and learning more about these people who unfortunately were unable to point our country in the right direction in 1910. [mathematical statistician]

Finally, and ineluctably, the long-term historical awareness that this narrative instills saps the very life source of the master narrative, urging the consciousness of the narrators steadily toward questioning their relationship to Africa, the continent itself. Recognizing their ambivalent relationship to the continent, acknowledging the extent to which they have held it an "other"—this is the process of decolonizing of the mind of the colonizer. The process requires renouncing the role of the white master on the continent, foregoing the assumption of a God-given place on the continent, recognizing the legitimacy of Africans in Africa, dismantling the edifice of South African whiteness and finding humility:

- We have an "imported" culture which comes from overseas, rather than one which has developed naturally in South Africa. [physiotherapist]

- Deep down I also feel I have to justify my right to live here, because I am not black. [director, management consulting company]

This recognition leaves no option but to acknowledge that one has lost one's home, the place of a "safe," homogenous identity[7] to which one can return. There is no other way, the logic of this narrative presses, but to enter into a new relationship—dialogic, appreciative, committed—with the continent that whiteness came to conquer. Opening up space to receive from Africa and from what is African, and to take this Africanness into previously "pure white " identity, enables the narrators to find their commonality with this "other"[8] that has, in many ways, been held at a distance for centuries:[9]

- My friendships have since made me aware of how black and white socialization has been different because of Apartheid. But at the same time I have also begun to realize how much common ground we share. I have discovered that, despite Apartheid, I have more in common with black South Africans than with other whites be they British, Dutch, French, or American. . . . When I first went overseas in 1986, I thought because of my colonial British background I would find Britain home. Instead I became increasingly aware that I was not British, and that I was African. This is how I came to see myself as white African. [lecturer]

There are tones of expectancy, anticipation about the process of personal synergy, in this narrative:

- I think that I, and white South Africans in general, will assimilate more black/African culture and become more Africanized. [secretary]

Hybridizing does not mean renouncing a place in the country. Instead it offers the potential for new exciting ways of being, as well as the possibility of a more stable, grounded identity for a psyche that looks to a future in Africa:

- When encountering or experiencing relationships one looks for commonality rather than difference—I have taken on more Africanness through my friendships and become less "white." Through this process I am becoming more aware of my own identity, and my internal/less obvious/developed racism and prejudices. I am acquiring more of a feel about who I WANT to be in the New South Africa. [consultant]

- I realize that I need to understand and identify with different cultures of people I meet and marry it with my own. I certainly feel part of a richer culture now than ever before. [psychologist]

- My experiences have developed and reinforced my perceptions of myself as a white African and I would like this to continue. I see myself moving further in the direction of a white African whatever consequences that may have for my actions, behavior, and attitudes. [Lecturer]

For those narrators who want "the whole story" there is a sense of becoming a cultural amphibian, of acquiring the complexity of a hyphenated identity. Here churns the perpetual restlessness of multiple subjectivity, a personal borderland where shifting binaries are held in tension through continual play:

- The term "white African" captures my dual personality, because Africa presents challenge but insecurity (partly because of the associations of whiteness with Apartheid, partly because of the oppression, cruelty, and instability within many African countries in the twentieth century) while Europe represents security but without the same challenge. [lecturer]

A subjectivity forming in accordance with the narrative of *Hybridization, That's the Name of the Game* has to deal with mixed rewards and losses. It involves a commitment on the narrator's part to his or her own potential for growth, and a trust in having a place in postcolonial, postapartheid South Africa. It involves balancing inner obstacles ("the fear and sadness of accepting that things will/must change. Not knowing what lies ahead," the young secretarial student says) with a sense of challenge and even fun ("we are loosening up and getting more adventurous," she confides) and the willingness to look around one with courage and awareness ("everything is always changing, and as long as I'm aware of the changes I am satisfied that I can work with them," the lecturer settles). In truth, those who trust this narrative also *Don't Know What to Do,* but they do know it isn't *Being White.*

Hybridization, That's the Name of the Game deconstructs the master narrative of "whiteness." No longer "pure," this whiteness is blended, blatantly contradictory, and complex. Once hyphenated, it does not have the power to abuse. Because this narrative is dialogic in its mode of construction, it can, logically, only unfold as it is co-authored with the "other." An African whiteness, it has acquired a hue. Acting in the face of, indeed reaching into, the colonialist fear of finding the African within the European ("the horror, the horror"[10]), this narrative concludes that while it is certainly true that *Whiteness Just Isn't What It Used to Be,* cultural miscegenation may yet furnish a congruent identity for those who live *Under African Skies.*

Chapter 9

⌢

Conclusion:
Whiteness Just Isn't What It Used to Be

You don't have to leave home to become a refugee. This dispossession does not have to happen, but it can and it does—and will—happen in many cases as old belief systems erode, as old bases of personal and social identity change.

—Walter Truett Anderson, *Reality Isn't What It Used To Be*

One of the more general lessons of history is that human groups can sometimes transcend the past and adapt to circumstances in unanticipated ways. If enlightened self-interest can induce whites to abdicate their privileged position, they may still be able to call themselves South Africans twenty-five, fifty, or even a hundred years hence.

—George M. Fredrickson, White Supremacy:
A Comparative Study of American and South African History

[B]oundaries, to those who have experience crossing them, become a matter of play rather than an obsession.

—Jan Nederveen Pieterse and Bhikhu Parekh,
The Decolonization of Imagination

In line with the growing interest in the racialization of white people, this book has told a story about whiteness within a changing South Africa. In trying to pinpoint the "open space" nature of this moment, the book takes as a theoretical assumption that postcolonialism and critical postmodernism are not so much at odds with each other as implicated in each other:

149

> Decentered, allegorical, schizophrenic . . . —however we
> choose to diagnose its symptoms, postmodernism is usually
> treated, by its protagonists and antagonists alike, as a crisis
> of cultural authority, specifically of the authority vested in
> Western European culture and its institutions. That the
> hegemony of European civilization is drawing to a close is
> hardly a new perception; since the mid-1950s, at least, we
> have recognized the necessity of encountering different cul-
> tures by means other than the shock of domination and con-
> quest. (Owens, 1992, p. 166)

When the Western center is tipped, as has happened quite dramatically in the New South Africa, encounters between those of European stock and the previously colonized have to take place on a
different footing. The extent to which these relationships change de-
termines the extent to which the postapartheid[1] era brings South
Africa to fully-fledged postcoloniality.[2] Layers of colonialism have
been shed at different stages since 1910, much as layers of colonialism were acquired after 1652. Certainly, the white norm that the
master narrative enforced has lost its statutory centrality.

Different aspects of society are held together now by different
centers. Politically, the power has been transferred to the majority
black population; economically, whites still call the shots. Different
cultural constructions have become more visible, thrown into relief
in an unprecedented way. People are more likely to detect cultural
frameworks *as* relative constructions, not absolutes, providing discourses from which South Africans may "mix and match" new subjectivities. The old boundary-keepers for social groups and for monological personal identities are becoming visible as frames, the partisan
interests served by how we have been enframed much more exposed.[3] This turn of events has major implications for whiteness, for
the discourses of identity, for the assumptions of positionality around
which the people of European descent within South Africa ardently
have constructed their identities since they first settled in Africa.

Postmodern Whitenesses

Whiteness was a modernist construction, central to the colonization project, and achieved through the exorcism of everything
"black," particularly African, from white identity. The construction,
depended primarily on the ideological fixing of a Manichean alle-

gory, drawing on and adapting various discourses available at the time. Utilizing the Enlightenment notions of universal progress and the supremacy of reason, it established "scientifically" the white "race" as superior. They were therefore fit to take a dominant role in relation not only to nature, but also to the non-European world, which was usually construed as an extension of nature. The historical construction of this narrative of whiteness has been traced in this book, and dubbed the master narrative of whiteness: the conception of whiteness as "absolutely centered, unitary, masculine" (Owens, 1992, p. 168). Owens draws together many of the characteristics of such a master narrative:

> For what made the *grands récits* of modernity master narratives if not the fact that they were all narratives of mastery, of man seeking his telos in the conquest of nature? What function did these narratives play other than to legitimize Western man's self-appointed mission of transforming the entire planet in his own image? (p. 175)

This master narrative of whiteness was inflected in the course of South African history. In acquiring its particularly tenacious South African articulation, the relationship between the two white groups played a major role, as well as the legal enforcement of minority white supremacy—"baasskap"(mastership)—by means of the Apartheid state. With the demise of the Apartheid government in April 1994, however, this master narrative fell apart in South Africa.

It requires force, even violence, to hold binaries in a fixed ideological hierarchy. It took a great deal of violence—systemic oppression and brute force—to organize South African society along a system of white minority supremacy. In the present state of political and social fluidity, the signifiers are at play. For white South Africans this has made it necessary to renegotiate their identities. Although this historical moment is certainly confusing for all South Africans, the energy previously allocated to enforcing modernist whiteness can now be expended in creative energy, choosing more varied options of personal and social redefinition.

Drawing on a repertoire of discourses, white South Africans are indeed constructing a range of "*petit* narratives" of whiteness, each of which is competing to explain, and to promote, a view of how being white should be construed in the new dispensation. Some of these stories have points of overlap with some of the others. Then again there are ideological aspects that are quite incompatible between stories, ways in which they react against each other. The essential points about the constructions are that (a) they do not add up to one, unified story of whiteness and (b) they have to contend with a new reality that does not support, and indeed is hostile to, many of the taken for granted assumptions of superiority and entitlement which the master narrative belief system had inculcated. The postmodern condition, the upsetting of "the reassuring stability of that mastering position" (Owens, 1992, p. 168) has caught up with South African whites.

A change in the flow of cultural information is one of the most defining aspects of the New South Africa. For the first time white South Africans are getting to know about African ways from Africans. Knowledge is circulating in the society generated from a different center; Eurocentric knowledge is now thrown into relief. All of postmodernism, Anderson (1990) tells us, can be summarized as looking at beliefs, including one's own (p. 256). Whereas the modern era was characterized by a political spectrum of *beliefs* ranging from "left" to "right," the postmodern era is characterized more by different *ways of believing*. The "new" spectrum ranges from fundamentalist—those who believe that their beliefs are true in an absolute sense—to constructivist—those who see beliefs as discursive options from which they can choose (pp. 12–13). In the face of all the information in the contemporary world about other belief systems, people's identities will either become more fluid or revert to fundamentalism. This means that fundamentalists have to deal with "troublesome information through psychological denial and/or political repression" (p. 249). As Anderson puts it:

> Information makes life difficult for anyone who would like to hold onto a story in its pure form. Information acts upon stories as rain acts upon sand castles. It discredits them, deconstructs them, refutes their prophesies, and complicates their lives. (p. 249)

Seen in this way, the five narratives outlined in the preceding chapters vary epistemologically to the extent that they are more, or less, fundamentalist in their relationship to the master narrative. The "right wing" narratives cling to the master narrative as a law of nature, a "total social fact" (Berger and Luckman, 1966, p. 187) in the face of a world that has "gone crazy." The "left wing" narratives, on the other hand, lean toward a more liberatory attitude. The present reality is seen as an opportunity to deconstruct past conceptions of whiteness and reconstruct identities along new, more appropriate lines.

The Narratives

My analysis identified five narratives that white people are constructing in this time of political and social transition. These narratives reflect a range of investment in, or disinvestment from, old style whiteness. The first narrative, *Still Colonial after All These Years*, is the most fundamentalist. The people who tell this story have not altered the plot or characters to bring them in line with the realities of the change in power. They seem to believe that the old relationships to the "other" can be magically retained, or even more magically, recovered. While both versions *(The Hardliner* and *The Altruist)* of this story are paternalistic, they differ in the degree of idealism and goodwill they show toward the "other."

The name of the second narrative, *This Shouldn't Happen to a White*, suggests that people who tell it still believe in the Manichean binaries of master narrative, but find them "illogically" inverted by the new order. Seething with racial envy, these people experience what is happening in terms of reversal and victimization—the new order is "out to get them." By contrast, the third narrative, *Don't Think White, It's All Right*, is told by whites who regard whiteness as integral to their identity, but are more pragmatic about their new position within the country. This narrative consists of two versions, *Whites Are Doing It for Themselves*, which tends to retreat to cultural roots, and *We Can Work It Out*, which looks for practical ways to survive and maintain a white influence in the New South Africa.

Another group of whites, by contrast, are convinced that they are completely unracialized. They react to the highly racialized South African society by protesting personal innocence. I have called the story these people are telling *A Whiter Shade of White*, and described some of the appeals they use to establish racial innocence. This story is told by left wing liberals who feel that they have never been implicated in the system and would also like to deemphasize group affiliation, but it is increasingly being picked up by a wider circle of white South Africans. There are obvious, self-serving reasons why it should suit whites in South Africa to be colorblind now that the politics in the country have changed. This is a tale of evasion.

The fifth narrative is *Under African Skies*, or, *White, but Not Quite*. This narrative also separates into different versions. The first version, *I Just Don't Know What To Do, Being White* testifies to the difficulty experienced by whites who are convinced what is happening is right, and support the Africanizing of the country. But they don't know how to negotiate their own personal place in the changes. The second version, *I Don't Wanna Be White no More* is an attempt to evade the pain of confronting whiteness, by appropriating blackness. People who are deeply identified with white guilt tell this tale. They cope with their guilt in different ways, either through manipulating their identities, taking on a pastiche of blackness, or through living a life of penance.

The final version of this narrative is *Hybridization, That's the Name of the Game*. Those who tell this tale are inclined to call themselves [White] Africans. These are people who are adopting a completely different stance: they do not deny their racialization, but do problematize their race. By holding onto both ends of the binaries that have constructed race, incorporating blackness into whiteness, Africanness into Europeanness, their undertaking deconstructs whiteness, undoes the dynamics that originally constructed the master narrative. For these people the present situation does not speak as much of defeat as of opportunity to relinquish the master's construction wisely.

This range of narratives (and probably new variations of them) is likely to continue into the future as competing stories, some becoming more dominant, others more subjugated, depending on how political and material events intersect with these discourses. All these stories draw on, react to, or subvert the sedimentation of the master narrative in some way or another. However fragmented, the master narrative is realistically likely to remain part of the political unconscious in South Africa for some time. All the narratives analyzed in this book quote the master narrative, even as they rearticulate whiteness and draw on other discursive repertoires. Once more, Anderson (1990) helps to envisage what is happening:

> [T]he systems of value and belief do not immediately disappear—people simply inhabit them in a different fashion, and sometimes the old ways have a surprising amount of life left in them. The human mind has a great repertoire of ways to accept and honor social constructions of reality without swallowing them whole. . . . We can see in many parts of the world signs of a postmodern attitude emerging in a tentative way, as people find it possible to retain some sense of their connection to older traditions and at the same time to create new arrangements. (pp. 25, 27)

Nor should we conclude that the fragmentation of the master narrative means that whiteness in South Africa has inevitably lost all power in the new dispensation. It is a modernist fallacy (much touted in the old regime) that only the unified is powerful. Different versions of whiteness contain enough commonalities, or family resemblances, to be able to act in joint interest through strategic coalition-building, rather than essential unity. It seems reasonable to speculate, though, that each of these narratives will continue to be influential in some way, directing the diversification of white identity now that conditions are less prescribed than before. Given that identity-building does not occur in a vacuum, and that all these narratives are being constructed in relation to other population groups in the country, different narratives also lend themselves to coalition-building with those "others" whose interests are perceived to be most similar. One can expect that narratives delineating the boundaries of the privileged fold, previously protected by the master narrative, will attract alliances with members of the previously semiprivileged groups in the country, such as the colored and the Indian peoples.

Postmodern Displacement

The story I tell, the story of how *Whiteness Just Isn't What It Used to Be* for white South Africans, relates the fragmented and ideologically contradictory constructions of whiteness within the country. These constructions are being told by people who are sharing a dramatic change in their life world; they are unmistakably stories of crisis, however diverse their interpretations of the crisis:

> The collapse of a belief system can be like the end of the world. It can bring down not only the powerful, but whole systems of social roles and the concepts of personal identity that go with them. Even those who are most oppressed by a belief system often fear the loss of it.[4] People can literally cease to know who they are. . . . There are many people who have been thus dispossessed. (Anderson, 1990, p. 27)

Whiteness Just Isn't What It Used to Be is therefore also a story about displacement, about the subjective experience of dispossession. While not an essence, there is a definite "structure of feeling"[5] in the narratives associated with the loss that inevitably accompanies change. White South Africans are grieving for what *just isn't what it used to be.* The narratives each give a different spin to the feelings of loss, but all the narratives contend with these feelings. The "fundamentalist tales" stoke up the feelings of loss; the more pragmatic tales try to come to terms with the feelings as matter of factly as possible; the tellers of *A Whiter Shade of White* don't own up to them; and the narrators of *Under African Skies* see them, at least to some extent, as gains. How the narratives orientate white South Africans to deal with these losses is an important indicator of the role the narratives are likely to play in the future. Because certain losses emerge most powerfully in the narratives, I should like to point them out, and comment briefly on how the narratives position themselves in relation to the losses.

Loss of Home

Having left Europe, and settled permanently in Africa, white South Africans, at a very literal level, made the southern tip of Africa their home. But, of course, "home" was predicated upon the master narrative. It was not only a physical space, but a cultural and psychological space. Most of the white people who are leaving the country now are doing so not only to find a different location that they perceive to be physically safe and economically predictable, but also to settle in a region more likely to remain culturally congruent and supportive of white identity. The changes in the country have suddenly made whites feel "out of place." Believing for several centuries that they were feudal lords, they woke up to find they had actually been squatters all along. There is an acute sense of loss of the familiar, loss of certainty, loss of comfort, loss of privilege, loss of well-known roles. The anxiety concomitant with uncertainty about the future is unmistakable in comments like the following:

> The braindrain which is occurring is worrying, the incorporation of Cuban doctors is also a matter of concern. The education system is undergoing problems and white South Africans are worried that standards will have to drop inevitably. White children may well face discriminatory practices when their education is complete.
>
> —respondent, study questionaire

The homesickness whites are experiencing is reflected in the number of respondents who expressed a desire for "a time when things would settle down." As one woman put it, "I long for homeostasis."

Martin and Mohanty (1987) analyze the concept of "home" in a way that provides a more complex understanding of such comments. They point out that home has to do with a place that provides the comfort of a secure, safe, familiar, protected, and *homogenous identity*. But, as they insist, such unified and "secure place[s] from which to speak, within which to act" (p. 206) are established only through denials, exclusions, and blindnesses. These places of "home" are a "repressive fiction" (p. 204). From this perspective, it is clear that the master narrative was a mechanism for converting Africa into a psychological home "fit for the white man." What whites are confronted with (mostly at lesser levels of consciousness) is that the collapse of the master narrative has exposed pure whiteness to have been the adult equivalent of Santa Claus or the Easter Bunny. The delusional structure of a cultural identity based on projections is being challenged by the new reality. Home has become unfamiliar, even alien, and for some, dangerously populated with the phantasmagoria of previous repressions. The narratives can be distinguished by the extent to which they promote learning about the "other," get past bogies into perspective, and create a more complex self that can deal more competently with a multivocal future. Tales such as *Still Colonial after All These Years* may offer simulacra of home. *This Shouldn't Happen to a White* will, in all probability, continue its by now legendary tale of exile and adversary within the promised land. *Don't Think White, It's All Right* will acquire aspects of Africanization as it becomes necessary and unavoidable. *A Whiter Shade of White* may find at some stage that far from being ahead of the pack, it hasn't kept up with the Africanization going on in other white identities. In encouraging a greater identification with Africa, while yet not insisting that whites give up aspects of Europeanness, *Hybridization* is the most promising tale to urge personal heterogeneity. But it quite specifically rules out the possibility of returning to a home that was abusive of self and other.

The realities of South Africa now are such that white South Africans may just have to become comfortable with the inevitability of learning to leave home. One of the difficulties is that moving out is often experienced as a betrayal of parent figures. From the comments of some young respondents, it is clear that they experience this guilt of betrayal as a major deterrent to experimenting with new selves. Yet the fear of "going too far" and running the risk of deserting one's culture, or having to deal with ostracism or censure is not confined to the young. It is something with which everybody who leaves the safe space of a monologic identity has to contend.

Loss of Autonomy and Control

Closely linked with the above is the sense of a loss of autonomy. Whereas previously white dependence on blacks was repressed and kept out of sight (largely through unfair labor practice), dependence upon Africans in the new dispensation is undeniable and public knowledge. Acknowledging interdependence requires learning humility, letting go of ungrounded feelings of self-sufficiency. Whites need to learn to trust what they have been taught to fear most. Fear of the loss of control comes out in references to possible chaos or increasingly "Third World" standards, of being swamped by the financial demands of Africa. Rian Malan (1990) writes about these anxieties in his autobiography:

> [For] me it was a question of being white in Africa, the continent of cruel dictators and endless famine, of collapsing economies, crumbling infrastructures, starving refugees and perpetual civil war. It seemed risky to lower one's defenses on such a continent, and yet the price of dominating it was too— in terms of the damage we were doing to black people, but also to ourselves. Two centuries of keeping them down had left us spiritually deformed, rotten with fears and greed, and yet we still couldn't find it in ourselves to trust. (p. 412–13)

Given such socialization, vast quantities of trust may be unrealistic to expect on a large scale—only those who are "game" for *hybridization* are really going to take risks in a comprehensive way. The signs are evident in comments of the respondents in this study that more whites in South Africa may prefer to withdraw in selected areas of their lives, creating axes of autonomy that will help them still to feel safe and in control. This is particularly evident in both versions of *Don't Think White, It's All Right*. The first version, *Whites Are Doing It for Themselves* seems to be heading toward creating pockets of "authentic" European culture (some entertaining alliances with "Europeanized blacks"). The reaccentuation on European heritage was a noticeable trend in the study. Both this version and *We Can Work It Out* point to an economic withdrawal into private entrepreneurship. For those "fundamentalist whites" who equate separateness from blacks with "self-respect,"[6] as their Voortrekker ancestors did before them, the withdrawal is likely to be a fairly thoroughgoing psychological great trek into enclaves of increasingly irrelevant and impracticable white separateness.

Loss of a Sense of Relevance

Another loss that whites are trying to come to terms with is the loss of a sense of importance and relevance. This is reflected in the widespread tendency to refer to their position as "marginalized." While it is true that whites have lost total political power, they still hold many key positions in the country, both in the civil service and private sector, and control most of the economy. The term reflects the experience of loss of a dominant position, subjectively translated as oppression.[7] The acute feeling of irrelevance is a function of how accustomed whites have been to power, rather than a true measure of the reaches of their peripherality. The feelings of irrelevance can also be seen to be linked to the subjective experience of being excluded from the main arena of history-making, an arena previously reserved for whites, specifically white males.

In the face of what can more accurately be termed relativization than marginalization, the narratives encourage different approaches to establishing relevance. As can be expected, the "right wing" narratives that define the bottom line as total power and perfect centrality encourage feelings of irrelevance to the mainstream social process. Reconstruction is not their concern. These people are more likely to seek feelings of relevance in resistance, which will (seemingly) promote self-interest. The most successful narratives at engendering feelings of relevance to the mainstream process are more modest about power-sharing. This suggests that relevance does not mean having all the say, and at all times. Moreover, the narratives that encourage an appreciation of what is emerging as an inclusive, syncretic history will be most successful in helping whites cope with widespread feelings of irrelevance.

Loss of Guaranteed Legitimacy

Although consciously articulated by only one respondent, whites are definitely also confronting a sense of loss of guaranteed legitimacy. Perhaps more than anything else, the master narrative was a legitimizing device. Whites were needed in Africa, precisely because they were of European stock. This is not quite so self-evident anymore. A great deal of energy in the narratives is expended on providing proof of how whites were needed in South Africa in the past, and how they can contribute to the future. The stakes in this issue are high, and the need to make an emphatic claim to the right of a continuing place in the country is evident. Most white South Africans *do* feel that they have a legitimate claim to their place in the country, both through birth and through the contribution they have made, and their presence is not contested by most African leaders. What has been lost, therefore, is the guarantee that the *interpretation* and *terms* of their legitimacy, previously unilaterally determined, will remain unchanged. The past contribution made by whites (particularly because of the means of its achievement) is more ambivalent, though not totally discounted, when regarded through the eyes of "other" South Africans.

The narratives that reject the current changes insist on the old style legitimacy, willing it in the face of a growing anxiety. The narratives that are characterized by greater involvement in the reconstruction process indicate that the contradictions of white presence in the country are being dealt with at a more conscious, and therefore potentially useful, level. There seemed to be an increased, though not monolithic, sense of past illegitimacy, as well as an increased, but not monolithic, sense of legitimacy since the advent of the new order. The difference seems to arise from a desire for a legitimacy earned in a way that is morally self-affirming through a redefinition of the relationship between self and "other."

Loss of Honor, Loss of Face

One of the most difficult of all the losses to deal with, however, is the feeling that there is very little on which to pin self-respect now that the previously voiceless are telling their stories. The Truth and Reconciliation Commission has provided a sympathetic forum for excavating these previously subjugated stories, many of which had been only vaguely known through rumor, others not at all. The sense of having been "found out" is acutely uncomfortable. In South Africa everybody can see that bloodstained Banquo has turned up to sit at the banquet table. Many whites are seeing him for the first time themselves; some still refuse to look. In the old South Africa massive official rationalization retarded the conscious confrontation of white guilt. However they may handle the feelings, whites have to deal with having shared a positionality that wronged others, of having benefited at others' expense. The issue pervades the entire spectrum of narratives, although the level of willingness to deal with this collective guilt varies greatly. The *desire* for innocence is overwhelmingly evident in all the narratives, though again some narratives are more able to separate the desire from the actuality.

This Shouldn't Happen to a White has hardly raised this issue of guilt to the level of consciousness. Innocence is achieved through projection. Many, but not all of those who tell *Don't Think White, It's All Right,* have tried to shrug off guilt as quickly as possible. The alacrity with which the guilt is shed is probably a good measure of how deeply the person still buys into the master narrative, and does not question racial exploitation when it occurs the right/white way round. The colorblind *Whiter Shade of White* is quite explicitly a story of face management, at whatever level of consciousness.

By contrast, a number of white South Africans felt a genuine and enormous unburdening of guilt when the transition of power occurred, relieved at no longer being associated with a formal system with which they had disagreed. Yet a greater level of awareness about the past and of the layers of unconscious complicity initially deepens the sense of guilt. This is what some of those who are *Under African Skies* are dealing with. While being gripped by a dysfunctional guilt complex is clearly not going to take white South Africans forward, grappling with the pain of knowing that privilege was wrested in one's name, and had real and debilitating consequences on the lives of others, cannot be discarded prematurely. Knowing this pain is intimately linked to the development of consciousness, of conscience, and leads to a responsible sense of accountability. Without this honesty, whites will deny themselves the opportunity for growth, and their relationship with other South Africans will still be based on denial and half-truths. In general, then, the extent to which the narratives are prepared to acknowledge responsibility for the past, and from that position create a different future in which whites can live with self-respect, will determine the quality of the contribution that each narrative makes to the New South Africa.

Feelings of anomie, disorientation, grief, nostalgia, excitement, freedom, vertigo—the range of feelings that accompany the failure of a belief system, the demise of "certain certainties"—these are feelings that are likely to be part of the experience of being white in South Africa for some time. The narratives provide options for what to salvage from the past, what to let go of, and perspectives that may provide new bearings. There is a freedom to create new social identities, using discourses that were previously unthinkable, either because the discourses were not readily available, or because they were not regarded highly enough to be cultural resources. This postmodern moment provides the opportunity to reevaluate past discourses of self and "other," to reframe the past, and to adopt different stances toward the future.

The narratives that are least bought into the old modernist construction of whiteness are in the best position to draw on the new resources, and to create more pluralistic, complex identities. Such social identities are best poised to help white people adjust to change by making the boundaries of whiteness more complex. From the perspective of a more inclusive, multimodal identity, the losses are seen as gains. It is the choice of complexity over homogeneity,[8] and it deconstructs whiteness in the very place in relation to which whiteness was originally constructed, Africa.[9]

> We must . . . be prompted to think the once unthinkable: that whites . . . be intellectually *and* culturally influenced by thought of black people; that whites and blacks think through the conditions of possibility . . . for whites to be black. (Goldberg, 1993, p. 218)

Far from being an absence, with nothing to offer, Africa is seen as a source of meaning, invited to influence the European. What whiteness was constructed to deny is acknowledged. Otherness becomes difference. In thus deconstructing the logic of domination of white over black that has been one of the lasting heritages from the Enlightenment, the very fact that some white South Africans are choosing the narrative of *Under African Skies* has implications well beyond the boundaries of South Africa. There are thus two related, though not identical, postmodern circumstances that have theoretical implications: (a) the fact of the fragmentation of the master narrative, and (b) the fact that becoming *White Africans* is a choice being seriously considered by some white South Africans.

Polycentric, Polivocal Whitenesses

As set out in the Introduction, whiteness has been theorized as the racial norm, the invisible center that deflects attention from itself by racializing the margins, and constructing them as the problem. Whiteness then believes in its own homogenous neutrality. Whites are described as generally unaware of their own racialization, unconscious of their privilege, or of how their implicit assumptions of white entitlement are a consequence of certain historical relations, not something essential about whiteness itself. The ideological power of the discourse about whiteness is demonstrated by the fact that it has helped white people to maintain a dominant position in the organization of global relations, and to keep much of the world hegemonically in its grip to this day. The critical thrust of the interest in whiteness has been to render this norm visible, by showing its embeddedness in historical and material relations, and by bringing in voices from the margins to create a multiplicity of centers.

In looking at one specifically located experience of whiteness, this book links in with this postcolonial project. However, what the argument presented here also shows is that the invisibility of whiteness only holds under certain circumstances. Even before April 1994, white South Africans were acutely aware of their whiteness— that it was a position of privilege, the absolutely defining factor in their life chances. The extreme version of the master narrative, its economic consequences for the different races where First and Third World conditions exist side by side, and very decidedly, the demographic anomaly of whites being a small minority within the country, all contributed to a whiteness that was highly visible to self and other.

Particularizing whiteness in this context indicates the danger of generalizing theory from one specific geographical and historical positionality. The world's populations are dispersed and fragmented. Ethnic loyalties and national allegiances are less and less isomorphic and homogenous, and global tribes span the continents. If we are to understand whiteness in all its guises and morphs, we probably also need to study "white" diaspora. These are places where "whiteness" is removed from the Euro-American center, and may also be displaced and have less power, but still shares cultural narratives, that may become more and more creolized with the passing of time. Whites in South Africa form part of such an imagined community,[10] linked by what Cohen (1992) calls "founding texts." These are stories that tend to blur disparate histories and provide a sense of sharing a special history. Just as in theorizing other issues, it is important to bring the margins into the theorization of whiteness—to prevent universalizing from the center. What happens at the margins often has much that is instructive to the center.

Ironically, perhaps, some of the more recent writings about whiteness in North America describe a whiteness closer to the "old" South African attitudes. Family resemblances are apparent in the acute awareness of belonging to a "besieged" racialized group to whom one's destiny is aligned, along with feelings of defensiveness, victimization, and even defiance. Whiteness, it seems, is only invisible to those it privileges while its entitlements are reasonably secure. In such circumstances, it can experience itself as benign, even generous, toward those who are on the other side of the coin. Its propensity for reactionary behavior is concealed. Aggression emerges once the task of defending white privilege is perceived to have become necessary, when privilege is challenged while the ideological assumptions of entitlement are still firmly in place.

The disruption of power in South Africa, where whites are continuing to seek their livelihood in a situation where they have neither numerical nor political power, is unusual in the history of whiteness. Most groups of whites left the countries they had colonized if they had not attained numerical majority as settlers, and could not retain political dominance. By definition, therefore, the circumstances in the New South Africa problematize the way whiteness was constructed as the social positionality of domination. Whiteness is clutching for power, along with the whites.

The crucial difference for whites now is that they no longer have the power to define themselves unilaterally. Whatever stories they tell about their whiteness and the changes it is undergoing, will take place in a context that is largely determined by Africans, and geared toward African interests. The "projects of African kingdoms" that Unterhalter (1995) maintains were in progress before colonization, and continued in subjugated forms after colonization, are now reconfiguring once again at the center of the political arena. This manifestation of the characteristically postmodern "return of the repressed" means that the question "What do blacks want?" will no longer be shrouded in superstition, but will be one of the defining factors in white identity. This places whiteness in a completely different relationship to the "other." The stories that articulate whiteness in ways that are perceived to be inimical to African interests will have greater difficulty maintaining themselves in the New South Africa. The New South Africa may be the site of the construction of a new whiteness, too.

Yet there is a family resemblance between what is happening in South Africa and other domains from which whiteness has exercised power. Globally, whites are a numerical minority (as are men and the middle classes), and the ideology of white superiority, constructed at a time when Europeans thought the world belonged to them (literally and metaphorically) is being challenged both at a material and conceptual level. As the world shrinks and power balances shift, whiteness is less and less likely to retain its privileged position. The very fact that whiteness has become visible as a construct of academic study shows that it is losing its ideological hold on intellectuals globally. Within "white countries" such as the

United States, the difficulty of organizing so as to remain white is proving difficult. The issue is perhaps more immediate to specific institutions, such as the Catholic Church, which is controlled by white men, though its following is predominantly nonwhite.

The South African example has demonstrated in technicolor and digital sound the unsustainability of whiteness under such circumstances as it becomes more trenchantly contested, positioned in a different relationship to rival discourses. Whereas it is very difficult to get in touch with the realities of oppressive structures when one is in power, and the voluntary renunciation of such a social positionality is exceptional behavior,[11] the exigencies of changing power must increasingly cause a fragmentation of modernist whiteness in other contexts. The reconfigurations that emerge will also be influenced by the competing stories whites tell about their loss of domination.

Stories are important not just because of what they say, but because they are used to achieve social purposes, and have tangible effects. The master narrative had the purpose and effect of social control and domination. In the new dispensation, whites will be shopping around for stories that seem to serve their interests best now that they have less control. It is useful to consider some of the ways in which the different stories of whiteness may function within the new South African context: in other words, to ask questions such as "Why would 'whites' want to tell this story?" and "What is this story likely to *do* in the changed society?" The answers are important because (a) a similar range of stories may be found in other contexts where whiteness loses control, influencing the outcomes in those contexts, and (b) they point to ways in which the theorization of whiteness can be rendered more complex by taking the margins of whiteness into account. There may be "other" ways to be white, nonnormative ways that are constructed in, and as a consequence of, the *presence* of the "other."

Whiteness as Resistance

In the face of a growing Africanization of the country, whiteness may certainly become a discourse of resistance. Although narratives such as *This Shouldn't Happen to a White* that brim with blatant hostility toward black people are likely to become increasingly irrelevant to the mainstream of South African society, the underlying logic could be mobilized to encourage a mentality of sabotage in relation to the new regime. The binary split on which the master narrative depended could be kept active in the political unconscious of the white population. They may even be invoked as discursive resources for mobilization of white struggle, even at a later date. The danger of racial polarization raises its head again if this narrative can form alliances of indignation with the most unconscious elements from other narratives, such as *A Whiter Shade of White.*

Narratives such as *Whites Are Doing It for Themselves* also have the potential to be a discursive resource for resistance and subversion, but in a less hostile, and probably more successful, way. Tropes such as "standards," "merit," and "fine arts" may be employed to the purpose, used to ensure that the continuation of liberal European values and attitudes (and thus lifestyle) do not get submerged in the new order.

Ironically, the accentuated sense of being besieged may achieve what being in power never quite did—drawing English and Afrikaans white South Africans into a much closer, united front. Their deepest bond is their whiteness.

Whiteness as Strategic Abdication

There are indications, referred to earlier, that many whites are poised to withdraw in a variety of ways from active, committed involvement in shaping the society they don't see as theirs anymore. This is a strategic abdication, a position that advocates keeping a low profile, just quietly "minding your own business." The word "business," of course, carries its multiple meanings, for this is very much a discourse that settles for affluence if there is to be little influence. Cohen (1992) points out that racism can go underground, perpetuated in coded ways.

A good deal of "damage control" could be achieved through ring-fencing more modest interests, particularly if they are rearticulated or co-articulated through discourses of multiculturalism and even nonracialism. The African National Congress's policy of nonracialism lends itself to strategic misinterpretation, making colorblindness a respectable option. This position engages the "politics of forgetting," (Rodriguez, 1998) and therefore *A Whiter Shade of White* may actually become quite a popular story, though *We Can Work It Out* will probably also do the job. In an inverted way *I Don't Wanna Be White no More* also belongs in this category, because although it associates with the mainstream, it is still a discourse of abdication. It renders whiteness invisible, while not acknowledging that it is still really looking after the interests of the white person.

Whiteness as Resource

"There are as many modes of decolonization as there are modes of colonization and ways of conceptualizing them," Nederveen Pieterse and Parekh (1995) remind us. Even though we may have a decolonized, multipolar world, "most centers of power and influence ... operate within an occidental orbit" (p. 4). To the extent that Westernization is conflated with internationalism, white South Africans will be able to position themselves as the custodians of valuable cultural and experiential resources. As long as the tropes of whiteness remain desired objects for many black African people of South Africa, while it is perceived to hold the key to prosperity, modernization, and access to a wider world (especially the world of capital) whiteness is likely to retain significant cultural hegemony. This is clearly linked to the global longevity of Western cultural hegemony. It is also linked to how well contesting narratives, such as nativistic Africanism, woo the "nonwhite" population and to how well their expectations of change are met by the new regime. All the narratives, except the *Hardliner Colonial* and *This Shouldn't Happen to a White* can continue to contribute to South African society in such a climate. I exclude these two narratives, because even though they are the ones that insist most on white authority, they would achieve the opposite effect, antagonizing through an attempt to retain a relationship of domination. Narratives such as *Don't Think White, It's All Right,* however, will do very well in this climate, offering whiteness as a consultative resource, using tropes such as "progress," "development," "modernization," and also drawing on discourses of multiculturalism. In this way, the advantages acquired through the spoils of colonialism can be made available to people historically disadvantaged by it, and white prosperity can be seen to be linked to that of blacks.

Should "nonwhite" South Africans become less hegemonically enamored with white culture, it is possible that whiteness may still become a discourse of support, playing a complementary role to the discourses that have become more socially attractive to the majority. In this way European customs, attitudes, and values can still remain a component, one idiom of South African society, a modifying influence on the mainstream. The more "left-wing" strains of *We*

Can Work It Out, and *Under African Skies* will clearly cope best with this situation.

What the above discussion points to therefore is that a fragmented whiteness may develop different functions in society, depending on what white people perceive to be in their best interests. The narrative that departs most radically from the master narrative in respect of what it *does,* is, of course, the *Hybridization* narrative. The narrative is important because of its content within the context of the New South Africa. Once again though, there are implications for the broader theorization of whiteness in other contexts. Much discussion in Critical White Studies is currently focused on rearticulating whiteness in socially meaningful ways, on encouraging positive, affirmative, and progressive racial reinvention.[12] Examining the manner in which this narrative operates to move whites forward in its context, reinforces once again that, just as the construction of whiteness needs to be examined contextually, so the way out of oppressive identities can only be undertaken with a sound grasp of the local and the particular.

Hybrid Whitenesses: An Open-ended Field

The significance that this narrative has for dismantling whiteness and creating heterogeneous identities is paramount. The identity of White African deconstructs not only a unitary ethnic identity, but a unitary "racial" identity. The particularities of the South African situation make it eminently suitable as a position for such a deconstruction. One can expect that the more complex the society becomes through the freer contribution of different cultures, the more congruent hybridized identities will become with the society, reducing the feelings of race betrayal discussed earlier.[13] A sign of successful South Africanism is likely to become versatility in both white and black aspects of the society. Whereas in the past code-switching versatility was a survival strategy for "nonwhites" because of their subordinate position, greater interdependence in the New South Africa will exert such pressure toward bicultural and tricultural identities on all citizens. The stakes for making new articulations of whiteness work in South Africa are very high. Excepting echoes of the master narrative, survival is cast in terms of adjustment in all the narratives. This means that if what is required is a certain amount of *hybridization,* a significant number of South African whites are likely to move, albeit gradually, toward this narrative.

Moreover, ironically, certain aspects of white heritage can be turned to advantage for developing hybridity, such as the schisms in white psyches left by the colonial system (Memmi, 1990; Pollock, 1994). Several respondents commented on early experiences with nannies and playmates as places of "splitting." Another fundamental split in the psyches of many whites in Africa is their love of the earth and sky of Africa, but the historical hatred of its people. Apartheid legislation perpetuated a blindness to this schism. The postmodern sensibility leans toward seeing this bifurcation as providing potential for more complex identifications. Berger and Luckman (1966) regard this type of primary socialization in which a child has two different worlds available to him or her, as providing the child with "hidden identities" (as well as the potential for a lifetime fraught with internal conflict and guilt). As they point out, the possibility of the question, "Who am I?," the potential for conscious identity construction, is directly linked to the choice between discrepant realities and identities.[14] They also discuss the less painful situation where the alternative worlds appear in secondary socialization, enabling the individual to opt for alternative identities in a conscious, even manipulative, manner. They conclude:

> A society in which discrepant worlds are generally available on a market basis entails specific constellations of subjective reality. There will be an increasingly general consciousness of the relativity of *all* worlds, including one's own, which is now subjectively apprehended as "*a* world," rather than "*the* world." It follows that one's own institutionalized conduct may be apprehended as "a role" from which one may detach oneself in one's own consciousness, and which one may "act out" with manipulative control. (pp. 172–73)[15]

The required material (discursive and psychological) to make a conscious choice to *hybridize* is clearly present. What would facilitate it is an ethos that celebrates syncretism, and is supportive of the choice not to fix an identity in a homogenous category, or according to one axis; an ethos that commends the creolized, the multiple, the blurred boundary, the strategic coalition rather than the ideologically predetermined. South Africa needs an ethos that applauds the many shades of brown that constitute the human race.

While this may sound romantic, the issues that confront this *hybridizing* white community are tough. Protecting the privilege of a few needs to give way to promoting development for all. The process requires coming to terms with a different sense of one's place in history. In particular, the participation of white South Africa's heritage in imperialism and even genocidal acts toward Africa and its people has to be acknowledged. The intimate role that the denigration of Africa has played in the identity construction of whiteness on this continent cannot be evaded. This lies at the deepest heart of all whiteness, and was carried across the Atlantic with the African slaves. Whereas it may be sufficiently far away for whites in North America not to have to confront this aspect of the white shadow, whites in South Africa cannot move forward without dealing with it. Deracialization on African soil cannot take place without an open heart toward Africa. South African whites can play a part in creating a postcolonial South Africa only if they themselves, their own identities, become postcolonial spaces.

A Final Comment

The rousing tones of the previous paragraph make me mindful of the irony that in writing about the demise of a modernist narrative, my book tells a neat modernist story itself. It centers my center, South Africa. Like the stories some of my respondents told that raised a wry smile, it even has a teleological plot—"progress" away from the Enlightenment, modernist master narrative, toward emancipation through postmodern fragmentation and hybridization. There is something in the nature of a story that wants closure, and desire plays a part in all our understandings. I draw consolation from the fact that I am not alone in this inconsistency. It is a well-known criticism that in deconstructing a concept, deconstructionism posits "a concept whose truth value is being questioned"; it "relapses into the error it denounces" (Owens, 1992, p. 78); or, similarly, that "the postmodern debate itself, which advertises its commitment to indeterminacy, openness, and multiplicity . . . provides in itself the discursive means to limit the force and implications of such questions" (Connor, 1989, p. 18).

Cohen (1992) argues:

[All social theories are] traversed by narrative structures which form a hidden thread running through the argument. . . . in the case of *theoretical ideology* it constitutes the main organizing principle. For here a particular epistemology is subsumed within a rhetoric of special pleading for a chosen reference group. . . . Such groups are constructed as the bearers of privileged knowledge or agency, by virtue of their social location. As such they are invested with a unique role as makers of history, or as critics of society. This is above all a narrative role, a role within a storyline which is unfolded as a teleology, that is a narrative moving towards a preordained conclusion, which structures the logic of preceding events. (pp. 70–71)

I cannot talk myself out of this one. Shall I express the hope that in centering South African whiteness, I have at least in some way contributed to a more multicentered approach to whiteness, and that the desire for a better future for my country and my people that seems to drive my thinking may counter other narratives by and about South African whites that are driven by different desires? The role of the unconscious in theorizing race is as powerful as anywhere else that the issue arises. As Cohen observes:

the issue of race is not only a minefield of vested interests, but a site where powerful structures of feeling—anger, hatred, pain and envy—are inevitably at play, and subject to strategies of sublimation and disavowal. (p. 97)

In the end, it is in the interplay, the overlaying, of many different stories of whitenesses, from plural sources, that our understanding of the phenomenon is made more complex, and freer from monological thinking. If nothing else, my sojourn in the United States has infected me with a bad case of terminal consciousness. I offer my construction in full consciousness of the fact that it is a construction, my story about the stories my respondents are telling in their attempt to find more relevant stories about a story that drew on other stories at the time of colonialism:

"It isn't so funny. . . . take it back. Call that story back," said the audience by the end of the story, but the witch answered: "It's already turned loose/It's already coming./It can't be called back." A story is *not* just a story. Once the forces have been aroused and set into motion, they can't simply be stopped at someone's request. Once told, the story is bound to circulate; humanized, it may have a temporary end, but its effects linger on and its end is never truly an end. (Trinh, p. 133)

My hope is that if the story of whiteness is not going to end without trace, its fragments may at least be reshuffled in ways that can work for a better life for all. May our stories never again cause suffering as the master's story used to.

They are of spirit which is like the wind
Mind them
When you touch them
When you hurt them
When you kill them
When you are unkind to them
When you are cruel to them
Mind them
They will live in you
And you in them
Like a story which does not end. . . .

Mongane Wally Serote
"Freedom Lament and Song"

Appendix 1

༺༻

Methodology

Method of Collecting Data, and Response to the Survey

As with the general choice of method, the logistics of this study directly affected the method of data collection. Because of time constraints, it was not possible to arrange for a pilot study in South Africa to test the effectiveness of particular questions. The questionnaire was given to a student at Arizona State University who was from New Zealand, and would probably be closer to a South African in terms of experience than a North American. At her suggestion some of the questions were clarified.

Copies of the questionnaire were posted and faxed to family and acquaintances in South Africa, and they were asked to "snowball" the questionnaire to people in their work environments and social circles. Questionnaires were sent to fourteen people in all, and ten gathered responses, albeit only one response in the case of one contact. Four contacts did not return any questionnaires, and this merits some comment.

Kauffman (1992) correctly draws attention to the fact that negotiations over how the research will proceed "are part of the data, not merely contextual variables for which the researcher must account" (p. 187). As she points out, subjects in interviews are also "busy constructing accounts of the interaction and using them as currency in their own social milieu" (p. 198). Given the tiered structure of this method of data gathering and the obviously "touchy" nature of the research topic, each stage of the data collection was infused with political negotiations of the kind to which Kauffman refers. Drawing on an understanding of the context in which each of these acquaintances was collecting data, one can infer that their lack of success has different implications.

One contact had recently changed employment, and I asked her to try and get responses in the business sector that she was entering. The subject matter was probably perceived to be too risky for her to approach contacts with whom she still had to establish secure business links. The second

173

contact volunteered enthusiastically to distribute the questionnaire among his friends, but once he had received it, never "got around to it." Again, I feel this reflected his discomfort with the self-disclosing nature of the responses required, and his unwillingness to impose questions that he felt might be offensive to his friends. The third "nonproducing" contact was in a very interesting position. He is a black South African, who had recently taken a position of considerable seniority in a government funded research organization, at this stage still employing mostly researchers who speak Afrikaans as their home language. Although this friend clearly had the official capacity to influence his white colleagues to respond, either he did not feel comfortable pressuring them, or they were not prepared to disclose such information when requested by him. The fourth person was my daughter, who lost the questionnaire in a major move. I'll refrain from analyzing this turn of events in terms of filial politics.

The most successful collectors of responses were those who were in a position of influence over the respondents who completed the questionnaires. For example, one was a school teacher who asked a senior class for volunteer respondents. A few contacts headed up departments at a university or in a business. One was a director of a company who hosts fortnightly business breakfasts and has a great deal of credibility with those who attend.

At the level of the relationship between myself, as the researcher, and the respondents, several respondents asserted their own power through writing notes along with their responses. Two, for example, qualified their participation in the project by commenting on how they wanted to participate in the research, but could not relate to the subject matter, as they did not think in terms of "race." (They had completed the questionnaire, nevertheless.) Two respondents showed some intensity of feeling by commenting in the course of their responses that they appreciated the opportunity to voice their feelings, and be listened to. (The fact that this research was being conducted in the United States probably led the respondents to feel someone "out there" needed to know about their outrage.) In one case responses were gathered from people who knew each other. It was clear that there had been some discussion about the project. A message emerged from several of these respondents that the questions were considered "difficult" and required more explication. I regard this as an example of "collective bargaining"; resistance to the "othering" involved in being a research subject. There were also comments on the research process, per se, a political move that placed some distance between the respondents and the results. One respondent, who is a clinical psychologist, rapped me over the knuckles because my method of data collection would "skew my results" and not be representative of the general population of the country. (She did not approve of qualitative methods of research.) In a more helpful tone, a researcher from the Medical Research Council wrote a letter explaining that he felt interviews would have provided more accurate and in-depth information. Finally, there were notes wishing me well with the project, and expressing the desire that their responses had been helpful, and the wish that the question of "race" could be resolved in a constructive manner.

Of course, the most crucial political statement that a person approached to answer such a questionnaire could make, would be to refrain from participating. Unfortunately, there is no record of how many people were approached, compared to how many completed the form.

Fifty-nine responses were received, most by mail, though some were faxed by the contact person. One additional respondent was actually a "colored" senior at school, and although his responses to the questions were fascinating, they clearly could not be used. Most respondents completed the questionnaire in full, writing complete sentences to all questions, except the first, which did not necessarily require it. Five responses were answered briefly, with answers sometimes consisting of only single words. On the other end of the scale, however, several respondents had taken the time to answer in a great amount of detail, volunteering a considerable amount of self-disclosure, and clearly intending to be as helpful as they could.

The question that respondents had most difficulty with required them to recall an incident from as early in their lives as they could, and to comment on how they had understood the meaning of their "whiteness" in the incident. This was the question most frequently left blank. Those who did make the mental effort to respond to this question gave valuable information. One of the questionnaires faxed to Cape Town had an indistinct question (question 3), and the respondents approached by this contact person did not fill in this question.

Breakdown of the Sample

An effort was made to obtain a range of responses, by approaching contacts in different parts of the country, and in different walks of life to circulate the questionnaire in their environments. Of the ten contacts who returned responses, three were faculty members at universities, two were in business, one was a school teacher, one was a secretary, two were professional medical researchers, and one was a student.

The following summary of the demographics of the sample gives an indication of the range and diversity of respondents. Not all respondents answered all the demographic questions, so the totals in the following information do not always add up to fifty-nine.

Gender:
Of 54 respondents, 23 were male, 31 female.

Age:
The breakdown in terms of age was as follows: 18–30 years old, 18 respondents; 31–40 years, 14 respondents; 41–50 years, 8 respondents; 51–60 years, 12 respondents.

Ethnicity:
In cultural terms, 29 of the respondents were English-speaking; 18 were Afrikaans. Less numerous "white" ethnic groups were also represented, in that there were two German-speaking respondents, one Polish person, and one Czechoslovakian.

Area of Residence:
By far the greatest number of respondents was from the Cape Town area, a total of 24. From the northern part of the country, two respondents lived in the area known as Northern Province since the April 1994 elections, and five were from Gauteng (the name now given to the Pretoria-Johannesburg-Vereeniging industrial complex). Ten respondents were from the inland Karoo region (a rural desert area), one was from Kwazulu-Natal, and three were from the Eastern Cape. One respondent said she regarded the whole country as her home.

Level of Qualification:
The range in level of qualification was as follows: not yet left school, 9; junior certificate, 1; senior certificate matriculation, 7; tertiary level diploma, 7; university degree, 11; masters' degree, 8; doctorate, 6.

Occupation:
professional, 21; corporate business, 3; self-employed, 8; administrative assistants, 7; scholars, 9; artist, 1; NGO employee, 1; retired, 1.

Income:
The income of the respondents reflected the following range: no income, 10; up to R30000, 12; R30000-R60000, 9; R60000-R90000, 5; over R90000, 12. One respondent was unemployed.
(Exchange value as of May 1996: R4.25 to the American dollar)

Involvement in Transformative Work:
This information was asked as a way of judging orientation toward the "New South Africa." The implications and interpretations of various answers are discussed more fully in the analysis; only the figures will be given here.
    Of 54 respondents, 19 replied that they had no involvement in any activity related to societal reconstruction. The remaining respondents all felt that were making a contribution in some way, though whether this in fact was to try to bring about a new dispensation, or to salvage what they could of the old, became clearer in the context of the entire response. Moreover, those who were really committed to change tended to be involved in more than one arena of society, hence the numbers do not tally exactly. Several (9) respondents felt that their work in education had a transformative dimension to it; nine were involved in the restructuring of their professions; ten

were involved in religious activities that they regarded as significant for change; three were facilitating workshops directly related to issues of race, gender, or personal growth of some form or another. Another person did voluntary work, two respondents were political activists (one a feminist activist) and one was involved in restructuring a state department. Two respondents felt that they facilitated change through their manner of personal contact, one had traveled to one of the "homelands" earlier and done some work there. Finally, one respondent believed his contact with the laborers on his father's farm was transformative. As mentioned, these figures require interpretation and should not just be taken at face value.

Upon return to South Africa, the completed work was given to several white South Africans to read, as a form of "member check." They were asked to comment on anything that struck them, but in particular any point that jarred. The instruction was that they did not have to agree with the analysis, but should be able to recognize themselves, and their compatriots, in the text. All the readers felt that the narratives as analyzed were insightful reflections of "whiteness" in the New South Africa.

Appendix 2

⌒

Brief Chronology of South African Political Events

1899–1902: Second Anglo-Boer War. British aspire to controlling lucrative Witwatersrand goldfields. A scorched earth policy decimates Boer farms, and forces the women and children into concentration camps.

1909: Eight-person delegation of African and colored politicians travel to London to protest draft South Africa Act (constitution for the union).

1910: Union of South Africa established consisting of four provinces: Transvaal, Orange Free State, Natal, and Cape Province (two former British colonies, and two Boer republics).

1912: Formation of South African Native National Congress; in 1923 it becomes the African National Congress.

1913: Natives' Land Act passed, allowing Africans to own a bare 7 percent of land in the Union. This was extended to 13 percent in 1936.

1914: National Party formed.

1940s: New generation of young militants go up the ranks in the ANC; develop the Program of Action for resistance.

1948: National Party comes into power.

1950s: ANC forms alliance with other non-African resistance movements.

1955: Freedom Charter presented to the Congress of the People consisting of various organizations fighting for the rights of black South African citizens.

1956–1961: 156 activists tried for treason.

1959: Some disaffected ANC members and others form the Pan-Africanist Congress (PAC).

1960: After escalating confrontations between the government and the resistance organizations, they are banned and those leaders who did not escape to exile are put in jail. Every opponent to the government is branded a "communist."

1960: Sharpeville shootings.

1960: National all-white referendum in October gives narrow support (52 percent) to the formation of the Republic of South Africa in May 1961.

1961: The ANC decides that its hitherto peaceful strategies have no more teeth, and that it is time to strategize an armed struggle. Both ANC and PAC set up military wings.

1963: Rivonia Trial leads to Nelson Mandela's imprisonment.

1969: Black consciousness movement emerges under Steve Biko.

1960s: As the decade drew to a close, international strategies of economic, sports, and cultural boycotts start having some effects in the country. White South Africans return the Nadienalist Party to power with increasing support.

1974/5: Socialist coup in Portugal leads to decolonization of Mozambique and Angola.

1976: Schoolchildren in Soweto resist the use of Afrikaans in schools. International pressure mounts against South African government causing economic downturns.

1976–1990: Spiraling resistance is met with ever-increasing repression and violence from the Nationalist Party government such as inhumane legislation backed up by the armed forces in the townships.

1983: Attempt to create Tricameral Parliament with Colored and Indian representation. United Democratic Front unites hundreds of organizations opposed to apartheid.

1985–86: States of Emergency declared almost countrywide. Repressive laws and heavy censorship escalate. Economy slumps as international disinvestment campaigns start biting.

1986–89: South Africa becomes ungovernable. Civilian organizations such as churches, white women's organizations, and anticonscription campaign become more visible in their resistance campaigns. The Progressive Federal Party meets ANC leaders in Dakar. The National Party negotiates with Nelson Mandela in prison.

1989: F.W. de Klerk succeeds P.W. Botha as Prime Minister. Allows antiapartheid marches to take place, and releases several political prisoners.

1990: Historic speech by F.W. de Klerk in parliament unbanning banned organizations. Nelson Mandela released.

1992: About 70 percent of white electorate vote yes for De Klerk's program of reform negotiations.

1994: First democratic elections in South Africa vote the ANC into power. Nelson Mandela becomes South Africa's first indigenous African president.

Notes

∽

Introduction

1. See B. Dervin, for her analysis of the importance of the "gap" for communication scholars, in "Comparative theory reconceptualized: From entities and states to processes and dynamics." *Communication Theory,* 1, 59–69, 1991.

2. A. Bonnett in "Who was white? The disappearance of non-European white identities and the formation of European racial whiteness," *Ethnic and Racial Studies,* 21(6) 1029–55, 1998, challenges the conflation of European and white identity. He discusses other premodern white identities in China and the Middle East that have been marginalized by modern European whiteness as a marker of difference.

3. R. Thornton provides a perceptive alternative analysis of the intersection of the postcolonial and postmodern in contemporary South Africa in "The potentials of boundaries in South Africa: Steps towards a theory of the social edge," R. Werbner and T. Ranger (eds.). *Postcolonial identities in Africa* (London: Zed Books, 1996). His chapter appeared after the completion of my thesis.

4. Technically, the white group cannot be called a "minority group" in the sense in which the term is used by many sociologists. J. Stone in *Racial conflict in contemporary society* (Cambridge: Harvard University Press, 1985) argues:

> the concept of a minority group must include both the numerical and the power dimensions as recognized by a comparative sociologist such as Richard Schermerhorn who has developed a fourfold typology. . . . This includes not only *majorities* and *minorities,* dominant and subordinate in terms of both numbers and strength, but also *elites* and

subordinated masses, where numerical superiority and power do not coincide. (p. 44, emphasis in the original)

5. GEAR is the acronym for the strategy of "Growth, Employment and Redistribution."

6. According to the *Race Relations Survey 1994/95,* published by the South African Institute of Race Relations, the net result of immigration and emigration was a loss of 2,857 persons in the first five months of 1994, compared to an estimated gain of 2,185 persons in the first five months of 1993. This "braindrain" consists mainly of highly qualified white professionals.

7. Japan and Korea are examples.

8. The extent to which the ideology of whiteness has held sway over our imaginations is reflected in the fact that although theorists have challenged the grip of modernist thinking in relation to many concepts, "whiteness" has until recently quite successfully eluded deconstruction.

9. The distinction between the set of political and social circumstances (as signified by the suffix "ity") and the theorization of these circumstances (as signified by the suffix "ism") is useful in mapping out the "posts." Postmodern theory (postmodernism) was ushered in by the fact of postcoloniality, in that the "New Philosophers" were students in the 1968 riots in France. The Algerian war of independence and the growing understanding within France of the implications of its colonial past occasioned these riots. As the theorization of the condition of postcoloniality, postcolonialism is one of the many "narratives" which attempt to make sense of (and strive to become the dominant explanatory framework for) the social and political conditions of postmodernity (see Anderson, 1990).

10. In theorizing the "incipient or actual dissolution of those forms associated with modernity" (Sarup, 1993, p. 130), postcolonialism attempts to decenter Western narratives. This includes the narratives of "mainstream" postmodern theorists such as Lyotard and Baudrillard, who theorize from the experience of the developed First World. Nevertheless, postcolonialism shares with most postmodern discourses the emphasis on discontinuities and also resists the homogenization of geographical, historical, and cultural specifics. As a theoretical perspective, it draws on the same philosophical roots as postmodernism, i. e. the work of poststructuralists like Foucault, Barthes, Derrida, and Lacan, but, in addition, postcolonial theory also draws on the neo-Marxist tradition, particularly the work of Gramsci and Althusser. This uneasy marriage is necessitated by the need for a stronger theory of agency that enables political action, and the need to be more grounded in the material realities of imperialism than the more textual postmodern positions allow (Ebert, 1985). Like feminism, postcolonialism absorbs some internal incongruities in the interests of the larger political objective. And like cultural studies, most articulations of postcolonialism insist on a connection to an

external world (Brantlinger, 1990). Few postcolonialists are prepared to follow the Baudrillardian disconnection with "real life," or, along with Lyotard,
to lose a vision of the historical, economic, and social connections between different groups, connections that provide coherent social understanding, particularly at a global level. Culture is not seen to be free-floating, severed from
the world of labor, politics, and ideology.

11. Foucault's phrase for the task of the intellectual.

12. See, for example, Allen, 1994; Bartolome and Macedo, 1997, Crenshaw, 1997, Delgado and Stefancic, 1997; Dyer, 1997; Fine et al., 1997;
Frankenberg, 1993, 1997; Gross, 1998; Hill, 1997; Harris, 1993; Ignatiev,
1995; Lipsitz, 1998; Mahler and Tretreault, 1997; Martin et al., 1996;
Nakayama and Krizek, 1995; Roediger, 1991, 1994, 1998. A brief overview
of some studies in the area of whiteness gives an indication of the work
being done toward the ends described above. Nakayama and Krizek (1995)
draw on de Certeau's notion of strategic rhetoric, Foucault's concepts of discursive practice and power, and Deleuse and Guattari's notion of assem-
blage, to reveal how whites have constructed their social location of whiteness, and the rhetorical strategies that they use to maintain its central
position. Martin et al. (1996) use a multiperspectival approach to examine
the self-identifying labels used by white Americans in the United States.
They found that the lack of variation in the results and the choice of the
least historically specific label indicate the desire for universalizing the position of white, and a resistance to historical, geographical, or cultural
specificity (p. 23). Roediger (1991, 1994) has done important work in showing how the white working class in the United States established its "whiteness" by rejecting alliances with black working class people, and has analyzed how ethnic immigrants negotiated their way into becoming North
American by behaving "white." For example, they engaged in racist activities and adopted a capitalistic work ethic. Giving an account of her own ethnic family's history, Di Leonardo (1992) recounts how they were lifted into
"homogenous" whiteness, instead of being played off against other ethnic
groups, through a "government-funded leg up during and after the war, that
wasn't there for minorities" (p. 33). Frankenberg (1993) has described how
whiteness shaped the lives of thirty North American women and their varying levels of awareness of its influence. Her analysis shows how the material and discursive dimensions of whiteness are always interconnected. As
she points out: "Discursive repertoires may reinforce, contradict, conceal,
explain, or "explain away" the materiality of the history of a given situation.
Their interconnection, rather than the material life alone, is in fact what
generates "experience"; and given this, the "experience" of living as a white
woman in the United States is continually being transformed" (p. 2). In his
analysis of how policy decisions, particularly by the Federal Housing Ad-
ministration, have widened the gap between the resources available to
whites and those available to other racial communities, Lipsitz (1995)
shows how white identities have been structured in the United States

through "disciplined, systematic, and collective group activity" (p. 383) which the language of liberal individualism covers up. White privilege, he argues, is hidden when it is attributed to "family values, fatherhood, and foresight—rather than to favoritism" (p. 379).

13. See M. Omi and H. Winant *Racial formation in the United States: From the 1960s to the 1990s.* (New York: Routledge, 1994) on the issue of racially evasive as opposed to racially cognizant discourse.

14. See C. A. Gallagher, 1999, for detailed discussion of this issue.

15. Milton Bennett's (1993) developmental model of intercultural sensitivity proposes progressive stages of readiness to deal with difference, and appropriate interventions for each stage of his model.

16. "White identity in context" in T. K. Nakayama and J. N. Martin, *Whiteness: The communication of social identity,* Thousand Oaks: Sage, 1999, also reflects on this intersectional positioning.

17. C. Geertz, 1983, "From the native's point of view": On the nature of anthropological understanding, in *Local knowledge: Further essays in interpretive anthropology* (New York: Basic Books), cited in P. P. Chock, "Irony and ethnography: On cultural analysis of one own culture," *Anthropological Quarterly, 59*(2), 87–96, 1986.

18. Fairclough (1992) comments on the confusion around the term "discourse" that arises as a result of the "many conflicting and overlapping definitions formulated from various theoretical and disciplinary standpoints" (p. 3). Fairclough distinguishes between discourse analysis as linguistic analysis of either spoken or written language, and the social theory approach (as exemplified in the work of Michel Foucault). In this latter approach, the term "discourse" refers to "different ways of structuring areas of knowledge and social practice" (Fairclough, p. 3). Discourses in this sense are "manifested in particular ways of using language and other symbolic forms such as visual images," and do not just reflect or represent social entities and relations, they construct or constitute them. Discourses therefore have social effects, constituting people in different ways as social subjects. This conception of discourse values a historical perspective that develops insight into how "different discourses combine under particular social conditions to produce a new, complex discourse" (Fairclough, pp. 3–4). It is this second sense, i. e., a social theory understanding of discourse, that describes the work of this book.

19. C. K. Riessman (1993), *Narrative analysis,* Qualitative Research Methods Series, vol. 30 (Newbury Park: Sage), outlines different methodologies for researching personal narratives. My methodology is in some ways a hybrid, as the questionnaire provided for a type of guided narrative at the level of personal account giving.

20. In postmodern criticism "narrative" is used to challenge the modernist belief in foundational knowledge, and stems from a grasp of the extent to which our understanding of reality, including the legitimization of that understanding (Berger and Luckman, 1966) is always socially constructed. Theorists such as Lyotard and Jameson have contributed the insight to contemporary literary theory that the narrative is not specifically a literary form, but in fact an epistemological category (Sarup, 1993). The world comes to us in the shape of stories (Sarup, p. 178).

21. "[W]orldmaking . . . always starts from worlds already on hand; the making is always a remaking" (Schwandt, 1994, p. 126).

22. As Mumby, 1993, puts it: "[T]he social construction of meaning does not take place in a political vacuum but rather is a product of the various constellations of power and political interests that make up the relationships among different social groups" (p. 5). The ideological aspect of narrative is captured in the following quotation from Schwandt, 1994, p. 179: "[E]very narrative simultaneously creates or makes up a reality and asserts that it stands independent of that same reality." In other words, narrative seems at once to reveal or illuminate a world and to hide or distort it.

Chapter 1. A Master Narrative of Whiteness

1. This is not an attempt to capture all the permutations and complexities of such a monstrously vast topic. To attempt that would be naive beyond words. Nor do I wish to homogenize the complex heterogeneity within whiteness or suggest a seamlessness in whiteness across the globe (which would run counter to the argument of the book). We need to recognize both overlapping general, recurrent, and continuous operations along the axis of power between the West and its others that informs the construction of whiteness, as well as the particularities, disjunctures, and multiplicities. Losing the former leaves us without political teeth, and neglecting the latter leads us into dangerous essentializing. Young, 1995, makes a similar point in relation to postcolonial analysis in general:

[A]t this point in the postcolonial era, as we seek to understand the operation and effects of colonial history, the homogenization of colonialism does also need to be set against its historical and geographical particularities. The question for any theory of colonial discourse is whether it can maintain, and do justice to, both levels. (p. 165)

In using the term "master narrative" I wish rather to communicate the ideological grip the logic of whiteness gained globally. I also hope to communicate the sense of what Lyotard has called "grand narratives," i.e.,

totalizing thinking that rests upon notions of universal history and absolute knowledge (Connor, 1989). These narratives present themselves as
having achieved closure across space and time, disguising the fact that
they are social constructions—and inevitably put a rhetorical "spin" on reality. This in turn implies that there can be no ultimate validation for notions such as race or ethnicity, and that the reasons for constituting such
categories of social identity around markers of difference must be rooted
within the power dynamics of social relations—which discourses hold
sway, and how they "subject" us.

   2. Of course it is a feature of creation mythology in all cultures to position their own social grouping at the beginning or center of human creation,
but the dynamics of power are played out differently depending on their
concept of relationships with self and other (Sanday, 1981).

   3. Some of the complexity of social identity can be explicated by drawing on postmodern, or more specifically, poststructuralist, insights into how
meaning is formed *within* discourses. Meaning is not seen to arise from a
correspondence between language or signification, and reality or reference.
Instead, it resides in the play of differences between signifiers. The belief
that there is a fixed structure of relationships between signifiers and signi-
fieds is typical of modernist thinking, reflected in the faith that discourse
"mirrors the reason and order already 'out there' in the world" (Cooper and
Burrell, 1988, p. 97). This is the binary thinking on which Western knowledge has largely been constructed, and which leads to the increasing differentiation associated with modernism. The vicissitudes in the ascription of
meaning to blackness by Europe demonstrate this fluidity of signification
very well.

   4. In contrast to "foundational" explanations of social identity, social
constructionist explanations rest upon the acceptance of the fact that social identity is constituted within the world of meanings and symbols, the
"reinterpretation of our predecessors' reinterpretation of their predecessors' reinterpretation" (Rorty, quoted in Fish, 1995, p. 221). By this view, individuals become social subjects by being interpellated (hailed) into the
discourses of their societies, through a process of "self-recognition" (Althusser, 1971). In other words, one is not "white" because one partakes of
white "essence" (genetic, ethnic, or otherwise) but because one is defined by
certain ways of conceptualizing a "white" identity, with all the consequences, material and otherwise, that this may entail. Social identity con-
ceived in this way is complex, crisscrossed by intersecting and often contradictory (or mutually reinforcing) discourses, which may be more or less
influential within a society. Viewing social identity in terms of discourse
does not mean that a social being is nothing *but* discourse, rather that it is
through discourse that the body and its desires are "bounded" and given
definition (see Goldberg, 1990b, p. 310). Nor does this conceptualization
mean that these discourses are disconnected from the material world. On

the contrary, discourses arise out of complex material circumstances (Foucault's preconceptual level) and in turn have a constituting and regulating effect on the material world. From this point of view, there is "a relationship of constitutive reciprocity . . . between the "objects" and "statements" within any discourse," and linkages between "power, knowledge, institutions, intellectuals, the control of populations, and the modern state as these intersect in the functions of systems of thought" (Bové, 1995, pp. 54, 57). In other words, the ideological is always already present within discourse about social identity.

5. Significantly, the attempt to fix meaning into a binary in which one signifier is hierarchically preferred over the other is the way in which ideology is constituted. "Ideologies like to draw rigid boundaries between what is acceptable and what is not, between self and not-self, truth and falsity, sense and non-sense, reason and madness, central and marginal, surface and depth" (Eagleton, 1983, p.133). Instead of plural sources of difference, ideologically charged discourse encourages people to see social relations as the function of a single source of difference that clearly places some people in a dominant position over others.

6. It is not just social identity, but the actual racial or ethnic groups that are socially constructed and maintained. Both within and between social groups, shifting forms of "division and alliance" (Rattansi, 1992, p. 39) emerge in relation to differences in power as "highly complex, contextually variable and economically and politically influenced [processes of] drawing and redrawing of boundaries [take] place in encounters" (Rattansi, p. 39). Social groups are fluid, socio-historical creations (Thiele, 1991). See H. L. Gates, "The hidden face of racism," *American Quarterly* 47:3 (1995): 395–407 for a discussion of how this dynamic of redrawing and consolidating boundaries operates in the present day United States. D. R. Roediger's theory in *The wages of whiteness: Race and the making of the American working class* (New York: Verso, 1991) of splitting the workers in the United States also follows a similar logic. A. E. Coombes in *Reinventing Africa: Museums, material culture and popular imagination in late Victorian and Edwardian England,* presents a wonderful account of how the social identity of the British nation was galvanized through manipulation of cultural representations of Africa (New Haven: Yale University Press, 1994).

7. In his discussion of ethnicity, Sollors (1995) points out that "it makes little sense to define "ethnicity-as-such," since it refers not to a thing-in-itself but to a relationship . . . Ethnic, racial or national identifications rest on antitheses, on negativity, or on . . . their "dissociative" character. Ethnic identity, seen this way, "is logically and historically the product of the assertion that "A is an X because he is not a Y" (Sollors, 1995, p. 288). Sollors further points out that the notion of ethnic purity is a modern invention, and serves to intensify group consciousness or prepare for hostile confrontations (Sollors, p. 303). In narratives of "race," difference has been fixed in a way

that is particularly "sticky"—namely, through appeals to biology. That a dominant group should benefit from fixing social identities in this way is self-evident.

8. See, for example, J. M. Yinger, "Intersecting strands in the theorisation of race and ethnic relations," in *Theories of race and ethnic relations,* ed. J. Rex and D. Mason (Cambridge: Cambridge University Press, 1986).

9. Y. Y. Mudimbe, in *The idea of Africa,* shows how degrees of savageness and remoteness were directly correlated in Greek thinking. The unmarked space of the Greek center is also the organizing principle of knowledge (Bloomington: Indiana Press, 1994).

10. Compare the notion of the "noble savage" (Montaigne) and the "good savage" (Montesque) with the view of natural man as aggressive and chaotic (Hobbes). J. Nederveen Pieterse, *White on black: Images of Africa* (New Haven: Yale University Press, 1992) provides an interesting discussion.

11. Brantlinger (1985) quotes a source from 1870 indicating this belief.

12. Again, it is the attempt to arrest the play of difference by such processes of definition that provides a sense of structure, of fixed social identity. Such structure is always a temporary stability, the outcome of prevailing power dynamics, not the "natural order of things" (though it may seem that way). As Ferguson (1994) expresses it, "Stasis and predictability can . . . be seen as interruptions requiring explanations" (p. 83). In terms of the argument of this book, we construct "narratives" in order to create a significant and orderly world, a world that is stable and predicable. Such self-validating narratives "construct a center around which certain kinds of social relations form" (Mumby, 1993) and have as their function

> the affirmation and reinforcement . . . of the most basic assumptions of a culture about human existence, about time, destiny, selfhood, where we come from, what we ought to do while we are here, where we go—the whole course of human life. (Miller, 1995, p. 71)

13. The debate about the relationship between whiteness and economic ideology arouses heated emotions. See, for example, the debate between G. Horne and S. Resnick in *Science and Society, 63(2),* 1999, 232–35.

14. I use this phrase in the Barthian sense of "text" as the field in which the meaning of a work, in this case Christian myths, are negotiated. K. E. Ferguson, "On bringing in more theory, more voices and more politics to the study of organization," *Organization 1:1* (1994): 81–99, explains:

> A text comes into focus in relation to a background of rules (named or implicit) that define the established, legitimated perspective on the

topic at hand. The text can either subvert or support this background of rules; it often does both, in somewhat different ways. (p. 87)

15. Of course, Africans have been driven to similar acts of desperation in dire circumstances. Edgecombe (1991) describes the destruction of organized Sotho chiefdoms during the period of Zulu expansion in the 1820s and 1830s, known as the Difiqane:

> Thousands of people became refugees and fled in all directions. . . . Those who sought shelter in the mountains and bushes were forced to live a hunter-gatherer type of existence. Those who died were either killed, had starved to death, or had been eaten by wild beasts and human beings. Cannibalism was, as Leonard Thompson has observed, "the ultimate proof that a society had disintegrated and its norms had collapsed." (p. 121)

16. See, for example, Brantlinger, 1985; hooks, 1990; Nederveen Pieterse, 1992; Segrest, 1994; Trinh, 1989

17. J. Nederveen Pieterse, *White on black,* 1992, comments that it was part of the "common sense" of Victorian ideology that Africans wanted to be white. He mischievously comments that one could be tempted, given these images, to ask whether it isn't more to the point that Europeans wanted to be black. P. Brantlinger, "Victorians and Africans: The geneology of the myth of the dark continent," *Critical Inquiry* 12 (1985): 166–203, quotes Dominique Mannoni:

> the savage . . . is identified in the unconscious with a certain image of the instincts . . . And civilized man is painfully divided between the desire to "correct" the "errors" of the savages and the desire to identify himself with them in his search for a lost paradise (a desire which at once casts doubt upon the merit of the very civilization he is trying to transmit to them.) (p. 196)

18. A. R. JanMohamed in "The economy of Manichean allegory: The function of racial difference in colonialist literature," *Critical Inquiry 12* (1985): 59–81, argues that as a result of their sense of superiority, colonialists did not enter into the self-other dialectic essential for the formation of identity. Most colonial discourse remains at the level of Lacan's imaginary identification, and therefore functions at an emotive level, rather than at the level of intersubjectivity (Lacan's symbolic order). For a more detailed psychoanalytical analysis, see H. Bhabha, "Interrogating identity: The postcolonial prerogative," in *Anatomy of racism,* ed. D. T. Goldberg (Minneapolis: Minnesota University Press, 1990) and "Remembering Fanon: Self, psyche and the colonial condition," in *Colonial discourse and postcolonial theory: A reader,* ed. P. Williams and L. Chrisman (New York: Columbia University Press, 1994).

19. A good example of an analysis of othering in terms of presence and absence is in T. M. Trinh, *Woman, native, other* (Bloomington: Indiana University Press, 1989).

20. See H. Bhabha, "Interrogating identity: The postcolonial prerogative," in *Anatomy of racism*, ed. D. T. Goldberg (Minneapolis: Minnesota University Press, 1990) and "Remembering Fanon: Self, psyche and the colonial condition," *Colonial and postcolonial theory: A reader*, ed. P. Williams and L. Chrisman (New York: Columbia University Press, 1994); F. Fanon, "The fact of blackness," in *Anatomy of racism* and "On national culture," in *Colonial discourse and post-colonial theory: A reader*; and A. Memmi, *The colonizer and the colonized*, (London: Earthscan Publications, 1990). All these authors argue for the interdependence of white and black psyches as a result of the colonial experience. The process of dissociation by which we construct our identities logically entails that the "other" which we aim to expel is constitutive of what remains within our "boundaries." The narratives that we construct about our identities are "existentially dependent" (Connor, 1989, p. 234) on the "other." Social identity is never pure. The issue is the extent to which we are conscious of how we project our shadow selves. I am not exploring the dependence of black identity on whiteness. Although it is clearly co-constructed, the dynamic is different as a result of the different position in relation to power.

21. Once the notions of "race" had been elevated in credibility by achieving "scientific" academic status, self-conscious theory, observations, and specialized vocabularies disguised the traces of medieval thinking which inform the notion of "race" as a scientific paradigm (Stepan, 1990). In Kuhn's (1970) theory, scientists conduct "normal" science under a dominant paradigm. This consists largely of solving anomalies that are not susceptible to explanation through the framework offered by the paradigm. Eventually, through the pressures caused by intractable conundrums, the paradigm is thrown into crisis (Chicago: University of Chicago Press).

22. See Trinh, 1989, *Woman, native, other*, for an excellent discussion of this issue. (Bloomington: Indiana University Press.)

23. S. R. Clegg in L. Rouleau and S. R. Clegg, "Postmodernism and postmodernity in organization analysis," *Journal of Organizational Change Management* (1991) maintains that, characteristically, the modernist theorist desires:

> to give a definite answer, a definite story, a definite narrative. The modernist theorist and the modernist theory are about what is true and what is not true, what is good and what is not good, what is uplifting and what is not uplifting. . . . It is to refer to an index of the world composed in terms of unproblematic high culture, low culture, of moral objects, immoral objects, of verities and absolute falsehoods. (pp. 8–15)

24. Narratives are always constructed in relation to other possible constructions. The referent of a discourse is always a discourse (Dickens and Fontana, 1994, p. 65). And the question of which discourse gets to dominate out of all the possibilities is patently political. Also see Hall, 1985.

25. P. Brantlinger in "Victorians and Africans: The geneology of the myth of the dark continent" (*Critical Inquiry, 12:* 166–203, 1985) cites the wars of resistance as offering the best evidence of the attitudes of Africans to their "savior-invaders." He also mentions the negritude movement, and modern nationalistic writings (p. 199). Similarly, B. Davidson, in *The Search for Africa* (London, James Currey, 1994) looks at African resistance from the point of view of Africanism. See also M. E. Steyn, "Who are you and what have you done with the real Hottentots?: The legacy of contested narratives of settlement in the New South Africa" in *Readings in cultural contexts,* ed. J. N. Martin, T. K. Nakayama, and L. A. Flores (Mountain View: Mayfield, 1998). J. Nederveen Pieterse in *White on black: Images of Africa and blacks in Western popular culture* (New Haven: Yale University Press, 1992) points out that the "accusation of cannibalism has come from both sides," and that Western domination has often been described by Africans and Third World peoples generally as a form of cannibalism. Also see N. L. Stepan and S. L. Gilman, "Appropriating the idioms of science: The rejection of scientific racism," in *The bounds of race: Perspectives on hegemony and resistance,* ed. D. La Capra (Ithaca: Cornell University Press, 1991) for an interesting discussion of some writings of minority groups in resistance to the claims of scientific racism. E. W. Said in *Culture and imperialism* (New York: Vintage Books, 1994) comments that:

Never was it the case that the imperial encounter pitted an active Western intruder against a supine or inert non-Western native; there was *always* some form of active resistance, and in the overwhelming majority of cases, the resistance finally won out. (p. xii, emphasis in the original)

26. Composed of complex combinations and shifting articulations of the discursive resources available to an individual or group of individuals within specific contexts, social identity is always open to "the possibility of tension, inconsistency and contradiction within and between sites" (Rattansi, 1992, p. 37).

Chapter 2. "White" South Africans

1. This is not true of the San (Bushmen) who were hunted like animals. The Khoikhoi, the original inhabitants of the Cape area, were driven inland. Those who remained in the Cape are in part the ancestors of the colored people of this area.

2. The question of the anxiety present in whiteness in South Africa, and the role being on the continent of Africa has played in this anxiety, are discussed in M. E. Steyn, "White Identity in Context," in T. K. Nakayama and J. N. Martin *Whiteness: The communication of social identity,* 1999 (Thousand Oaks: Sage).

3. I regard the dynamics of the civil war, and the relationship between the WASPS and the "other" ethnic groups as significantly different from what I have described here, though white unity is obviously not "seamless," even in the United States.

4. They did not want to be "slaves to the company" according to M. de Villiers in *White tribe dreaming: Apartheid's bitter roots as witnessed by eight generations of an Afrikaner family* (New York: Penguin, 1987). Working in employment was evidently associated with slavery. Part of being white was being able to allocate one's own labor as one chose. Although not identical, a family resemblance between this dynamic and the dissociation of whiteness from slavery in the American south is obvious. See D. R. Roediger, *The wages of whiteness: Race and the making of the American working class* (London: Verso, 1991).

5. See S. Clingman, "Beyond the limit: The social relations of madness in Southern African fiction," in *The bounds of race: Perspectives on hegemony and resistance,* ed. D. La Capra (Ithaca: Cornell University Press, 1991) for an interesting discussion of "the return of the repressed" in South African literature. Since 1994, there has been a marked increase in the number of Afrikaners who are beginning to claim back this hybridity, as a symbol of their legitimacy in the New South Africa.

6. This was already true during the time that the Dutch East India company controlled the Cape, but was even more pronounced after the British had taken over control of the Cape. The early Dutch settlers regarded the British, whom they perceived to be indifferent to their needs, with the utmost distrust.

7. The Boers did not develop "scientific" explanations for their superiority until the implementation of Apartheid, when they relied on the discourses of social science to justify organizing the country in the basis of "groups." See, for example, D. T. Goldberg, *Racist culture: Philosophy and the politics of meaning* (Oxford: Blackwell, 1993) and G. Schutte, *What racists believe* (Thousand Oaks: Sage, 1995). However, as S. Dubow in *Illicit union: Scientific racism in modern South Africa* (Johannesburg: Witwatersrand University Press, 1995) points out:

> For a white public seeking to rationalise its social supremacy, it was not always necessary to have direct access to or understanding of the details of scientific debate; a broad awareness of the existence of a body of knowledge justifying racism was sufficient. Thus, claims by farmers to

"know the native mind" did not depend on intimate familiarity with psychological and anthropological projects designed for the purpose. . . . Popular prejudice may not have relied on theoretical expositions, but it was certainly sustained by knowledge of their availability. (p. 9)

8. This was the name given to the Afrikaner pioneers who undertook the arduous and dangerous trek into the interior of the country in ox-drawn, covered wagons.

9. The assumption that the victory indicated God's blessing on the white enterprise in South Africa was, of course, deeply insulting to the defeated Africans. For this reason, the African National Congress chose 16 December, the anniversary of the battle, to launch the armed struggle against the Apartheid government more than a century later. In his autobiography, *Long walk to freedom* (London: Abacus, 1994), Nelson Mandela explains the symbolism:

> We chose 16 December, Dingane's day, for a reason. That day, white South Africans celebrate the defeat of the great Zulu leader Dingane at the Battle of Blood River in 1838. Dingane, the half-brother of Shaka, then ruled the most powerful African state that ever existed south of the Limpopo River. That day, the bullets of the Boers were too much for the assegais of the Zulu *Impis* and the water of the nearby river ran red with their blood. Afrikaners celebrated 16 December as the triumph of the Afrikaner over the African and the demonstration that God was on their side, while Africans mourned this day of the massacre of their people. We chose 16 December to show that the African had only begun to fight, and that we had righteousness—and dynamite—on our side. (p. 337)

10. A. Césaire in "Discourse on colonialism," *Colonial discourse and post-colonial theory: A reader,* ed. P. Williams and L. Chrisman (New York: Columbia University Press, 1994) points out in his discussion of Nazism that the Christian bourgeois of the twentieth century cannot tolerate that the "Europe colonialist procedures," reserved exclusively for Europe's "others," be applied against "the white man." My grandmother was interned in one of these concentration camps as a child. Even as an old lady, she would have difficulty talking about it and would become tearful if we asked her questions.

11. These fears provided excellent sites of intervention for the resistance movement. Mandela in *Long walk to freedom,* 1994, gives an example of how he manipulated white fears during his trial in 1962:

> I had chosen traditional dress to emphasize the symbolism that I was a black African walking into a white man's court. I was literally

carrying on my back the history, culture and heritage of my people. That day, I felt myself to be the embodiment of African nationalism, the inheritor of Africa's difficult but noble past and her uncertain future. The *kaross* [blanket] was also a sign of contempt for the niceties of white justice. I well knew the authorities would feel threatened by my *kaross* as so many whites feel threatened by the true culture of Africa. (p. 385)

12. Tensions within the labor movement were rampant. The Communist Party urged nonracist labor action for higher wages; the Afrikaner Nationalists and Labour Party sought protection of the interests of white workers against black encroachment. The militancy of the Nationalists gained ground, though, and in the 1922 worker's strike the banners proclaimed: "Workers of the World Fight and Unite for White South Africa." See S. B. Spies, 1992, "Unity and Disunity, 1910–1924, in T. Cameron and S. B. Spies, Eds., *A new illustrated history of South Africa,* 2nd ed. (Cape Town: Southern Book Publishers)

13. To cite an example, Schutte in *What racists believe* (Thousand Oaks: Sage, 1995) observes that the failure of the homelands policy was ascribed to African incompetence.

14. The cultural division between the English and Afrikaans whites provided opportunity for the resistance movement to exercise its own versions of the "divide and conquer" technique. Mandela in *Long walk to freedom,* 1994, provides insight into how the language issue was perceived:

The Afrikaner was traditionally hostile to Africans learning English, for English was a foreign tongue to the Afrikaner and the language of emancipation to us. (p. 195)

15. Also see, for example, the personal accounts given by Carl Niehaus in *Fighting for hope: His own story* (Cape Town: Human and Rousseau, 1993), and Rian Malan in *My traitor's heart* (New York: Vintage Books, 1991), of their struggle to reconcile themselves with their cultural and political heritage.

Chapter 3. Things Bad Begun

1. Carole King's phrase.

2. A domestic worker paid by the hour.

3. Afrikaans for "rural areas." The word is accepted in South African English.

4. A corruption from the word "Hottentot." It is still sometimes used colloquially in racist discourse to refer to the Cape colored population, and is decidedly derogatory in connotation. The fact that the farm worker uses it himself shows the degree of internalized oppression. He could also have been using the term manipulatively, of course—a strategy used by the powerless to get what they want by mimicking the oppressor's language about themselves.

5. As Nadine Gordimer has said in a television interview with Bill Moyers, it is really mysterious why some children growing up in the Apartheid environment embraced brutality, whereas others instinctively recoiled from it.

Chapter 4. Narrative One

1. The name for the Pretoria-Johannesburg-Vereeniging area since the change of government. It is derived from the Africanisation of the Afrikaans term for "gold."

2. The derogatory word for "blacks" that would be the equivalent of the U.S. American "nigger." The word is derived from the Arabic for "unbeliever." It was used by Muslims to refer to peoples of southeastern Africa. See B. Davidson, *Africa in history: Themes and outlines* (New York: Touchstone, 1991, p. 95). In the early colonial days it was applied to all the indigenous people of South Africa.

3. The word boer is used here in the sense of "Afrikaans farmer." Literally, the word means "farmer," but in the time of British colonial rule it came to be used for Afrikaners in general, and connotes a lack of sophistication. During the struggle, activists called the police "boere."

4. Afrikaans for "mastership," and part of Apartheid discourse.

5. The schoolboy is translating directly from Afrikaans. The expression glosses as "previous generations" or "how things have always been done."

6. Many interesting discussions explore the relationship of the colonialist unconscious to the adventure stories about "darkest Africa." Good examples are P. Brantlinger, "Victorians and Africans: The geneology of the myth of the dark continent," in *Critical Inquiry, 12* (1985): 166–203, and L. Chrisman, "The imperial unconscious? Representations of imperial discourse," in *Colonial discourse and post-colonial theory: A reader,* ed. P. Williams and L. Chrisman (New York: Columbia University Press, 1994).

Chapter 5. Narrative Two

1. Known as the Northern Transvaal until 1994; traditionally a stronghold of "white" conservatism.

2. This is not entirely delusional; affirmative action has challenged the career expectations of many "whites." What is unrecognized by these respondents is that their expectations were unreasonable, and framed within a broader historical context of the generations of systematic disadvantage experienced by "blacks."

3. While the spin given to the fact of the high crime rate is clearly racist, it is fair to note that South Africa is experiencing an alarming crime rate.

4. The word "respect" is inflected through Apartheid discourse. It was held to be the appropriate demeanor for interracial contact, and implies keeping one's distance. It is also not symmetrical. When describing the appropriate behavior of "nonwhites" toward "whites," it included connotations of subservience.

5. South Africa now has a constitution which guarantees individual rights, somewhat similar to that of the United States. Again, the use of "rights" in this narrative has been inflected through Apartheid discourse, where it has included the "right" to dominate.

6. These words are reminiscent of those of the Voortrekker woman quoted in chapter two. I will return to this point in the final chapter of the book.

7. In *White supremacy: A comparative study of American and South African history* (New York: Oxford University Press, 1981), G. M. Fredrickson points out that there was no need for this type of informally organized violence—the state saw to the subordination of the "nonwhite" groups through legislation. With a state that now outlaws racial discrimination, white supremacists may feel the need to take matters in their own hands.

Chapter 6. Narrative Three

1. I am borrowing Audre Lorde's imagery.

2. Afrikaner nation. Literally, "boer" is "farmer," and "volk" is "nation."

3. In this sense, the ANC is certainly modernist. S. During, "Waiting for the last post: Some relations between modernity, colonization, and writing," in *Past the last post: Theorizing post-colonialism and post-modernism,* eds. I. Adam and H. Tiffen (Calgary: University of Calgary Press, 1990) agrees

with J. Derrida, *Psyché: Inventions de l'autre* (Paris: Galilée, 1987) that Nelson Mandela is "the most charismatic figure of the Enlightenment" (p. 27). During argues that "Universalism can advance the struggle of the colonized against those who would limit access to the law," and continues:

> Black South Africans can embrace the Enlightenment all the more readily because, forming the national majority, democracy will help them control their own destiny. Their identity is consolidated by those oppressive apparatuses that, using racist and culturalist discourse, discriminate against—and fix them—as blacks. . . . This problematic is much less relevant in countries in which the colonized form a minority, however large, to whom democracy offers little. (p. 29)

Chapter 7. Narrative Four

1. See M. W. Murphree, "Ethnicity and Third World development: Political and academic contexts," in *Theories of race and ethnic relations,* ed. J. Rex and D. Mason (Cambridge: Cambridge University Press, 1986) for a discussion of the salience of ethnicity in the postcolonial state.

2. The reader will recognize the colonial claim of noncotermineity— "others" are stuck in traditional, eternal past, while Europeans live in the modern present.

3. For a full discussion of this aspect of Afrikaner settlement, particularly the role of the religious belief in the "Promised Land," see G. M. Fredrickson, *White supremacy: A comparative study of American and South African history* (New York: Oxford University Press. 1981).

4. The British colonial history in South Africa was thoroughly racist, but it was executed in different, usually more subtle, ways (see Frederickson, 1981). Also, in the heyday of Apartheid, English-speaking South Africans benefited economically from the policy. Many chose not to be "involved" politically, distancing themselves from the Apartheid government. Of course there are many degrees of opposition. It did not really follow that by not voting for the Nationalist Party they were making a principled stand against racism. A few did involve themselves actively in the extraparliamentary liberation struggle against Apartheid.

Chapter 8. Narrative Five

1. The respondent's comments allude to the contemporary Afrocentric discourse of writers such as Molefi Asante. See *The Afrocentric Idea* (Philadelphia: Temple University Press, 1987.) Exposure to this discourse is becoming more frequent through training courses on multiculturalism, presently popular in corporate South Africa. Both Biko (see note 2) and Asante follow in the

tradition of nativistic discourses such as the negritude movement. See, for example, L. S. Senghor, "Negritude: A humanism of the twentieth century" in *Colonial discourse and post-colonial theory: A reader,* eds. P. Williams and L. Chrisman (New York: Columbia University Press. 1994).

2. Steve Biko was a leader of black consciousness in South Africa, who died while in detention as a consequence of police brutality. I do not ridicule reading this book as a way to understanding "whiteness." On the contrary, I think it is extremely important for white South Africans to educate themselves about the struggle from a black African perspective. Doing so certainly does counter the generally accepted (white) "facts" that were propagated by the Apartheid government propaganda machines. Nevertheless, in the context of the rest of the response, I feel justified in interpreting this comment as an indication that something else is going on in this narrative. Some comments in *Hybridization, That's the Name of the Game* will also provide perspective on this issue.

3. One of the "Independent Homeland States" of the Apartheid system. All these "homelands" have been reincorporated into South Africa since the 1994 elections.

4. At least not that have been regarded as "respectable."

5. Whites did (do) have a role to play in the struggle for democracy, of course. Striving for subjectivities that are not driven by power and a need for dominance creates a healthier, safer society for all. Injustice and oppression damage us all.

6. The comment still reveals a bias toward "Westerncentrism".

7. See B. Martin and C. T. Mohanty, "Feminist politics: What's home got to do with it?" in *Feminist studies: Critical studies,* ed. T. de Lauretis (Bloomington: Indiana University Press, 1987) for a discussion of "home" and identity.

8. Many writers have commented on the "othering" of Africa, the continent. Particularly pertinent to this discussion is G. Schutte's comment in *What racists believe* (Thousand Oaks: Sage, 1995) on the fear of Africa he observed in white South Africans.

9. Both English and Afrikaans-speaking South Africans have indeed done this, but in different ways. English-speaking South Africans have tended to retain a largely Eurocentric worldview, and thus have had a fairly obviously bifurcated relationship to the continent all along. On the other hand, one can question the Afrikaner "love" of Africa that is passionate about the "land" but despises her people. G. Schutte (1995) (note 8) makes a similar observation in his study:

> Most of their statements about Africa were extremely negative. The examples they used to illustrate black mismanagement and incompe-

tence in government and economic affairs all came from Africa. The "African" components of these whites' self-identification seems to have much more to do with geography, climate, animal and plant life, and white colonial lifestyles than with African culture.

10. Kurtz's last words in J. Conrad's *Heart of Darkness.* He had "partaken" too deeply of Africa, and discovered that the "savage" was within the heart of himself, a man regarded as the paragon of European enlightenment.

Chapter 9. Conclusion

1. There is some debate about whether the term "postApartheid" should be used to the exclusion of the term "postcolonialism" in the South African context, given that white South Africans do not see themselves as colonialist. See A. Carusi, "Post, post and post. Or, where is South African literature in all this?" in *Past the last post: Theorizing post-colonialism and post-modernism,* ed. I. Adam and H. Tiffin (Calgary: University of Calgary Press, 1990). As should be clear, I align myself with those who argue that this does not invalidate postcolonial studies as an analytical framework for South Africa. The discourse of postcolonialism has placed itself in a position to counter, with varying degrees of success, imperialistic strategies, be they in the political, economic, or cultural sphere.

2. Jan Nederveen Pieterse and Bhikhu Parekh, 1995, trace the process of decolonization at a cultural level through three main stages: decolonization, internal decolonization, and postcoloniality. Postcoloniality is the stage characterized by border crossings and bicultural social forces (London: Zed Books, p. 11).

3. Ferguson, 1993, provides an excellent discussion of this notion of *enframing* (Berkeley: University of California Press).

4. As the narrative *I Just Don't Know What to Do, Being White* has shown, even people who wanted the old system to collapse can be without bearings once it goes. We grieve for what has been familiar.

5. Stuart Hall's phrase.

6. The reader will recall the words of one respondent who believes *This Shouldn't Happen to a White:*

[The injustice] has prompted many whites to start a business in the private sector and maintain their self-respect. (p. 138)

7. For example, the common translation of any attempt to attain *equal* rights for disadvantaged "others" into the granting of *special* rights. See M. Segrest, *Memoir of a race traitor* (Boston: South End Press, 1994).

8. Some postmodernists might say it is a choice of schizophrenia over paranoia.

9. The particular fervor with which white South Africans held onto "whiteness" probably had to do with the fact that they were on the territory of the "other." See M. E. Steyn, "Whiteness in context: A personal narrative" in *Whiteness: The communication of social Identity*, ed. T. K. Nakayama and J. N. Martin (Thousand Oaks: Sage, 1999).

10. An example of how this imagined community operates is provided by E. Unterhalter, "Constructing race, class, gender and ethnicity: State and opposition strategies in South Africa," in *Unsettling settler societies: Articulations of gender, race, ethnicity and class,* ed. D. Stasiulis and N. Yuval-Davis (London: Sage, 1995). She recounts how, historically, there has been a strong influence of ideologies of improvement in South African women's organizations, with "indigenous women aspiring to an ideal embodied by settler women, and . . . settler women aspiring to an ideal embodied by a woman living in metropolitan Europe" (p. 220).

11. G. R. Bucher discusses this issue with Linder in *Straight / white / male* (Philadelphia: Fortress Press, 1976):

the liberation we are talking about involves a process of uprooting. We are speaking of breaking away or renouncing certain sources of identity and meaning in our lives as demonic, corrupt, and the essence of oppressorhood. . . . Power usually responds only when threatened . . . it doesn't give up on itself except when forced. . . . Renunciation is initiated out of one's own quest for a freer self. (pp. 131, 138–39)

12. See J. L. Kincheloe, S. R. Steinberg, N. M. Rodriguez and R. E. Chennault (eds.), *White reign: Deploying whiteness in America* (New York: St. Martin's Press, 1998).

13. The phrase "an open ended field" is taken from J. Nederveen Pieterse and B. Parekh (eds.), 1995, *The decolonization of imagination: Culture, Knowledge and Power* (London: Zed Books). They see the postcolonial as a field of bicultural and bilingual forces.

14. P. L. Berger and T. Luckman, in *The social construction of reality: A treatise in the sociology of knowledge* (New York: Doubleday, 1966), actually regard this as an example of "unsuccessful socialization."

15. Other theorists provide useful frameworks for thinking about the ways in which a country like South Africa could be at an advantage for complicating "white" identity. Pêcheux's concept of "disidentification" is one. See D. Macdonell, *Theories of discourse: An introduction* (Oxford: Basil Blackwell, 1986).

References

Alcoff, L. (1991). "The problem of speaking for others." *Cultural Critique, 20,* 5–32.

Allen, T. W. (1994). *The invention of the white race. Vol. 1: Racial oppression and social control.* New York: Verso.

Althusser, L. (1971). *Lenin and philosophy.* (B. Brewston, trans.). New York: Monthly Review Press.

Anderson, W. T. (1990). *Reality isn't what it used to be.* San Francisco: Harper & Row.

Antaki, C. (Ed.). (1988). *Analysing everyday explanation: A casebook of methods.* London: Sage.

Appiah, K. A. (1990). "Racisms." In D. T. Goldberg (ed.), *Anatomy of racisms* (pp. 3–17). Minneapolis: University of Minnesota Press.

——— (1991). "Is the post- in postmodernism the post- in postcolonial?" *Critical Inquiry, 17,* 336–57.

——— (1995). "Race." In F. Lentricchia and T. McLaughlin (eds.), *Critical terms for literary study* (pp. 274–87). Chicago: University of Chicago Press.

Apple, M. W. (1998). Foreword. In J. L. Kincheloe, S. R. Steinberg, N. M. Rodriguez and R. E. Chennault (eds.), *White reign: Deploying whiteness in America.* New York: St. Martin's Press.

Asante, M. K. (1987). *The Afrocentric idea.* Philadelphia: Temple University Press.

Baldwin, J. (1884). "On being white and other lies." *Essence,* April, 90–92.

Balibar, E. (1990). "Paradoxes of universality." In D. Goldberg (ed.), *Anatomy of racism* (pp. 283–94). Minneapolis: University of Minnesota Press.

Banton, M. (1987). *Racial theories.* Cambridge: Cambridge University Press.

Bartolome, L. I., and Macedo, D. P. (1997). "Dancing with bigotry: The poisoning of racial and ethnic identities." *Harvard Educational Review,* 67(2), 222–46.

Bennett, M. J. (1993). "Towards ethnorelativism: A developmental model of intercultural sensitivity." In R. M. Paige (ed.), *Education for the intercultural experience.* Yarmouth, ME: Intercultural Press.

Berger, P. L. and Luckman, T. (1966). *The social construction of reality: A treatise in the sociology of knowledge.* New York: Doubleday.

Bhabha, H. (1990). "Interrogating Identity: The postcolonial prerogagive." In D. Goldberg (ed.), *Anatomy of racism.* (pp. 283–94). Minneapolis: University of Minnesota Press.

Bhabha, H. (1994). "Remembering Fanon: Self, psyche and the colonial condition." In P. Williams and L. Chrisman (eds.), *Colonial discourse and post-colonial theory: A reader* (pp. 498–516). New York: Columbia University Press.

Biko, S. (1996 [1978]). *I write what I like: A selection of his writings.* London: Bowerdean Press.

Billig, M. (1988). "Methodology and scholarship in understanding ideological explanation." In C. Antaki (ed.), *Analysing everyday explanation: A casebook of methods.* London: Sage.

Blaut, J. M. (1993). *The colonizer's model of the world: Geographical diffusionism and Eurocentric history.* New York: Guilford Press.

Bonnett, A. (1998a). "How the British working class became white: The symbolic (re)formation of racialized capitalism." *Journal of Historical Sociology,* 11(3), 316–40.

——— (1998b). "Who was white? The disappearance of non-European white identities and the formation of European racial whiteness." In *Ethnic and Racial Studies,* 21(6) 1029–55.

Boulton, A. O. (1995). "The American paradox: Jeffersonian equality and racial science." *American Quarterly,* 47(3), 467–91.

Bové, P. A. (1995). "Discourse." In F. Lentricchia and T. McClaughlin (eds.), *Critical terms for literary theory,* 2nd ed., pp. 50–65. Chicago: University of Chicago Press.

Brantlinger, P. (1985). "Victorians and Africans: The geneology of the myth of the dark continent." *Critical Inquiry, 12,* 166–203.

——— (1990). *Crusoe's footprints: Cultural studies in Britain and America.* New York: Routledge.

Brantlinger, P. (1995). "Dying races: rationalizing genocide in the nineteenth century." In J. Nederveen Pieterse and B. Parekh (eds.), *The decolonization of the imagination: Culture, Knowledge and Power,* pp. 43–56. London: Zed Books.

Bucher, G. R. (ed.). (1976). *Straight / white / male.* Philadelphia: Fortress Press.

Bulkin, E., Pratt, M. B., and Smith, B. (1988). *Yours in struggle: Three feminist perspectives on anti-Semitism and racism.* Ithaca: Firebrand Books.

Bunting, B. (1964). *The rise of the South African reich.* Harmondsworth: Penguin.

Cameron, T. and Spies, S. B. (eds.). (1991). *A new illustrated history of South Africa,* 2nd ed. Cape Town: Southern Book Publishers.

Carusi, A. (1990). "Post, post and post. Or, where is South African literature in all this?" In I. Adam and H. Tiffin (eds.), *Past the last post: Theorizing post-colonialism and post-modernism.* Calgary: University of Calgary Press.

Césaire. A. (1994). "Discourse on colonialism." In P. Williams and L. Chrisman (eds.), *Colonial discourse and post-colonial theory: A reader,* pp. 498–516. New York: Columbia University Press. (original work published 1972)

Chafe, W. (1992). "Sex and race: The analogy of social control." In P. S. Rothenberg (ed.), *Race, class, and gender in the United States,* 2nd ed. New York: St. Martin's Press.

Chock, P. P. (1986). "Irony and ethnography: On cultural analysis of one's own culture." *Anthropological Quarterly,* 59(2), 87–96.

Chrisman, L. (1994). "The imperial unconscious? Representations of imperial discourse." In P. Williams and L. Chrisman (eds.), *Colonial discourse and post-colonial theory: A reader,* pp. 498–516. New York: Columbia University Press.

Clingman, S. (1991). "Beyond the limit: The social relations of madness in Southern African fiction." In D. L. La Capra (ed.), *The bounds of race: Perspectives on hegemony and resistance,* pp. 231–54. Ithaca: Cornell University Press.

Coetzee, J. M. (1987). "Blood, flaw, taint, degeneration: The case of Sarah Gertrude Millen." In C. Malan (ed.), *Race and literature,* pp. 26–47. Pinetown: Owen Burgess.

Cohen, P. (1992). "It's racism what dunnit: Hidden narratives in theories of racism." In J. Donald and A. Rattansi (eds.), *"Race," culture and difference,* pp. 11–48. Newbury Park: Sage.

Connor, S. (1989). *Postmodernist culture: An introduction to theories of the contemporary.* Oxford: Blackwell.

Conrad, J. (1989). *Heart of darkness: A case study in contemporary criticism.* R. C. Murfin (ed.), Boston: Bedford Books of St. Martin's Press.

Coombes, A. E. (1994). *Reinventing Africa: Museums, material culture, and popular imagination in late Victorian and Edwardian England.* New Haven: Yale University Press.

Cooper, R. and Burrell, G. (1988). "Modernism, Post-modernism and Organizational Analysis: An introduction." *Organization Studies, 9*(1), 91–112.

Crenshaw, C. (1997). "Resisting whiteness' rhetorical silence." *Western Journal of Communication,* 61(3), 253–78.

Davidson, B. (1991). *Africa in history: Themes and outlines.* New York: Touchstone.

—— (1994). *The search for Africa: A history in the making.* London: James Currey.

De Villiers, M. (1987). *White tribe dreaming: Apartheid's bitter roots as witnessed by eight generations of an Afrikaner family.* New York: Penguin.

Delgado, R. and Stefancic, J. (eds.). (1997). *Critical white studies: Looking behind the mirror.* Philadelphia: Temple University Press.

Derrida, J. (1985). "Racism's last word." *Critical Inquiry,* 12, 290–99.

—— (1987). *Psyché: Inventions de l'autre.* Paris: Galilée.

Dervin, B. (1991) "Comparative theory reconceptualized: From entities and states to processes and dynamics." *Communication Theory,* 1, 59–69.

Dickens, D. R. and Fontana, A. (1994). *Postmodernism and social inquiry.* New York: Guilford.

Di Leonardo, M. (1992). "White lies, black myths: Rape, race and the black underclass." *Voice,* Sept. 22, 29–36.

Dubow, S. (1995). *Illicit union: Scientific racism in modern South Africa.* Johannesburg: Witwatersrand University Press.

During, S. (1990). "Waiting for the last post: Some relations between modernity, colonization, and writing." In I. Adam and H. Tiffen (eds.), *Past the last post: Theorizing post-colonialism and post-modernism.* Alberta: University of Calgary Press.

Dyer, R. (1988). "White." *Screen,* 29, 44–65.

—— (1997). *White.* London: Routledge.

Eagleton, T. (1983). *Literary Theory: An introduction.* Oxford: Blackwell.

Ebert, T. L. (1985). "Writing in the political: Resistance (post) modernism." In J. D. Leonard (ed.), *Legal Studies as Cultural Studies.* Albany: State University of New York Press.

Edgecombe, R. (1991). "The Mfecane or Difacane." In T. Cameron and S. B. Spies (eds.), *A new illustrated history of South Africa* 2nd ed., pp. 115–126. Cape Town: Southern Book Publishers.

Fairclough, N. (1992). *Discourse and social change.* Cambridge: Polity Press.

Fanon, F. (1990). "The fact of blackness." In D. Goldberg (ed.), *Anatomy of racism* (pp. 108–26). Minneapolis: University of Minnesota Press. (original work published 1952)

——— (1994). "On national culture." In P. Williams and L. Chrisman (eds.), *Colonial discourse and post-colonial theory: A reader* (pp. 498–516). New York: Columbia University Press.

Ferguson, K. E. (1993). *The man question: Visions of subjectivity in feminist theory.* Berkeley: University of California Press.

——— (1994). "On bringing in more theory, more voices and more politics to the study of organization." *Organization,* 1(1), 81–99.

Field, B. (1990). "Slavery, race and ideology in the United States of America." *New Left Review, 181,* 95–118.

Fine, M. (1994). "Working the hyphens: Reinventing self and other in qualitative research." In N. K. Denzin and Y. S. Lincoln (eds.), *Handbook of qualitative research* (pp. 70–82). Thousand Oaks: Sage.

Fine, M., Weis, L., Powell, L. C. and Wong, L. M. (eds.). (1997). *Off white: Readings on race, power, and society.* New York: Routledge.

Fish, S. (1995). "Rhetoric." In F. Lentricchia and T. McClaughlin (eds.), *Critical terms for literary theory* 2nd ed., pp. 203–24. Chicago: University of Chicago Press.

Fishkin, S. F. (1995). "Interrogating 'whiteness,' complicating 'blackness': Remapping American culture." *American Quarterly,* 47(3), 428–66.

Frankenberg, R. (1993). *White women, race matters: The social construction of whiteness.* Minneapolis: University of Minnesota Press.

——— (1997). *Displacing whiteness: Essays in social and cultural criticism.* Durham: Duke University Press.

Fredrickson, G. M. (1981). *White supremacy: A comparative study of American and South African history.* New York: Oxford University Press.

Frye, M. (1983). *The politics of reality: Essays in feminist theory.* New York: Crossing Press.

Gallagher, C. A. (1997). "White racial formation: Into the twenty-first century." In R. Delgado and J. Stefancic (eds.), *Critical white studies: Looking behind the mirror,* pp. 6–11. Philadelphia: Temple University Press.

Gallagher, C. A. (1999). "Researching race: Reproducing racism." *The Review of Education / Pedagogy / Cultural Studies,* 21(2) 165–91.

Gates, H. L. (1995). "The hidden face of racism." *American Quarterly,* 47(3), 395–407.

Geertz, C. (1983). "From the native's point of view: On the nature of anthropological understanding." In *Local knowledge: Further essays in Interpretive Anthropology.* New York: Basic Books.

Gergen, M. M. (1988). "Narrative structures in social explanation." In C. Antaki (ed.), *Analysing Everyday Explanation: A casebook of methods.* London: Sage.

Giddens, A. (1979). *Central problems in social theory.* Berkeley: University of California Press.

Ginwala, F. (1991). Women and the elephant: The need to redress gender oppression. In S. Bazilli (ed.), *Putting women on the agenda,* pp. 62–74. Johannesburg: Raven Press.

Giroux, H. A. (1992). *Border Crossings: Cultural workers and the politics of education.* New York: Routledge.

——— (1997). "Rewriting the discourse of racial identity: Towards a pedagogy and politics of whiteness." *Harvard Educational Review,* 67(2), 285–320.

——— (1997). *Channel surfing: Race talk and the destruction of youth.* New York: St. Martin's Press.

——— (1998). "Youth, memory work, and the racial politics of whiteness." In J. L. Kincheloe, S. R. Steinberg, N. M. Rodriguez and R. E. Chennault (eds.), *White Reign: Deploying whiteness in America,* pp. 123–36. New York: St. Martin's Press.

Goldberg, D. T. (1990a). (ed.). *Anatomy of Racism.* Minneapolis: University of Minnesota Press.

——— (1990b). "The social formation of racist discourse." In D. T. Goldberg (ed.), *Anatomy of racism,* pp. 295–318. Minneapolis: University of Minnesota Press.

——— (1993). *Racist culture: Philosophy and the politics of meaning.* Oxford: Blackwell.

Gonzales, A., Houston M. and Chen, V. (eds.). (1994). *Our voices: Essays in culture, ethnicity, and communication.* Los Angeles: Roxbury Publishing Company.

Goodwin, J. and Schiff, B. (1995). *Heart of whiteness: Afrikaners face black rule in the new South Africa.* New York: Scribner.

Gordimer, N. (1987). "Living in the interregnum." In C. Malan (ed.), *Race and literature*, pp. 209–25. Pinetown: Owen Burgess.

Gramsci, A. (1971). *The prison notebooks: Selections* (Q. Hoare and G. N. Smith, trans.). New York: International.

Gross, A. J. (1998). "Litigating whiteness: Determination in the nineteenth-century South." *Yale Law Journal*, 108:109, pp. 109–88.

Guillaumin, C. (1995). *Racism, sexism, power, and ideology*. New York: Routledge.

Hall, S. (1980). "Race, articulation and societies structured in dominance." In UNESCO *Sociological theories: Race and colonialism*. Paris: Unesco.

—— (1985). "Signification, representation, ideology: Althusser and the post-structuralist debates." *Critical Studies in Mass Communication*, 2(2), 91–114.

—— (1994). "Cultural identity and diaspora." In P. Williams and L. Chrisman (eds.), *Colonial discourse and post-colonial theory: A reader*, pp. 392–403. New York: Columbia University Press.

Harris, C. I. (1993). "Whiteness as property." *Harvard Law Review*, 106(1701), 1709–91.

Hartigan, J. Jr. (1997). "Establishing the fact of whiteness." *American Anthropologist*, 99(3), 495–505.

Hasian, M. A. Jr. (1995). "When rhetorical theory encounters post-colonial theory." Paper presented at the national convention of the Speech Communication Association, San Antonio.

Hickman, M. J. and Walter, B. (1995). "Deconstructing whiteness: Irish women in Britain." *Feminist Review, 50*, Summer, 5–19.

Hill, M. (ed.). (1997). *Whiteness: A critical reader*. New York: New York University Press.

—— (1998). " 'Souls undressed': The rise and fall of new whiteness studies." *Review of Education / Pedagogy / Cultural Studies*, 20(3), 229–39.

Hodge, J. L. (1990). "Equality: Beyond dualism and oppression." In D. T. Goldberg (ed.), *Anatomy of racism*, pp. 89–107. Minneapolis: University of Minnesota Press.

hooks, b. (1990). *Yearning: Race, gender, and cultural politics*. Boston: South End Press.

Horne, G. (1999). "Response to Resnick." *Science and Society*, 63(2), 234–35.

Hyde, C. (1995). "The meanings of whiteness." *Qualitative Sociology*, 18(1), 87–95.

Ignatiev, N. (1995). *How the Irish became white.* New York: Routledge.

JanMohamed, A. R. (1985). "The economy of Manichean allegory: The function of racial difference in colonialist literature." *Critical Inquiry,* 12, 59–87.

Kauffman, B. J. (1992). "Feminist facts: Interview strategies and political subjects in ethnography." *Communication Theory,* 2(3), 187–206.

Kincheloe, J. L. and Steinberg, S. R. (1998). "Addressing the crisis of whiteness: Reconfiguring white identity in a pedagogy of whiteness." In Kincheloe, J. L., Steinberg, S. R., Rodriguez, N. M. and Chennault, R. E. (eds.), *White reign: Deploying whiteness in America.* New York: St. Martin's Press.

Kincheloe, J. L., Steinberg, S. R., Rodriguez, N. M. and Chennault, R. E. (eds.). (1998). *White reign: Deploying whiteness in America.* New York: St. Martin's Press.

Krippendorf, K. (1989). "On the ethics of constructing communication." In B. Dervin, L. Grossberg, B. O'Keefe and E. Wartella (eds.), *Rethinking communication: Vol. 1: Paradigm issues,* pp. 97–122. Newbury Park: Sage.

———— (1993). "Conversation or intellectual imperialism in comparing communication (theories)." *Communication Theory,* 3, 252–66.

Kuhn, T. S. (1970). *The structure of scientific revolutions,* 2nd ed. Chicago: University of Chicago Press.

Lather, P. (1991). *Getting smart: Feminist research and pedagogy within the postmodern.* New York: Routledge.

Lipsitz, G. (1995). "The possessive investment in whiteness: Racialized social democracy and the 'white' problem in American Studies." *American Quarterly,* 47(3), 369–87.

———— (1998). *The possessive investment in whiteness: How white people profit from identity politics.* Philadelphia: Temple University Press.

Lyotard, J. (1993). *The postmodern condition: A report on knowledge.* Minneapolis: University of Minnesota Press.

Macdonell, D. (1986). *Theories of discourse: An introduction.* Oxford: Basil Blackwell.

Magubane, B. M. (1999). "The African renaissance in historical perspective." In M. W. Makgoba (ed.), *African Renaissance: The new struggle.* Sandton: Mafube/Tafelberg.

Mahler, F. A. and Tetreault, M. K. T. (1997). "Learning in the dark: How assumptions of whiteness shape classroom knowledge." *Harvard Educational Review,* 67(2), 321–49.

Makgoba, M. W. (ed.). (1999). *African Renaissance: The new struggle.* Sandton: Mafube/Tafelberg.

Malan, R. (1990). *My Traitor's Heart.* New York: Vintage Books.

Mamdani, M. (1996). *Citizen and subject: Contemporary Africa and the legacy of late colonialism.* London: James Currey.

——— (1999). "There can be no African Renaissance without an Africa-focused Intelligentsia." In M. W. Makgoba (ed.), *African Renaissance: The new struggle.* Sandton: Mafube/Tafelberg.

Mandela, N. (1994). *Long walk to freedom: The autobiography of Nelson Mandela.* London: Abacus.

Martin, B. and Mohanty, C. T. (1987). "Feminist politics: What's home got to do with it?" In T. De Lauretis (ed.), *Feminist studies: Critical studies.* Bloomington: Indiana University Press.

Martin, J. N., Krizek, R. L., Nakayama, T. N. and Bradford, L. (1996). "Exploring whiteness: A study of self labels for white Americans." *Communication Quarterly,* 44(2). 125–144.

Mbeki, T. (1999). Prologue. In M. W. Makgoba (ed.), *African renaissance: The new struggle.* Sandton: Mafube/Tafelberg.

McClintock, A. (1992). "The angel of progress: Pitfalls of the term "Post-colonialism" " *Social Text,* Spring, 1–15.

——— (1994). "The angels of progress: Pitfalls of the term 'Post-Colonialism.'" In P. Williams and L. Chrisman (eds.), *Colonial discourse and post-colonial theory: A reader,* pp. 291–304. New York: Columbia University Press.

McLaren, P. (1998). "Whiteness is . . . the struggle for postcolonial hybridity." In J. L. Kincheloe, S. R. Steinberg, N. M. Rodriguez and R.E. Chennault (eds.), *White Reign: Deploying whiteness in America,* pp. 63–76. New York: St. Martin's Press.

Memmi, A. (1990). *The colonizer and the colonized* (H. Greenfield, trans.). London: Earthscan Publications. (original work published 1957)

Miller, J. H. (1995). "Narrative." In F. Lentricchia and T. McClaughlin (eds.), *Critical terms for literary study,* 2nd ed., pp. 66–79. Chicago: University of Chicago Press.

Mohanty, C. T. (1994). "Under western eyes: Feminist scholarship and colonial discourses." In P. Williams and L. Chrisman (eds.), *Colonial discourse and post-colonial theory,* pp. 196–220. New York: Columbia University Press.

Morrison, T. (1992). *Playing in the dark: Whiteness and the literary imagination.* Cambridge: Harvard University Press.

210 *References*

Mudimbe, Y. Y. (1988). *The invention of Africa: Gnosis, philosophy, and the order of knowledge.* Bloomington: Indiana University Press.

—— (1994). *The idea of Africa.* Bloomington: Indiana University Press.

Mumby, D. K. (1993). *Narrative and social control: Critical perspectives.* Newbury Park: Sage.

Murphree, M. W. (1986). "Ethnicity and Third World development: Political and academic contexts." In J. Rex and D. Mason (eds.), *Theories of race and ethnic relations.* Cambridge: Cambridge University Press.

Nakayama, T. K. and Martin, J. N. (1993). "The white problem, or towards a postcolonial intercultural communication." Paper presented at the annual meeting of the Speech Communication Association, Miami Beach.

—— (1999). *Whiteness: The communication of social identity.* Thousand Oaks: Sage.

Nakayama T. K. and Krizek, R. L. (1995). "Whiteness: A strategic rhetoric." *Quarterly Journal of Speech,* 81(3), 291–310.

Nederveen Pieterse, J. (1992). *White on black: Images of Africa and blacks in Western popular culture.* New Haven: Yale University Press.

Nederveen Pieterse, J. and Parekh, B. (1995). "Shifting imaginaries: Decolonization, internal decolonization, postcoloniality." In J. Nederveen Pieterse and B. Parekh (eds.), *The decolonization of imagination: Culture, knowledge and power.* London: Zed Books.

Niehaus, C. (1993). *Fighting for hope.* Cape Town: Human & Rousseau.

Omi, M. and Winant, H. (1994). *Racial formation in the United States: From the 1960 to the 1990s.* 2nd ed. New York: Routledge.

Outlaw, L. (1990). "Toward a critical theory of race." In D. T. Goldberg (ed.), *Anatomy of racism,* pp. 58–82. Minneapolis: University of Minnesota Press.

Owens, C. (1992). *Beyond recognition: Representation, power and culture.* Berkeley: University of California Press.

Owomoyela, O. (1996). *The African difference: Discourses on Africanity and the relativity of cultures.* New York: Peter Lang.

Pêcheux, M. (1982). *Language, semantics and ideology: Stating the obvious.* H. Nagpal (trans.). London: Macmillan.

Pollock, G. (1994). "Territories of desire: Reconsiderations of an African childhood." In G. Robertson, M. Mash, L. Tickner, J. Bird, B. Curtis and T. Putnam (eds.), *Travellers' tales: Narratives of home and displacement.* London: Routledge.

Puar, J. K. (1995). "Resituating discourses of 'Whiteness' and 'Asianess' in Northern England." *Socialist Review,* 24(2), 21–53.

Race relations survey, 1994/5. Johannesburg: South African Institute of Race Relations.

Rattansi, A. (1992). "Changing the subject? Racism, culture and education." In J. Donald and A. Rattansi (eds.), *"Race," culture and difference,* pp. 11–48. Newbury Park: Sage.

Reader's Digest Association Ltd. (1994). *Illustrated history of South Africa: The real story,* 3rd. ed. Cape Town: Reader's Digest Association Ltd.

Resnick, S. (1999). "On white supremacy and anticommunism." *Science and Society,* 63(2), 232–33.

Rex, J. (1986). "The role of class analysis in the study of race relations—a Weberian perspective." In J. Rex and D. Mason (eds.), *Theories of race and ethnic relations.* pp. 64–83. Cambridge: Cambridge University Press.

Rex, J. and Mason, D. (1986). *Theories of race and ethnic relations.* Cambridge: Cambridge University Press.

Ridge, S. G. M. (1987). "Chosen people or heirs of paradise; trekkers, settlers, and some implications of myth." In C. Malan (ed.), *Race and literature,* pp. 102–115. Pinetown: Owen Burgess.

Riessman, C. K. (1993). *Narrative analysis.* Qualitative Research Methods Series, 30. Newbury Park: Sage.

Rodriguez, N. M. (1998). "Emptying the Content of Whiteness: Toward an understanding of the relation between whiteness and pedagogy." In J. L. Kincheloe, S. R. Steinberg, N. M. Rodriguez and R. E. Chennault (eds.), *White reign: Deploying whiteness in America.* New York: St. Martin's Press.

Roediger, D. R. (1991). *The wages of whiteness: Race and the making of the American working class.* New York: Verso.

——— (1994). *Towards the abolition of whiteness: Essays on race, politics and American working class history.* New York: Verso.

——— (1998). *Black on white: Black writers on what it means to be white.* New York: Schocken Press.

Rosaldo, R. (1989). *Culture and truth: The remaking of social analysis.* Boston: Beacon Press.

Roughley, A. R. (1991). "Racism, aboriginality and textuality: Toward a deconstructing discourse." *Australian Journal of Anthropology,* 2(2), 202–12.

Rouleau L. and Clegg, S. R. (1991). "Postmodernism and postmodernity in or- ganization analysis." *Journal of Organizational Change Management.*

Said, E. W. (1994). *Culture and Imperialism.* New York:Vintage Press.

Sanday, P. (1981). *Female power and male dominance: On the origins of sex- ual inequality.* Cambridge: Cambridge University Press.

Sapriya, K. E. (1995). "Postcolonial theory and intercultural communica- tions pedagogy." Paper presented at the Speech Communication As- sociation National Convention, San Antonio.

Sarup, M. (1993). *An introductory guide to poststucturalism and postmod- ernism,* 2nd ed. Athens: University of Georgia Press.

Schutte, G. (1995). *What racists believe.* Thousand Oaks: Sage.

Schwandt, T. A. (1994). "Constructivist, interpretivist approaches to human inquiry." In N. K. Denzin and Y. S. Lincoln (eds.), *Handbook of quali- tative research.* Thousand Oaks: Sage.

Segrest, M. (1994). *Memoir of a race traitor.* Boston: South End Press.

Senghor, L. S. (1994). "Négritude: A humanism of the Twentieth Century." In P. Williams and L. Chrisman (eds.), *Colonial discourse and post- colonial theory,* pp. 196–220. New York: Columbia University Press.

Shome, R. (1996). "Postcolonial interventions in the rhetorical canon: An other view." *Communication Theory,* 6(1), 40–59.

Sollors, W. (1995). "Ethnicity." In F. Lentricchia and T. McClaughlin (eds.), *Critical terms for literary theory,* 2nd ed., pp. 288–305. Chicago: Uni- versity of Chicago Press.

Stadler, A. W. (1991). "The period 1939–1948." In T. Cameron and S. B. Spies (eds.), *A new illustrated history of South Africa* 2nd ed., pp. 115–126. Cape Town: Southern Book Publishers.

Stasiulis, D. and Yuval-Davis, N. (1995). *Unsettling settler societies.* London: Sage.

Stepan, N. L. (1990). "Race and gender: The role of analogy in science." In D. T. Goldberg (ed.), *Anatomy of racism,* pp. 38–57. Minneapolis: Uni- versity of Minnesota Press.

Stepan, N. L. and Gilman, S. L. (1991). "Appropriating the idioms of science: The rejection of scientific racism." In D. La Capra (ed.), *The bounds of race: Perspectives on hegemony and resistance,* pp. 72–103. Ithaca: Cornell University Press.

Steyn, M. E. (1998). "Who are you and what have you done with the real Hottentots? The legacy of contested colonial narratives of settlement in the New South Africa." In J. N. Martin, T. K. Nakayama and L. A. Flores (eds.), *Readings in cultural contexts.* Mountain View, California: Mayfield Publishing Company.

——— (1999). "White identity in context." In T. K. Nakayama and J. N. Martin (eds.), *Whiteness: The communication of social identity.* Thousand Oaks: Sage.

Steyn, M. E. and Motshabi, K. B. (eds.). (1996). *Cultural synergy in South Africa: Weaving strands of Africa and Europe.* Johannesburg: Knowledge Resources.

Stone, J. (1985). *Racial conflict in contemporary society.* Cambridge: Harvard University Press.

Tanno, D. V. and Jandt, F. E. (1994). "Redefining the 'other' in multicultural research." *Howard Journal of Communication,* 5(1&2), 36–45.

Thiele, S. (1991). "Taking a sociological approach to Europeanness (whiteness) and aboriginality (blackness)." *Australian Journal of Anthropology,* 2(2), 179–201.

Thornton, R. (1996). "The potentials of boundaries in South Africa: Steps towards a theory of the social edge." In R. Werbner and T. Ranger (eds.), *Postcolonial identities in Africa.* London: Zed Books.

Trinh, T. M. (1989). *Woman, native, other.* Bloomington: Indiana University Press.

Unterhalter, E. (1995). "Constructing race, class, gender and ethnicity: State and opposition strategies in South Africa." In D. Stasiulis and N. Yuval-Davis (eds.), *Unsettling settler societies: Articulations of gender, race, ethnicity and class.* Sage series on race and ethnic relations, vol. 11. London: Sage.

Van den Berghe, P. L. (1986). "Ethnicity and the sociobiology debate." In J. Rex and D. Mason (eds.), *Theories of race and ethnic relations,* pp. 246–63. Cambridge: Cambridge University Press.

Van Sertima, I. (1999). "The lost sciences of Africa: An overview." In M. W. Makgoba (ed.), *African renaissance: The new struggle.* Sandton: Mafube and Tafelberg.

Ware, V. (1992). *Beyond the pale: White women, racism and history.* London: Verso.

Waters, M. C. (1990). *Ethnic options: Choosing identities in America.* Berkeley: University of California Press.

West, J. Y. (1993). "Ethnography as ideology: The politics of cultural representation." *Western Journal of Communication,* 57, 209–20.

214 *References*

Wetherell, M. and Potter, J. (1988). "Discourse analysis and interpretive repertoires." In C. Antaki (ed.), *Analysing everyday explanation: A casebook of methods.* London: Sage.

Williams, P. and Chrisman, L. (1994). *Colonial discourse and post-colonial theory.* New York: Columbia University Press.

Wittig, M. (1992). *The straight mind.* Boston: Beacon Press.

Wray, M. and Newitz, A. (eds.) (1997). *White trash: Race and class in America.* New York: Routledge.

Yinger, J. M. (1986). "Intersecting strands in the theorisation of race and ethnic relations." In J. Rex and D. Mason (eds.), *Theories of race and ethnic relations,* pp. 20–41. Cambridge: Cambridge University Press.

Young, R. (1992). "Colonialism and humanism." In J. Donald and A. Rattansi (eds.), *"Race," culture and difference,* pp. 243–51. Newbury Park: Sage.

Young, R. J. C. (1995). *Colonial desire: Hybridity in theory, culture and race.* London: Routledge.

Author Index

∾

215

Dubow, S., 30, 31, 42, 43, 192n. 7
During, S., 196n. 3
Dyer, R., xxvi, xxviii, 183n. 12

Eagleton, T., 187n. 5
Ebert, T. L., xxxi, 182n. 10
Edgecombe, R., 33, 189n. 15

Fairclough, N., 184n. 18
Fanon, F., 190n. 20
Ferguson, K. E., xxix, 12, 188n.14, 199n. 3
Fine, M., xxvi, xxviii, xxix, xxxiv, 183n. 12
Fish, S., 186n. 4
Fishkin, S. F., xxv, xxvi
Fontana, A., 191n. 24
Foucault, 182n. 10, 183n. 12, 184n. 18, 186n. 4,
Frankenberg, R., xxvi, xxviii, 183n. 12
Fredricksen, G. M., 23, 24, 26, 27, 28, 29, 31, 32, 33, 35, 149, 196n. 7, 197n. 4
Frye, M., 8, 9, 19, 20

Gallagher, C. A., xxvii, xxix, xxxii, xxxiii, xxxv, 184n. 14
Gates, H. L., 14, 187n. 6
Geertz, C., xxxvi, 184n. 17
Gergen, M. M., xxxviii, 48
Giddens, A., 18
Gilman, S. L., 191n. 25
Ginwala, F., xxii
Giroux, H. A., xxvii, xxviii, xxix, xxx
Goldberg, D. T., xxx, 23, 31, 38, 40, 41, 162, 186n. 4, 192n. 7
Goodwin, J., 42
Gordimer, N., 24, 195n. 5
Gramsci, A., 182n. 10
Gross, A. J., 183n. 12
Guattari, 183n. 12
Guillaumin, C., 5, 12, 18, 20, 27

Hall, S., 21, 23, 26, 191n. 24, 199n. 5
Harris, C. I., 183n. 12

Hartigan, J. Jr., xxxi
Hasian, M. A., xxviii
Hickman, M. J., xxx
Hill, M., xxvi, xxvii, 183n. 12
Hobson, J. A., 23
Hodge, J. L., 12
Horne, G., 188n. 13
Hyde, C., xxvi

Ignatiev, N., 26, 183n. 12

JanMohamed, A. R., 12, 14, 189n. 18

Kauffman, B. J., 173
Kincheloe, J. L., xxx, 200n. 12
Krippendorf, K., xxxiii
Krizek, R. L., xxvi, xxxiv, 183n. 12
Kuhn, T. S., 190n. 21

Lacan, 16, 182n. 10, 189n. 18
Laclau, xxxviii
Lather, P., xxxiv
Lipsitz, G., xxix, 5, 18, 183n. 12
Luckman, T., 152, 169, 185n. 20, 200n. 14
Lyotard, J., 182n. 10, 183n. 12, 185n. 12

Macdonell, D., 200n. 15
Macedo, D. P., 183n. 12
Magubane, B. M., xxii, 10, 11, 30
Mahler, F. A., 183n. 12
Makgoba, M. W., xxiii
Malan, R., 158, 194n. 15
Mamdani, M., xxii, xxiii, xxxi, 35
Mandela, Nelson, xxi, 193n. 9, 194n. 11, 197n. 3
Mannoni, D., 189n. 17.
Martin, B., 16, 157, 198n. 7
Martin, J. N., xxvi, xxix, 183n. 12, 184n. 16
Mbeki, T., xxii
McClintock, A., xxiii
McLaren, P., xxviii
Memmi, A., 10, 14, 16, 169, 190n. 20

Subject Index

༄

Subject Index